Cultural Memory
in
the
Present

Mieke Bal and Hent de Vries, Editors

THE IMPERTINENT SELF

A Heroic History of Modernity

Josef Früchtl

Translated by Sarah L. Kirkby

STANFORD UNIVERSITY PRESS

STANFORD, CALIFORNIA

2009

Stanford University Press
Stanford, California

The Impertinent Self was originally published in German in 2004 under
the title *Das unverschämte Ich. Eine Heldengeschichte der Moderne* © 2004,
Suhrkamp Verlag.

This book has been published with the assistance of Nederlandse Organisatie voor
Wetenschappelijk Onderzoek (NWO).

Library of Congress Cataloging-in-Publication Data

Früchtl, Josef.
  [Unverschämte Ich. English]
  The impertinent self : a heroic history of modernity / Josef Früchtl ; translated
by Sarah L. Kirkby.
     p. cm.—(Cultural memory in the present)
  "An abridged version of the German edition."
  Includes bibliographical references.
  ISBN 978-0-8047-5735-5 (cloth : alk. paper)
  ISBN 978-0-8047-5736-2 (pbk. : alk. paper)
   1. Heroes in motion pictures.   2. Heroes in literature.   3. Self (Philosophy)
4. Philosophy, Modern. I. Title. II. Series.
PN1995.9.H44F7813   2009
791.43'652--dc22

                                                  2008053010

Contents

Preface

This book is an abridged version of the German edition. The abridgement, in my opinion, allows for greater clarity. It aims to present a theory of modernity within philosophy, cultural history, and (to a lesser extent) social science by constructing parallels among the Self, as the philosophical principle of modernity, and the figure of the hero in certain movie genres. The book, therefore, takes its place in the ongoing discussion within the humanities and social sciences about modernity, a discussion started in the early 1980s with references to the Nietzschean tradition, on the one hand, and to the Hegelian tradition, on the other, all the while forgetting an important third tradition: romanticism. This book also assumes a new position within the tradition of critical theory, a field of study particularly concerned with analyses of the function of popular culture, and especially the function of film in modern society.

Regarding the translation, in principle we used available English translations of the philosophers and theorists featured prominently within the book. In places, however, we provided our own translation. Almost all the movie quotations are from the Internet movie database IMDb.

I would like to thank a few people for their support: Hent de Vries, for enabling me to publish this book in the series "Cultural Memory in the Present"; Hans Ulrich Gumbrecht, for bringing his influence to bear; Norris Pope and Emily-Jane Cohen, for having so much patience with me; Thomas Elsaesser, for being there in the background and for his fine manner of cooperation; and, finally, Natalie, for coming to Amsterdam and building a new life with me.

Introduction: Heroes Like Us

The Impertinent Self

"In many people it is already an impertinence to say 'I.'"[1] This utterance from Adorno's *Minima Moralia* was the philosophical impulse for this book. Indeed, in more than one sense, Adorno's comment can be said to have something impulsive or even repulsive about it. It could also undoubtedly have been included within a dictionary of cynicisms. It inspires spontaneous agreement, followed promptly by rejection; a fluctuation between fiendish joy and intellectual sublimity, on the one hand, and annoyance at its presumptuousness and high-handedness, on the other. This affective agreement may arise from depressing and seemingly irrefutable evidence to the effect that, upon saying "I," many, maybe even most people are expressing that they are individuals, unmistakable individuals; yet, in saying this, they are hardly lending expression to such unmistakability. They are far more likely merely saying what nearly everyone else is saying. Nevertheless, when an individual, a Self, calls others who say "I" without thinking impertinent, this comes across as equally impertinent.

Since Adorno wrote, we have obviously entered different times. Since the 1990s at least, there has been a definite shift regarding the nuances of impertinence. The ego now puffs itself up enormously, considers itself to be immensely important, presents itself shamelessly to the extent of obscenity (moral more than sexual), is unable to stop talking about itself, as if daily life were an endless series of talk shows, and displays itself generously, as if the body were a walking billboard sporting the same unchanging message: "I am the greatest. I am the most beautiful." The "shameless society," as newspaper arts sections have labeled it, partly in criticism and partly in affirmation, has entered the public stage, a stage primarily provided by television. Untiringly and (quite obviously) excitedly, the limits of our sensibility are being tested daily. If you want to know what the people of today wear not *as* underwear but *underneath* their underwear, you only need to turn on certain TV channels. You will be catered to in an atmosphere somewhere in between a comfy living room and a brothel, a healthcare report and a peepshow.

However, this diagnosis of a society equally shameless and impertinent stems not only from the concerned editors or arts sections of serious publishing houses, not to mention the Catholic Church and its corresponding guild of Christian and conservative politicians; sociologists and social psychologists got there long before them.

In 1976, for example, in *The Cultural Contradictions of Capitalism*, the American sociologist Daniel Bell put forward a theory that hedonism is the justification for capitalism. In his book, Bell perceives society no longer in the manner of Hegel and Marx, as governed by one principle, the "spirit" or "commodity form" (*Warenform*), but in the manner of Max Weber, as governed by several principles. For him these are the three principles of efficiency, equality, and self-realization, corresponding to the distinct realms in society of economics, politics, and culture. An overall structure of a contradictory nature has resulted, first, from the widening gulf between the economic and the cultural, more specifically the artistic, since the mid-nineteenth century, a gulf personified in the opposition between the bourgeoisie and artists who subscribe radically and antisocially to the precept of *l'art pour l'art*; second, from the fact that the principle of self-realization, which previously dominated only the artistic area of culture, is now asserting itself throughout society as a result of mass production and mass consumption, of an economic system that instills one new wish after another and then provides the means with which to satisfy those wishes. Since Bell equates self-realization with hedonism, with fulfilling desires as an overall lifestyle option, he arrives at the hypothesis that hedonism has become the modern justification for capitalism. This amounts to the same basic ethical standpoint that for Max Weber stood in direct contrast to accustomed to the fast pace of demonstrations, electrified by the rhythm of rock music, and united by the vibe of open-air concerts, the movement created from this spirit of self-realization a whole new dynamic for the pending cultural revolution. Such "beginning," laissez-faire optimism and relaxed confidence has never been seen since. Following the Second World War, the West had finally found something new.

In Germany this uprising was preceded by the decade of Adenauer, the 1950s, ruled under the slogan of the conservative CDU party: "No experiments!" Adenauer, who was born in 1876 and therefore socialized during Kaiser Wilhelm's empire, became the very first chancellor of the Federal Republic of Germany at the age of seventy-three, in 1949, and was then reelected three times, in 1953, 1957, and finally 1961. In this last election the CDU party lost the absolute majority it had finally attained four years previously in the wake of a constant upward trend since 1949. Willy Brandt stood as candidate for the social democrat SPD party for the first time. In 1963, after fourteen years in power and at the age of eighty-seven, Adenauer stepped down. That same year John F. Kennedy, the youngest-ever U.S. president (forty-four years old upon assuming office), declared his own solidarity ("Ick bin ein Berliner") and that of all the citizens of the free world with the divided city of Berlin, just two years after the Wall was erected, and in November, he was shot in Dallas.

The changes were also to be witnessed culturally. September 11 is a date now full of historical significance: on that date in 1962, Adorno marked his fifty-ninth birthday; in 1973, General Pinochet (and the CIA) overthrew Salvador Allende's freely elected socialist government in Chile; and in 2001, the terrorist attack on the World Trade Center, that outstanding symbol of western life, occurred. In September 1962, the Beatles finished recording their first single, "Love Me Do," their breakthrough coming one year later with "She Loves You." The acoustic trademark of youth in the 1960s, that cry of victory, that assaulting, screaming, cascading, hopping "Yeah, Yeah, Yeah" was born. And this "Yeah," this alone, not the far more conventional song it comes from, expressed so precisely the feeling within society that the Beatles initially represented: an ironic affirmation, a corrupted "Yes." It is an utterance in the affirmative, but it does not just mean "Yes"; as "Yeah," it sounds like it might have been bleated from the throats of sheep, as if the flock (that is, mass society) were standing in front of its shepherd and screaming with laughter what he can hear, but has no wish to hear: a big, sarcastic Yes to everything around him. "It is a conformism expressed through irony and a blatancy which here functions as conformism." The success of the Beatles is founded "in the sheer impertinence" with which they reacted to structures of authority. Their songs are, as John Lennon noted with a twinkle in his eye, "just a bit of fun."[2] The Beatles mark the birth of the fun society with their musical sound, but it was music that represented more than just a good laugh because it also had the critical, sociopolitical slant, first captured by Bob Dylan. No music expressed the youthful optimism of the 1960s, its *swing*, better than that of the Beatles. The impertinent Self had found its music.

Thus, the impertinent Self strides out onto the social and cultural stage. Sociologists and cultural scientists begin to pay attention to it. Philosophers also have a word or two to say about it.

The Hypothesis

Contemplating modernity means contemplating the Self. That is my point of departure. Hegel was the first to declare it a philosophical problem; in more recent times, philosophers with differing theoretical tendencies have readdressed it. Jürgen Habermas, for example, challenged by the advocates of "postmodernity" and weighing both camps, has come down decidedly on the side of modernity and its berated "master thinkers" Kant, Hegel, and Marx. One of his challengers, Richard Rorty, initially took up the cudgels for the other side, no less decidedly but also no less willing to enter into discussion, in a fulminant but, for German readers, not all that surprising appreciation of romanticism and its ideals of artistic self-creation. Moderating, but not moderately, between these two positions emerged Charles Taylor. Since his great monograph about Hegel, Taylor has emphasized the importance of the romantically accentuated, expressive aspect of subjectivity for our comprehension of modernity. Today, Habermas's tone has softened. The points of opposition have been clarified; now the points in common can be examined. This presents a good opportunity to compare them once more, especially as the previously warring factions also concur in describing *modernity* as an essentially *ambigu-*

ous phenomenon. Taking this aspect as key, the argument then becomes one of how to rate this ambivalence *appropriately*. The accentuation of the *romantic* in the notion of subjectivity here acquires eminent significance, standing as it does for an increase in the ambivalence, for an *insolubility* of the ambiguity, tense to the point of tragedy.

Contemplating modernity thus amounts to contemplating the Self. Contemplating the Self, however, means evaluating the relationship between its different dimensions. If we follow Habermas's lead, this means turning our attention to the three dimensions—following on from Kant's three *critiques*—of "self-knowledge," "self-determination," and, as I, unlike Habermas, would like to call it, "self-experience." And yet an inner opposition surfaces within the self-determination dimension, namely, that of autonomy and authenticity, of (deontological) morality and (eudemonistic) ethics, of self-determination in the narrower sense and self-fulfillment. Romanticism insists on self-fulfillment, self-creation, expression of the Self in its individuality. But it also brings into play the fundamental conflict existing between the two aspects mentioned. Current theorists react to this using various strategies: *extension, collision,* or *hybridization.* Both the collision and, in essential elements, the hybridization strategies are to be seen as versions of the general *romantic tension* idea, whereas the extension strategy is to be comprehended as a continuation of the *enlightening reconciliation* concept. Habermas, thus, transforms the fundamental conflict by introducing the new, extending principle of communicative intersubjectivity, but he can only dissolve it by acknowledging primacy to justice-oriented self-determination. Rorty pacifies it ironically, but also dogmatically, with the old principle of liberalistic sphere division. Taylor acknowledges the collision but hopes for a solution through a metaphysics salvaged aesthetically. A truly agonal concept that does not refute the romantic tension idea would ultimately retain the principal insolubility of the collision. Contemplating the Self, therefore, means attributing more weight to its aesthetic-expressive (Habermas), agonal-ironistic (Rorty), agonal-expressivistic (Taylor), and hybrid-creative (Foucault, Deleuze, and Guattari) or, more briefly and comprehensively, its romantic dimension. To this extent it is a matter of strengthening the *romantic* discourse of modernity, with the core hypothesis being: modernity is the battle of the ego (in concrete cultural historical terms, the male ego) with and against itself.

To prevent theoretically totalizing misunderstandings from arising, subjectivity here is the *philosophical*, and not the sociological, economic, political, and so forth, guiding principle. As in the tradition of Hegel and Marx, it can no longer be a case of wanting to attribute all phenomena within one society or one epoch to a single principle. Philosophically speaking, the only claim can be to open up a way of looking at our culture, marked by its own internal philosophical conceptual context. For this, particularly according to Hegel, the subjectivity category is key.

My book takes up the theory of the "transformation" (Habermas), "decomposition" (Lyotard), or "deconstruction" (Derrida) of the modern subject in order to subject it to a more differentiated, gradual observation, in other words to demonstrate in a new and detailed way just what "decomposition" and "deconstruction" (in this case) really mean. The Self then becomes the ambivalent (male) *hero* of modernity, whose tale is told at *three different, overlapping levels.* This hypothesis needs to be proven not only from a *philosophical* point of view, however, but also from a cultural historical one, and I shall do this using *film.* The philosophical observations will range *first* from Hegel via Lukács and Horkheimer/Adorno to Habermas—classic, self-justifying modernity; *second* from romanticism to Taylor and Rorty—agonal modernity in what are now more clearly two variations, namely, the tragic (Taylor) and the ironic (Rorty); *third* from Nietzsche to Foucault and Deleuze/Guattari—hybrid modernity. In cultural terms, these three traditional strands are reflected most significantly by the film genres: *Western, gangster movie,* and *science fiction.* Modernity and its philosophical principle, the Self, thus appear in three variations: *classical, agonal,* and *hybrid.*

Against this philosophical and cultural historical background, talk of a modernity and a *postmodernity* assigned or secondary to it proves to be as simplifying and unproductive as discussions on their different aspects over the past decades have adequately demonstrated. Instead of positioning a "postmodern" alongside or behind "the" modern, in my opinion it seems to be more helpful to subject modernity itself to a more differentiated analysis, splitting it into its underlying layers. This "archaeological" perspective precludes any attempts at historical-linear construction from the outset. There is no danger of conceiving of modernity as a monolithic unity and contrasting it with a postmodernity, a "second modernity," or any other succeeding epoch with a different title. Viewing modernity as a stratified phenomenon facilitates better comprehension of the overlappings, parallelizations, and shifting significance of its individual layers. Within itself, modernity then develops a relationship not only of opposition but also of compatibility and harmony. What is known as "postmodernity" is nothing other than modernity with its romantic and hybrid layers removed. The "heroic tale" of the Self, of course, no longer has a *telos*; the gradual model is not appropriate here. The Self as a hero is a precarious and ambivalent figure, and the tale of this ambivalence needs to be told. The battle of the ego with and against itself, shaped from a *romantic* perspective by modernity, is found on closer examination to exist already, at the classic self-justifying level; at the hybrid level, it changes completely to become a creative game of (wild) combinations with its own elements. The layers are mutually penetrating, and each marked aspect of modernity is predominated by one layer rather than the others.

Correspondingly, the assignation of film genres to the concepts of modernity cannot be handled strictly as classification. There are Westerns in which the agonal, the romantic-tragic, or the romantic-ironic layer is more pronounced than the classic one; thrillers that are constructed according to the hybridization principle; and science-fiction films that turn out to be Westerns in a futuristic guise. It will come as no surprise that authors who are cited as justification for one particular concept of modernity are also to be found as examples of a different concept, especially when they are authors who are as restless as Nietzsche and Foucault. Here, too, clean divisions are not possible. Moreover, the quantitative structure of my book is imbalanced. Its first part is extremely weighty compared with the second, which in turn is far weightier than the third, explained by the obvious circumstance that the classic layer of modernity provides the fundamental or justifying elements to which the other two layers necessarily refer, and that the hybrid layer, while developing independently, does share its romantic impregnation with the agonal layer, which is already essentially explicated in the second part of the book.

If the three layers of modernity correspond to three dimensions of the Self, and if these in turn are largely reflected in three subgenres of film, the mass medium dominating the twentieth century, then a philosophical analysis of modernity should also provide us with an analysis and critique of *popular culture*. If I were asked what I find so fascinating about the Western, the gangster movie, and the science-fiction film, or about the figures of the Westerner, the gangster (or his counterpart, the dubious private detective or fanatic cop), and the cyborg, then my answer would be: it is a fascination with the Self, the Self in three dimensions, the justifying-reasoning, agonal, and hybrid-creative dimensions. In movies we encounter the Self as constitutive, all-justifying, and grounded in reality most obviously in the Western; as agonal, contradictory, torn, and irreconciled most obviously in the gangster movie, with all its criminal passion; as creative and hybrid (in both senses of the word: in its hybrid, its pride as much as its bastardization) in the science-fiction film.

This narrow coupling of three film genres with the complex notion of modernity or subjectivity implies a certain precedence of these types of movie over others, for example, the comedy, the love story, the melodrama, the musical, the action movie, the war movie, erotica, or—categorically different from all of the above—the documentary (corresponding in literature to nonfiction *versus* all the different types of fiction). This coupling is to be seen, however, not as using the modernity theory to deduce aesthetic, and in particular cinematographic, genres according to the historical philosophical example of Hegel, but as using the modernity theory to focus. The layers constituting modernity or the Self could certainly be elucidated using another film genre, such as the comedy (which, in its ironic version of the agonal, would definitely be appropriate) or the melodrama (which, from Douglas Sirk via Rainer Werner Fassbinder to Lars von Trier, has been grasped, in the words of Stanley Cavell, as a tragically colored attempt by womankind to become the subject) or others. Some of them, such as the action movie, are diametrically opposed to the division proposed here because they can be combined with any of the three (meaning that the action movie would also be a suitable candidate for the hybridization of modernity). But the Western, the gangster movie, and the science-fiction film are far more exemplary than their challengers, particularly with regard to their treatment of the sexes. This alone justifies their methodical elevation, and not any other essentializing classification. They may not be the only genres essentially appropriate to modernity, but they are most appropriate for demonstrative purposes.

Theoretical Type and Method

From the point of view of philosophers who have subjected the myth to industrious examination, such as Horkheimer, Adorno, and Blumenberg, the Self is a new title or, rather less respectfully, *merely* a new title for old mythological concepts. Other possible titles are "history," the "unconscious," "being." They are mythical in their function. This is apparent in the fact that the Self has a history that, to cite Lyotard, has become a "great narrative" and is defined by the way in which it assumes a fundamental legitimizing function for modernity. The concept of the Self also maintains a mythical function in that, like every concept (design, notion, comprehension) used for explanation purposes, contributes to minimizing anxiety and to making readers feel more at home in the sense of the above-mentioned authors. But it also, in the sense of structuralism and psychoanalysis, leads to a precarious balancing act, a "knot" of opposing claims that requires untangling. This in turn always gives rise to another, albeit potentially more transparent and less complex tangle.

Thus the book traverses the fields of philosophy and cultural history with the intention of being a critique of images and myths, here the myths of the Wild West, of the gangster and his counterpart (the detective or cop), and finally of the cyborg or artificial human being. This book is a study of images that, as Wittgenstein put it, in more than one sense "imprison" us, fascinate us, and capture us, and in so doing determine not only our everyday convictions, but also, as Wittgenstein and countless others tell us, the majority of our philosophical convictions. It is impossible to end a myth and the "work" invested in it, so Blumenberg tells us; Heidegger, Derrida, and Rorty say it is impossible to "overcome" or destroy basic concepts of western philosophy. It is therefore also impossible to end the work lavished on the myth of the ego as characterized in popular culture within the characters of the Westerner, the gangster or detective, and the artificial human being.

The history of the Self as the hero of modernity has some major role models: Hegel's *Phenomenology of Spirit* and Horkheimer/Adorno's *Dialectic of Enlightenment*. Following what I said above about an "archaeological" manner of observation and its linked farewell to teleological thinking, it becomes clear that, bearing this aspect in mind, Hegel can no longer function as a role model, even though he is well suited with regard to other aspects, primarily that of the hero as a concept. In content as well as in form, with regard to its hypotheses as well as presentation, the *Dialectic of Enlightenment* comes closer. When I speak of a "history" of the Self, I mean that the narrative style required by histories has learned from modern narrative technique and no longer adheres to the continuity provided by the linear relating of events. In this case, learning from film means learning from its cutting technique. I would thus like to fulfill the good old methodological maxim of giving a presentation that is just as historical as it is systematic.

Early critical theory, with its linking of philosophy, individual sciences (especially sociology and psychoanalysis), and cultural or ideological criticism, is a useful paradigm for this, or at least a potential stimulus that remains important. As a named ideal, Adorno and Benjamin's "material philosophizing" remains exemplary. Following Nietzsche, however, critical theory, as a situative switching of critical perspectives, seems to me to be pragmatically more appropriate and is a fresh legitimization of the way in which I switch types of discourse among the fields of philosophy, sociology, psychoanalysis, and cultural history. This book is an attempt to employ a crossover method, a "transversal" method, to use the terminology of Wolfgang Welsch and Deleuze/Guattari, an alternating discursive perspectivism. This *crossover* of philosophy, individual sciences, and film analysis ultimately desires no less than to reformulate under altered conditions what more than fifty years ago Horkheimer and Adorno formulated as the "Dialectic of Enlightenment."

This history of the Self will be presented both *historically* and *systematically*. It will also practice *material philosophizing*; in other words, it will be both a construction and a phenomenological analysis. Wittgenstein's term "family resemblance," which he introduces in his *Philosophical Investigations*, is central in this respect. Accordingly, it makes sense for an argument to run not in a logical and deductive manner, like a chain, but in a closely woven manner, like a rope, like intertwined fibers, ultimately like that trusty image of woven textile (*textum*), the root of literary text. Fibers or arguments require overlapping. A fiber, an argument, may be weak when taken on its own, but in its tight connection to others, it contributes to the overall strength of the hypothesis. Of course, I have to admit at this early juncture that there will be no methodically sound rules to control the firmness of this connection. What I shall attempt to provide is a wealth of good reasons to substantiate my opinions. Whether they are good enough, convincing enough, will become clear from my readers' reactions.

HEGEL, THE WESTERN, AND
CLASSICAL MODERNITY

There's a feeling I get when I look to the west
and my spirit is crying for leaving.

—LED ZEPPELIN, "STAIRWAY TO HEAVEN"

1

The Myth and the Frontier

Our story starts with Hegel, the completer. His fundamental philosophical program was to reconcile the traditional dualisms of ancient ontology and modern, subject-based philosophy; of metaphysical-rationalistic and empirical thought; of objectivity and subjectivity; of political community and individual freedom, and so on. His guiding principle in this was self-consciousness. He believed the Self to be capable of dealing with the differences from itself and then to relinquish itself in order to return as an expanded Self, an ultimately infinite Self, in other words to be itself and at the same time to be its opposite.

Hegel explicates the principle of self-awareness in all its glorious capability, but it was Descartes, as Hegel himself repeatedly acknowledges, who discovered it. It was Descartes who clearly and ultimately revealed the Self to its full advantage as the *fundamentum inconcussum* of cognition, using a simple, nonskeptical thought borrowed from Augustine, namely, that we can doubt everything except doubting. Formally speaking, this means: except thinking itself. Hegel writes about him with unbridled pathos in his *History of Philosophy*: "René Descartes does indeed mark the true beginning of modern philosophy, in the sense that it makes thinking into a principle. . . . He is such a hero, taking the whole thing back to the beginning and constituting the grounds of philosophy afresh. . . . Here we have arrived home and, like a ship's captain after a long sea voyage in rough waters, can call out 'Land ahoy!'"[1] It is not so much Hegel's pathos as his choice of words that catches our attention. He relates the history of philosophy as an heroic tale in which, after many dangerous years at sea, the protagonist reaches safe land, *terra firma*, home, and home is where the philosopher says "I."

The basic pattern of this story, developed by Homer in his *Odyssey*, is well known in the occidental world. Yet, leaving land, in other words leaving home and the firm ground beneath one's feet, and venturing out into the unknown ocean is far more than just a philosophical metaphor. In their *Dialectic of Enlightenment*, Max Horkheimer and Theodor W. Adorno, with reference to the tale of Odysseus's wandering, take it to convey a basic experience of European civilization, namely, that of the bourgeoisie asserting themselves and thus becoming both self-educated and wayward. Hans Blumenberg goes even further. In his short discourse *Shipwreck with Spectator*, he pursues this metaphor as one of life for human beings per se, albeit employing examples from European spiritual history as well. Picturing existence as a sea voyage full of uncertainty does indeed appear to represent a Eurocentric perspective. The people of the "New World," who at the beginning of the "Modern Age" arrived there in ships—the first three settler ships landed on the coast of Virginia in 1607; the Puritan "pilgrim fathers" in their famous ship the *Mayflower* landed in 1620—later inspired their own great metaphor and myth, in which their own view of the world is concentrated. Any metaphor of this dimension, any—to use Blumenberg's words—"absolute metaphor" fulfills a metaphysical and, one might also say, mythical function: namely, the inference of a total horizon. This hypothesis remains correct even if there is good reason to doubt its anthropological and metaphysical justification by Blumenberg. For, in the words of Arnold Gehlen, to say that the human being, as "a creature of deficiencies" with a deficient biological nature, "compensates" through culture and compensates within culture his lack of meaning through metaphysical achievements, is a metaphysical assertion in two respects: explanation of a whole, and explanation from a single principle. The fact that, nowadays, an explanation of this kind is immediate cause for suspicion is, in the words of Lyotard, because it continues to spin the pattern of an integral "great narrative" based on fundamentalist principles, as if the conceptual work for more than a century on the dissolution of this narrative pattern had never taken place. The myth that has emerged in North America and that is understood as the oldest and most characteristic myth of this part of the world, indeed as the greatest modern myth of all time, is that of the *frontier*, the border as a confrontation with the new and the different, the myth of the Wild West.

The Myth of the Frontier

Westerns are movies about America's frontier.[2] The stars of this genre are cowboys and Indians, sheriffs and gunmen, saloon wenches and ranch girls, Quakers and cavalry soldiers: the stock figures of one country at one particular time, essentially the second half of the nineteenth century, of a time past. Yet the conflicts that occur between these stereotypical characters are conflicts typical within American culture and cultures under American influence (nowadays, that is most of the world). Their codeword, widely known and yet working in cryptographic ways, their guiding metaphor, is *frontier* or, expressed as an imperative: "Go West!" really meaning: "Go on!" "Go West!" is the appellation directed at pioneers ever since the first ships landed on the East Coast of North America; at the end of the twentieth century the same slogan was being used worldwide to advertise a brand of cigarettes. The country seems to be "without frontiers" in two senses. Fences and barbed wire appear misplaced, and where they are erected, the pioneers simply march on.

Westerns are thus movies about the *external*, geographical border that America has pushed on and away. The principle they demonstrate is that of territorial expansion. The country also appears to be "without frontiers" as a *social* space. The constraints of civilization, the constricting stipulations of morality, rights, and the law, here have no validity (yet). It is the land of "freedom and adventure." Or at least it is in the advertising slogan of another famous twentieth-century cigarette brand, its emblem a cowboy, a man equipped with all the relevant insignia identical to the cigarette brand and the country from which it emerged, the *Marlboro Man*.

Westerns are thus also movies about the internal, social, and sociopsychological frontiers of America, the acknowledgement of which America (and not just America) also continually pushes on and away. Hegel noted the political, antirevolutionary aspect of this continual frontier-pushing in his lectures on the philosophy of history. North America can avoid the "tension" between social classes because it has access to the "colonization solution." Social conflicts can be solved within the spatial dimension. In densely populated Europe this is no longer possible, and the consequences are enormous. If at the end of the eighteenth century, for example, "Germany's forests had still existed, the French Revolution would never have happened."[3]

The corresponding principle demonstrated by Westerns is, however, far more complex. Its most prominent guise is individualism, the figure of the individual who defies the challenges of nature and history and remains true to himself. The noun *frontier* comes from the same root as the verb *to front*. Henry David Thoreau, who as a social critic momentously proclaimed an obligation toward civil disobedience, who as a researcher and nature lover ethically taught that one can only really comprehend the essential things in life by breaking free from the artificial world of cities, money, and family ties, convictions that have been almost entirely forgotten in current philosophy (with the lucky exception of an oddball like Stanley Cavell, who chooses to remember them), coined the term frontier as the epitome of an attitude, of a conviction: "The frontiers are not east or west, north or south, but wherever a man fronts a fact."[4] Fronting facts—nobody can escape this ethical attitude in the land of Western pioneers.

Elements of the Myth

Westerns are movies about a frontier that is not merely a natural and geographical frontier, nor only a social and sociopsychological frontier. Its import, or even its national import, when seen through the eyes of U.S.-Americans, is far more the result of a different level altogether, namely, the *mythical* level. Westerns are movies about the frontier (of America), about confrontation (with the existent, the different, the new) in its mythical dimension, ultimately movies about the individual in its mythical dimension.

First of all and following common linguistic use of the term, "mythical" means something akin to "legendary," "phenomenal" ("epic" and "incredible"), "conceptually ungraspable," "fundamentally meaningful," "timeless." A consultation of philosophy and the sciences in the hope of finding a clear conceptual notion or even a definition leads more or less to embarrassment in the face of several familiar problems. A definition has as a prerequisite what can only be the result of exploring a tangible problem. Yet we can presume, at least according to the testimonial of the experts, that a correct, generally binding definition of myth, in other words "the" definition of myth, does not exist. This is for the simple reason that every definition depends on theory.[5] A person analyzing myths according to their content or historical motif will arrive at a different definition of the term from a person researching them according to their function. The definition arrived at by a person undertaking to do the latter will in turn depend on whether he addresses the function (psychologically) for the individual or (sociologically) for the community. The concept and therefore the matter of the myth changes with the epistemological perspective one assumes. One that integrates all possible, or at least all preceding factual epistemological perspectives, and that therefore delivers if not the only correct definition, then in overall terms the best definition, has to be categorized either as a theological relict, a secularized faith in the overriding divine perspective, or as a modest, albeit still pious scientific wish, for even the best definition remains relative regarding the (integrating) function it is to serve, namely, in pragmatic terms, the solving of a problem.

In order to solve this problem of definition, it is in turn clearly insufficient to cheat one's way around it and to start in a forced empiristic manner with an actual discussion, in this case about the mythical dimension of Westerns, as that would presuppose knowledge of the mythical. In a plain act of hermeneutic correctness, it is imperative to begin by clarifying one's own prior understanding. In the following deliberations I shall thus emphasize some different elements of the myth with the intention, independently of their theoretical origins, of combining them to form a concept that is viable for the Western, as well as for other movie genres. The theoretical role model that rises into view is early critical theory for its linking of philosophy, individual sciences, and cultural, as well as ideological criticism, for its attempt at integrating definitions of terms, which of course does not mean simply taking on board all that it proposes. Its attempt at conceptual integration is what is exemplary, not necessarily the result of this attempt. As a reminder, the following constellative attempt at a definition is primarily geared toward one function, which could be termed "culture philosophical": the explication of a movie genre (such as the Western, but also later on science-fiction and gangster movies) and thus, causally connected, also a decomposition of the fundamental concept of modern philosophy, namely, the Self.

Formally and etymologically, a myth is primarily a narrative, a related tale in the sense of a fable. It reports certain events by telling a story, not by entering into an argumentative philosophical context or by producing a scientific analysis. "Narrative" is a simplified term for "pictorial, vivid, expressive thought." It is thinking in ambiguous images instead of in abstracting and generalizing signs, in context and affect-related expressions instead of subsuming and differentiating concepts. In lieu of "image" and "expression" we can also speak of "symbol" and "allegory" if we take this as meaning a sign that lacks an unambiguous meaning not by being indistinguishable from all other, differently sounding signs within a grammatical system, but by having its meaning created for a purpose. The words "cross" or "lamb," for example, can also function as Christian symbols; the word "star" (in the context of a Western) can symbolize the law; the word "hat" (in the same context, as well as in an old European context) can symbolize a free man. But in myths, and incidentally also in magic, but not in art, the symbol is not only opposed to the (clear) sign but at the same time also stakes a direct and unbroken claim to its function. The myth employs a symbol as if it were a sign, uses an unclear entity as if it were a clear one, uses an allegory as if it were a true reproduction, uses an (unclear) indication as if were identical to the indicated, to reality. By calling himself Udeis (Nobody), Odysseus inlays the name with an intention, with a conscious orientation to a purpose, and thus he distinguishes between the word and the thing. In so doing, he removes language from the magical realm in which Polyphemus remains, as well as from the mythical realm with which he is only linked in content, to the extent that we are prepared to acknowledge that the myths have merely found expression in the layers of Homer's epic tale, whereas the linguistic articulation itself is directed at liberation from them along the transformation path.

This, of course, as we know today, does not mean that myths have to belong to the irrational camp. The formulation "from myth to reason" (mythos to logos) coined by classical philologist Wilhelm Nestle in 1940, the whole idea of the myth as a "prelogical entity" discussed three decades earlier (and later retracted) by Lucien Lévy-Bruhl, has meanwhile been replaced across the whole spectrum by a presentation that grasps the myth in its own logic or grammar as a "symbolic form" or an "enlightenment."[6] The myth is an autonomous, irreducible form of human self-comprehension, equal to religion, art, science, and—to employ Cassirer—language, ultimately technology. It cannot be translated completely into one of the other forms of self-comprehension, nor can it be "overcome." One can only continue to work on it. In the words of Hans Blumenberg, "work on myth" becomes an appropriate motto of an age that is enlightened in the matter of myths.

As far as content is concerned, a myth narrates events from a time long past known as "prehistory" because it was not historically recorded. This prehistoric reference is of little interest with regard to content, however. Arbitrariness plays a role here; as Roland Barthes recently postulated, anything can become a myth: origins, tales of gods, heroic sagas, fairy tales, but also worldviews, ideologies, modern everyday single and mass phenomena (Einstein's brain, Garbo's face, the new Citroën, hamburger and fries, and so on).[7] What is far more interesting about the prehistoric reference is its *legitimizing* element. Odysseus, Achilles, Oedipus, Cain and Abel, Abraham and Isaac, David and Goliath, the Nibelung, King Arthur—around all of these and some sparsely sown historical facts, stories are woven. As a result of these stories values emerge, together with a family, a clan, a tribe, a city, a people, a nation, which traditionally makes these stories and values its own, and which through them comprehends itself as a community. Myths, like all forms of culture that uphold tradition as a system of signs and symbols, are thus never private, instead serving social integration, in functional and especially sociological terms. They aid individuals in grasping themselves as part of a more comprehensive unit, a linking history, by literally authenticating or justifying a central value. Justifying something means being able to refer it to an intersubjectively noncontroversial point, in social contexts to refer it to a value, and in this case to refer it to something deemed holy, inviolable, and powerful. For Herder and the early romantics, this legitimizing power of the myth was foremost; following on from Émile Durkheim and Bronislaw Malinowski, Cassirer described it as the creation of a "unity of feeling" and "solidarity of life."[8]

After sociology and cultural anthropology, a further aspect is the psychoanalytical perspective. It, too, provides an explanation for the transhistoric suggestion generated by the myth. At the level of the species it fulfills a comparable function to that of the dream at the level of the individual, providing the collective with an imaginary replacement for the elementary needs and urges that in reality are denied satisfaction. Phylogenetically, in reality the chief denying body is nature, whose supremacy humankind strives to check by attempting to humanize it. Impersonal forces and occurrences are turned into creatures familiar to us from our interpersonal dealings. This cultural achievement is what helps us to feel "comfortable when discomfited." But culture itself also becomes a denying body. As Freud emphasized without illusion, if all culture encourages the suppression of urges, then the impulse to attain endless happiness, carried by the principle of desire, will always remain elusive. As a result of this, human beings never rid themselves of a certain uneasiness, behind which lurks an awareness of guilt, and behind that in turn a fear of the superego, of the conscience as an internalized authority. In this permanent state of discomfort under the cloud of self-destruction, the myth, just like the dream, helps to make life, that is, living with others, more bearable. It is a form of collective coping with culturally induced experiences of suffering, experiences that will return so long as we have culture.[9] As a young man, Nietzsche took a similar view in his *Birth of Tragedy*. He believed that human beings are kept from an unbearable truth, from an insight into the eternal suffering of individuation and from (Dionysian-ecstatic) self-destruction by the (Apollonian-beautiful) appearance of a dream world, which for the ancient Greeks assumed the guise of the "tragic myth." If the semiotic definition of the myth decrees this meaning to be invented, then the psychoanalytical definition provides a reason for this invention. A myth is expression of the sense interpreted by a collective into a sign referring to something indicated, to "reality." It is collective projection, intersubjectively shared desire, which stems from the suppression of elementary conflicts and at the same time appeases them.

Structuralism, developed by Claude Lévi-Strauss and further developed by Roland Barthes, moves within the framework of semiology. Accordingly, the myth is a statement form and is as logical as a grammar form. Like a natural language, myth is constructed according to rules. It is therefore important to analyze the connections made within myth narration. For this syntactical connection, according to Lévi-Strauss, the oppositional structure is essential. Like thinking itself, mythical thinking adheres to binary oppositions in an attempt to use repeating and varying oppositions to cope with the oppositions that haunt a society, for example, those between life and death, culture and nature, and so on. If in a myth a man is compared to a lion, this comparison expresses the binary opposition of human *versus* animal or culture *versus* nature. Any similarities that might exist between the two compared objects lose their significance within a binary structure, in both senses of the word. The simplicity of the differences stands out, facilitating an understanding that is as easy as it is general. A myth, a thinking in simplifying and generalizing oppositions, emerges about a social (cultural, psychological, political, and so on) contradiction, which turns out to be insoluble because the two contradictory sides appear to be equally necessary. Lévi-Strauss did not wish to uncover the structure of the myth in order to merely understand its social import, but also to understand its universal import. His famous formulation for the notion that binary structures are inherent to human thinking was that myths operate in men's minds without their being aware of the fact.[10] One can, of course, distance oneself from this anthropological-ahistoric consequence, but for the analysis of myths the crystallization of oppositional structures is indeed helpful.

The myth is not only a thinking in insoluble oppositions, a vivid and pictorial thinking, with a symbolic, invented meaning that assumes a sociointegrative, legitimizing, and compensating function; it is also a form of *coping with contingency*. This function has already been addressed in the psychoanalytical definition. It can also be verified with recourse to ethnological and structuralist research. However, it is only within the philosophical framework that it achieves certain lofty implications. The experience of contingency, of being at the mercy of an untamable environment without protection, is accordingly part of the basic experience of archaic, technologically underdeveloped societies, instilling within them a need to stem those contingencies befalling them, if not in reality then with the help of myths in their imaginations.[11]

Philosophically speaking, this plausible ethnological hypothesis can be developed further to form the hypothesis that "contingency" is not only a term to describe the historical and technological variations on the ungovernability of our world, but perhaps even more so to describe its principal irrationality. Blumenberg developed this hypothesis in great detail. He called being contingent being devoid of reason and purpose the "absolutism of reality." This is a reinterpretation and extension of the theological absolutism that formed the pivot for his work *The Legitimacy of the Modern Age*. To this extent, in the later Blumenberg, one could speak of a pantheism under negative precursors. If human beings used to have to assert themselves against the arbitrary god of the late Middle Ages, it is now against reality itself. "Human self-assertion," the second leading concept of Blumenberg's book, becomes a concern not just of the modern age, but of every age. It becomes anthropological self-assertion, and its method is not so much that of a reactional usurping, but of a distancing. In their thoughts, human beings attempt to keep reality in opposition to their search for reasons and purposes, their causal and teleological thinking, at arm's length, and to interpret the "supreme powerfulness" of reality as "supreme powers."

For Blumenberg, the myth is one of the "symbolic forms"—in the sense of Cassirer—which conduct this interpretation. They all have the function of creating a familiar, ordered, and accessible world; "reality" is, for Blumenberg, just another word for "foreignness" and "unearthliness," that is, "namelessness," definitely "conceptlessness," and ultimately a "source of anxiety." Those things for which we have no concepts or even names render us helpless and threaten our self-assertion. As Blumenberg infers with Freud and Ferenczi, complemented by Horkheimer and Adorno, this is as true for the individual as for the species; for both, there exists a kind of birth trauma. In the history of the species, the myth is the earliest processing of this fundamental experience of anxiety. Human beings need the myth because, or so long as, they are unable to explain the unknown as anything other than "different." The myth—not alone, but also and as the first instance to do so—liberates humankind from this anxiety. Turning this argument emphatically on its head, a society that is liberated and free of anxiety would no longer require myths. Yet the Enlightenment program of transforming the myth to reason proves impossible due to the insoluble human experience of contingency. The only processing possible is that which is aesthetic and metamorphosing, for Blumenberg ideally ironic, enlightening, and cheering. The myth knows no end because it satisfies the constitutive need of humankind "to feel at home" in the world, the state that cannot be substantiated.[12]

In Search of the Lost Home: *The Searchers*

The Western is a *Heimatfilm*, a German term for which there is no direct English translation,[13] but which is correctly circumscribed as a "sentimental film in an idealized regional setting." This would imply, however, that the Western is not a *Heimatfilm* after all, for only the numerous B-movie Westerns, standardized low-budget productions from the Hollywood film factory, are sentimental and idealized, and these movies do not define the Western. We can boldly state of its genre[14] what is true of all film genres, namely, that a dozen magnificent movies exist, followed by roughly the same number of very good ones, and then a multitude of others ranging from conventionally entertaining to simply idiotic. (This does not mean that the idiotic ones are of no interest, at least from a sociological point of view; in fact, the more people who watch them, the more sociologically interesting they become). Nevertheless, the Western *is* a *Heimatfilm*. The genre's most influential director is John Ford, and his most salient (multifaceted) movie is *The Searchers*.

A warlike soundtrack, orchestra music, Native Indian in both rhythm and tune. On the cinema screen a wall of red bricks; John Wayne appears. He stands there for just a few seconds, black, larger than life and as doom-ridden as the music, before the title appears in small red script: *The Searchers*. The music changes abruptly as other names begin to appear. A guitar leads into a pleasing melody enhanced by violins and then three male voices singing, "What makes a man to wander, what makes a man to roam? What makes a man leave bed and board and turn his back on home? Ride away. Ride away. Ride away." This lyric introduces the questions to be repeated in extenso throughout the movie and to be answered by the end of it, albeit leaving viewers to draw their own inferences.

The song, with its sedate rhythm reminiscent of a rocking chair, has just died away, the screen has just gone black, when suddenly, as if blown from behind by a gust of wind, a square appears in the center of the screen. A door opens toward us viewers, letting light into a room that is just as dark as the cinema. Almost at the same moment the rear-view silhouette of a woman becomes visible, walking out of the dark and slowly approaching the door. The camera stays behind her, so that our gaze follows her figure. We the viewers are drawn into the movie and the events it is about to relate. We are drawn in by being guided out of the darkness. With the opening of its story, the movie at the same time seems to be saying it will provide pictorial and mythological enlightenment: "Look, I am moving you out of the darkness and into the light. I am giving the old term *moving picture* (or *Lichtspiel*[15]) its due, and I am merely doing once more and specifically what all movies do, namely, bringing light into the darkness." But the initial sequence is also a clear exposition of the principle of representation used by Ford to comment formally on the theme *Heimat*: the principle of framing.

Framed by a wide, deep blackness and by the black female silhouette in the middle of the screen, we now see, half-hidden, an expansive, sandy-brown landscape against a deep blue sky. The woman steps outside. The dark picture frame recedes, but not entirely. For the woman is now standing on a veranda that forms a new dark frame for the bright landscape bathed in daylight. The woman looks into the distance and observes a man approaching on horseback. Gradually other people fill the screen, too: a man, an adolescent girl, a boy, a little girl, and a small dog. This family obviously knows the man on horseback, now standing before them in a coat and hat and carrying a saber, an officer from the South. It is Ethan Edwards, alias John Wayne, the brother of the father of the family. "Welcome home!" The woman greets him, and he kisses her, somewhat hesitantly, on the forehead. A strange moment, in which the violin and guitar, which have so far accompanied the scene, stop for a while before then starting up again in a faintly threatening tone, not regaining their harmony until they all go into the house. The house is the darkly encapsulating home that peacefully collects the family together.

This idyll is fleeting, however. In the house, during a joint meal, dark aspects surrounding the homecomer are rapidly revealed. The story is set in Texas in 1868, three years after the end of the American Civil War and the defeat of the Southern states. Ethan avoids questions as to where he has been in the meantime. A medal he gives his little niece allows us to conclude that he was in Mexico fighting on behalf of the Austrian archduke Maximilian, who became emperor in 1864, against the liberal

Mexican president Juárez, in which case, this would mean another battle ending in defeat.

The secret behind Ethan Edwards's behavior clearly has something to do with the woman. It was she who opened the door to that outside from which Ethan came; it was she who was the first to welcome him; it was for her that he displayed conspicuously hesitant behavior when he kissed her hello. It is also she who, inside the house, deflects any questions that Ethan might find awkward. This behavior follows that of the model bourgeois wife and mother, glossing over any emerging embarrassments and sweeping unpleasantries under the carpet, but she also has another, far more personal motive, which only the pastor and Rangers captain notices (and tactfully keeps quiet about): the way in which she strokes her hand over Ethan's uniform makes it clear that she loves him, just as he loves her. The reason behind Ethan's prolonged roaming, therefore, appears to be unhappiness in love, a love that in the given cultural circumstances, were it to be practiced, would inevitably lay blame at the lovers' door. The reason for Ethan's restlessness would be the near-tragic insolubility of this conflict. Whichever way he decided, to go or to stay, to relinquish publicly or secretly, to relinquish at all or to love openly—he would always be unhappy, having caused somebody, in most cases himself, to suffer.

The psychoanalytic and feminist explanation for this would be: when men go to war they flee from an inner antagonism represented by the female.[16] In the outside world they go in search of an enemy who is really inside themselves; they fight against an enemy with whom they are in truth standing back to back. And, for Ethan Edwards at least, this is evident. This is a man fleeing from the central antagonism of the cozy home and toward simple oppositions, or "abstract negations," as Hegel would say. When Native Indians kill all of his family except the two daughters, whom they kidnap, Ethan uninhibitedly gives himself up to an ideology based on opposites. The movie carries this further, with Ethan setting out to search for the girls with a group of men. The opposition role is assumed by the Native Indians and even acquires a name: Chief Scar. Representing "femininity," he is the inner enemy projected to the outside, and in his quest to defeat the chief, Ethan draws on the punitive powers of the Christian God, the strict laws of the patriarch. "The day will come" is a prophecy he repeatedly utters, the day of revenge for the Lord and his earthly champion, Ethan Edwards.

Ethan's Old Testament strategy of atonement collapses, however. It could only function in its entirety if he succeeded in murdering the murderer of the woman he loved and in bringing back at least the younger of her daughters "untouched" and "pure," as a kind of substitute for the one he loved so "purely." But, after years of searching in vain, this is no longer to be expected. Taking the psychological interpretation one step further, the desire for atonement, initially a desire for destruction directed against the other side, against the Native Indians, now becomes an open desire for destruction directed against one's own side, against one's (own) family. Ethan can act out this desire on his young niece. She is living with an Indian, meaning that she herself has become an Indian. For Ethan it is clear that it would be better for Debbie to die than to live in disgrace, the disgrace of having sullied her own race, and Ethan wants to be the one to extinguish her himself.

In Ethan love and hate are confounded in a way that Freud grasped using the term *ambivalence*: as the meeting of two opposing emotions toward one and the same object. He loves Debbie because she is the daughter of his (secret) love, and he hates her precisely because this love had to remain a secret, in other words because this love was coupled with the necessary suppression of physical urges. So long as he was able to see her as a desexualized girl, he loved her, but as soon as she becomes a sexual object belonging to a man who represents the other side of his inner self, he hates her. The psychological strategy that he unconsciously pursues thus appears to be as perfect as it is perfidious.[17] The warrior in him dissolves the Commandment preventing him from coveting his brother's wife by finding somebody else, the Indian Chief Scar, who takes the coveted woman by force. Ethan can now, first, clarify the battle line by squarely laying all the blame arising from such forbidden pleasure on the supposed other side, the red warrior, and thus legitimize his campaign of revenge. Second, Ethan himself can then devote himself to a replacement pleasure, namely, the romantic pleasure of eternal wandering through an orphaned world. True happiness, so the romantic notion, is lost happiness; true home is the one dreamt backward; it has been destroyed (by him) and can now be glorified in his memories. Ethan Edwards is a romantic, a man full of desire and sentiment in search of his lost *Heimat*.

Ultimately, however, the movie supports those who do not persist in clear battle lines and simple oppositions, for example the mongrel Martin, the white Indian squaw Debbie, and a quirky, bald-headed old man called Mose Harper, who immediately calls to mind the pertinent Shakespearean figure of the fool. Ford's movie does this by employing its symbolic leit-motif: the frame. The contrast between light and dark, present from the outset, does not correspond to that between civilization and wilderness, *Heimat* and foreign terrain, good and evil.[18] Far more, we realize that with this opposition the movie is already performing something that did not receive an established theoretical label (in the philosophical and literary sciences) until much later: it "deconstructs," as if, way before its time, it were party to Derrida's art. The initial scene sets up the familiar symbols: the civilized home is situated in the darkness harbored by the house, whereas the extensive wilderness, out of which the stranger emerges, is located outside in the bright light of day. The symbolic contrast between light and dark is then inversely accentuated following the assault on the family's house by the Native Indians: Ethan stumbles through the debris in desperation, and his gaze falls on a large black hole that used to be the front door. We see, from within, how he, darkly framed, approaches this opening and sinks to his knees when confronted with what he finds. Ethan, who uses brute force to prevent Martin from seeing what he has just seen, reacts so heftily that we may conclude that the woman has been brutally abused and raped. In this scene the significance of the frame has been reversed: from a protecting darkness to a darkness of pending doom. The barbaric is no longer "outside," but has now taken over the homely interior, the inside of the cozy home.

For John Ford, *Heimat* is a concept full of ambiguity. The final scene of the movie, following on from Debbie's liberation, underlines this in a very touching way. After the cavalry and the rangers have attacked the Indian camp, Ethan searches for Debbie, who has run into the prairie and onto the top of a cave. She has known that he wants to kill her ever since he raised a revolver to her at their very first reunion, several years after Ethan began searching. Debbie is running for her life, but for the man on horseback she is easy prey. He catches up with her, jumps from his horse, and strides up to her. Martin screams, begging him from behind: "Don't shoot, don't, Ethan! Don't! Don't!" We are positioned behind the camera in the darkness and safety of the cave that Debbie had been trying to reach, tensely waiting for what will unfurl outside. To our astonishment, Ethan does not do what he was threatening to do. Instead of shooting his niece, he grabs her and picks her up joyously as a father would his child, or a man his wife, or even an uncle his niece, and then carries her off in his arms: "We're going home, Debbie."

The tragedy has been warded off; the vicious circle of killing out of a desperation born of inner strife has been brought to a halt. An inexplicable moment, a completely unexpected turn of events. But even this rediscovered happiness is only a momentary lull. When Ethan and Martin return home with Debbie for the last time, the dark side of domestic bliss is once again revealed. They approach a ranch slowly on horseback. We as viewers are once more positioned behind the camera in the darkness of the interior, looking through the frame of the open door to the outside. With Debbie in his arms, Ethan comes straight toward us. On the veranda of the ranch, an elderly couple receives them and leads Debbie into the house. In a symmetric reversal of the initial scene of the movie, the camera now glides backward into the darkness of the interior. It is as if we are getting out of the way or making room for Debbie and her new parents to pass us as black silhouettes and disappear into the darkness. Ethan has stepped up onto the veranda, too. But then he lets Martin and his fiancée go first, also initially filling the screen as two-dimensional silhouettes, in order then to dissolve into its black frame. Ethan is still standing at the door. Since the sunlight is falling on him from behind, he too is partly silhouetted, prepared to be completely sucked in by the blackness of the interior. But he hesitates, then turns around and retreats into the dusty, inhospitable landscape, slowly disappearing into its expanse with every step he takes.

Off-screen the somewhat sad title song "What makes a man to wander? What makes a man to roam?" strikes up again. This time, unlike at the beginning of the movie, the song does not merely pose questions. Its lyric is no longer about the cozy home that the man is leaving behind, but about an entirely undefined, symbolic, religious, ethical place "up there." Its ultimate answer, therefore, necessarily remains indefinite. There is no real place in which the hero could feel at home. What is left to him is just that both weak and stubborn certainty called hope. By contrast, the question pertaining to the reason behind his restless searching has been answered. It is not about external factors, but about oneself, one's "heart and soul," one's "peace of mind." What moves the hero is not knowing who and what he really is: "A man will search his heart and soul, go searching way up there. His peace of mind he knows he'll find. But where, oh Lord, Lord where?" In the light of this question, the song then returns to the indefinite, and once again we hear the refrain, this time half affirmative, half resigned, as if it blew in on a gentle breeze: "Ride away, ride away, ride away." Ethan distances himself; the door closes; the screen turns completely black. Riding away, continuing his search, this is the *movens* that drives the lonely hero onward, he who has excluded himself from the community. While he wrestles with his ambivalences and the constant temptation to divide them into simple antagonisms, and while the veil of the indefinite settles over the place in which he could have begun to feel at home, it is clear that the community is not only a provider of security. It is also swathed in the shadow of the hushed, the suppressed, the barbaric.

Finally, the attitude of the viewer also has to be ambivalent. "Has to" means here that our reception of the movie cannot be unambiguously unbroken, or can only be with difficulty. When the screen becomes a black surface, the darkness of the film's interior and the darkness of the cinema momentarily conjoin. For an instant, fiction touches reality. One last illusion, for now we are clearly neither in the world of the settlers, nor in that of the lonely cowboy. Now *we* are excluded. "Simultaneously wistful and confident, we remain in that other provisional home which Hollywood, the dream factory, offers its viewers: the cinema seat."[19] Wistful because we have to go, have to leave that other life, an imaginary life full of people who in some ways have become familiar and in others have remained strangers. Especially wistful because the hero—maverick and crosser of frontiers—has been removed from our searching gaze, because he has left us with his problem of not knowing where one belongs, on the side of civilization or of the wilderness, the community or the individual. This problem is further reinforced by the fact that we can see the ambivalence on both sides, yet we can also feel Ford's melancholic sympathy for the man who, himself ambiguous, refuses to yield to ambiguous civilization. Yet we are also confident because we are allowed to come back again, because we know that "coming soon to this movie theater" will be another door of kinds that will be opened, and that light will fall onto the screen, and that we will be able to explore the postponed solution to our problem in a new constellation.

The relationship between individual and community *in* the movie turns into one the viewer has *to* the movie: the same ambivalence reigns at both levels. The framing of the house by the door at the beginning and end of Ford's movie reinforces the view that the world of the Western can be seen as both *epically rounded* and *orchestrated*. The beginning and end of his tale meet to form a circle as if wishing to establish a mythical version of time; at the end nothing is as it was at the beginning, yet this chosen version of time suggests that the end is once more the beginning, and that the beginning is the end. At the same time, the portrayed world is clearly recognizable as a stage production. The opened door that the movie employs so demonstratively is not only an iconic element cultivated in romantic paintings but in this case also serves to introduce a stage play. Through it we enter into an unreal world and a long-gone past. The Western, as Ford demonstrates so transparently, is a projection, the inventive representation of a three- and four-dimensional world using light beams, sounds, and moving pictures on a white surface. And it is this orchestrational aspect that enables us as viewers to adopt a consciously ambivalent relationship to the movie: we are supposed to be and want to be "inside" it, to be a part of the movie, yet at the same time not; then again we are supposed to be "outside," in the real world, yet at the same time not.

With the end of the movie we become again what the hero was during the movie. For now, until our next visit to the theater, until the next opening scene, we are not only excluded but also romantics. Wistful and confident, we temporarily sit in the movie theaters of this world. For us every movie is what the restless wandering was for the hero of *The Searchers*: a substitute for happiness. What is ambiguously fascinating about the hero also constitutes the fascination of cinema. It displays the same restlessness, and the principle of the series is also intrinsic to it. We are confident because the film genre demands sequels in the same way we do, calling for that sought-after happiness to be handed over, yet we are also wistful because the happiness depicted in movies refers us guiltily to a happiness (we ourselves have) thwarted. Cinema is per se romantic.

The Hero in the Epochs of the Mythical and the Bourgeois

The initial reaction of those present to Achilles' outrage
is shocked silence.
The appearance of the killer in the saloon has a similar effect.
The pianist stops playing,
and everybody freezes.

—SERGIO LEONE

The Self as a Myth

At the beginning of *The Searchers* the name "John Wayne" appears on the screen in big black letters, seemingly carved in stone. By the end of the movie, with his back turned on home, turned on us viewers, he has become a myth. He is no longer an individual, but something more universal, no longer a (lonesome) cowboy, but *the* ultimate (lonesome) cowboy. He has become a *symbol*, in the sense of a semantically condensed sign uniting apparently insoluble *contradictions*, ambivalences he strives to escape from by attempting to interpret them as simple pairs of opposites. His mythical dimension is embedded precisely in the sheer vanity of this attempt. The myth does not, to put it in psychoanalytical and Nietzschean terms, deny these repressed conflicts, but disguises, cloaks, appeases them, thus rendering them (more) bearable. This is also true of the myth of the Self. *"Heimat" is where Hegel and related philosophers say "I."* The Self is the *Heimat* of modern philosophers. According to Freud, Horkheimer, Adorno, and, most recently, Blumenberg, the function of the myth is also, however, to create *Heimat*. Finally, as shown by John Ford, *Heimat* is highly ambivalent. This ultimately means that *the Self is another name for a more modern and equally ambivalent "myth."* Hegel would not have said so, of course. He preferred another name for the entanglement of Self and myth: "hero."

Hegel's Heroes

Asked to define "hero," Hegel replied that a hero is somebody who artistically embodies the unity of individuality and universality in mythical or violent times.

Hegel's lengthiest deliberations on the hero are to be found in his *Lectures on Esthetics*, and there is a good reason for this. The aesthetic context provides a first layer of definition: heroes are located within art. It is art that primarily shapes heroes. This means that not only do we receive our knowledge about heroes solely from art, namely, from the ancient epos and from tragedy, but also that art (and here Hegel means the art of the ancient Greeks) and heroism formally agree in their realization of the unity of individuality and universality in "immediacy." For art this means: in the sensorial and the vivid, not—as in religion—in "conception" or—as in philosophy—in "thought." For the hero this means: in the "character" and the "mood." Just as an individual work of art presents an example of something universal, the hero *embodies* universality as an individual. And he embodies it predominantly as a *founder of laws and states*. Greek heroes are to be found in a "prelegal" or "mythical" epoch and often become "founders of states, so that right and order, law and morals come from them."[1]

The paradox of the original or founding political act, which Lyotard and Derrida have hair-splittingly dissected in postmodern times using the constitutions of modern states such as France and the United States, and which essentially consists in a founding of right on wrong, of legality on despotism, while simultaneously shrouding the proceedings in mystery, is also recognized by Hegel. He does not deny the voluntaristic, violent, unlawful character of the founding deed of heroes. But as a historical philosopher, a philosophical idealist, and a dialectic thinker, he views this deed merely as a first, founding act that has yet to prove itself as a true act of foundation.[2] The wrong of the archaic heroic deed is, like every wrong for Hegel, a necessary step in the development of the concept of right, which, like every development for Hegel, follows the principle of definite negation. The concept of right is defined in each case by negation of the corresponding wrong, in other words by the negation of the negation of the right, so that the latter reaches from its initial "being-in-itself" validity (that is, a validity merely set by the heroic deed) to "real" validity, that is, a validity achieving realization in the course of a process. Something is real if it can be preserved throughout its negation, and for Hegel this is also precisely what is reasonable, as fundamentally illustrated by the principle of subjectivity: the ego that knows itself to be an ego negates its simple, undivided unity and preserves itself (keeps and receives itself) truly as twofold, equating an "I" with an "I." Anyone saying "I" is already doubled; he is actually saying "I" twice.

Nevertheless, Hegel's definition of the hero does not depend deductively on his principle of subject-based philosophy. This, in turn, is not reduced to a philosophical reformulation of the central figure of Christian theological thought.[3] Something being itself and at the same time its own opposite, a "speculative basic figure" of a unity that splits itself in two and, in splitting, closes itself itself, unmistakably calls to mind the teachings of Christianity, according to which the universe assumes its validity as a *creatio ex nihilo*, as a creation from within itself, as a self-divestment of God that progresses to self-alienation through incarnation, the appearance of God's son in human form, while through the Holy Ghost remaining preserved within the divine unity. But the ego, which in order to identify itself as the ego has to be able to detach itself from itself, can also be removed from this speculative background and reformulated, at least partly, in nonmetaphysical conditions. The social psychology of George Herbert Mead represents one such condition, as does, with certain restrictions, the linguistic pragmatism of Jürgen Habermas. Yet Hegel's central thought can also be expressed with sober validity in terms of current philosophy, independently of these reformulations: "'True' is only what is not afraid of tackling actively that which is different from itself; only what speaks in order to reap contradiction; only what acts in order to have its words measured according to that action."[4]

Hegel's definition of the hero is not unequivocally linked to the premise of subject-based philosophy, and this becomes particularly clear from his historical analysis of the conditions and limitations of heroism. Hegel contrasts monolithically the prelaw or mythical epoch with the *bourgeois* or *modern* age. All individual definitions are classified according to this major division.

The Hero and the Bourgeoisie

A hero shoulders a universal burden single-handedly, whereas a member of the bourgeoisie distributes the load among his own kind. In so doing he unburdens himself in several respects, but he also makes himself dependent, relinquishing the autonomy that characterizes the hero. He does not do this voluntarily: the very society he has struggled to create forces him to assume this anti-heroic status. Hegel was the first witness to this ambiguous example of progress and remains the best. The "subordinate position" of the subject within bourgeois society and its chosen form of government is illustrated in the way that an individual subject is assigned "only an entirely specific and always restricted share in the whole," in the way that sociopolitical activity is "like activity in business, trade etc. in civil society subdivided in the most varied possible way." The punishment of a criminal, for example, is "no longer a matter of individual heroism and the virtue of a single person," Hegel explains, but divided up on several levels: investigation of the circumstances by the police, a verdict in court, and then execution of the sentence.[5] Bourgeois society and the modern state are characterized by their division of labor, responsibility, and power.

A state *under the rule of law* imposes the validity of a law and order that is autonomous, "being-for-itself," removed from the randomness of the individual, even if the individual does not wish it and opposes it in an injurious manner. Law and order entails a "compulsion," either simply to submit to it or to freely recognize its validity. Anyone violating a law, regardless of who he is, will feel the punishment, and this is precisely what demonstrates its universal validity or "public authority." In their actions individuals, therefore, provide "mere examples" of universality. They simply apply existing laws and do not, as the ancient heroes did, turn a single "case" into a law through their own action. Their actions have only an applicative and not an exemplary validity and are thus, "compared with the whole, insignificant."[6]

Hegel does not fail to point out the antidespotic political consequences of the significance of constitutionally pruned individuals. This significance also extends to those areas within the bourgeois constitutional state that stake claim to a special status deduced from tradition: the monarchy, the civil service, and the army.[7] In the bourgeois constitutional state, right and wrong, welfare and poverty, war and peace are not dependent on the random peculiarities of any one individual. Quite the reverse is true, in fact. Those with ruling powers, whether monarchic, administrative, or military, are not beyond the boundaries of the law.

Against this background the differences between heroes and the bourgeoisie gradually become apparent.

Since a hero is not familiar with a social division of labor, competence, and power, he is "undividedly" responsible for the consequences of his actions. In legal terms, he knows no mitigating circumstances, instead shouldering "the entirety" of an action and, like Oedipus, repudiates any division of guilt."[8] To a constitutional court, however, equally familiar with the differentiation between (good) intention and (converse) realization as it is with the need to take special situations into account, someone like Oedipus would come across as either a fundamental consequentialist with rigorous principles, or as a pathological case.

In a society that is not organized according to a division of labor, standing up entirely for one's own actions also means that the deeds of individuals are woven into the "substantial," the unquestioned supporting whole. Such a society does not know the differentiation between person and clan, or person and family, and the "guilt of the ancestor descends to his posterity, and a whole generation suffers of the original criminal."[9] Individuals are thus subject to a common fate; life appears to obey conditions that they themselves can neither influence nor dispel.

The guilt that the hero assumes is atoned either through fate as an anonymous consequence or through the "revenge" of another, who in turn becomes a hero. The revenge may be just, but it is based purely on the convictions and decisions of an individual placing himself "at the head of the real world" and thus establishing the direction reality is to take. The bourgeois constitutional state, by contrast, is founded on "organs of the public authority" and "universal norms." Here, persons, public prosecutors, judges, and enforcement officers are "incidental," exchangeable. Here, there is no revenge, just "punishment."[10]

As an insoluble part of an all-permeating whole, the hero is the stuff of mythology, whereas the bourgeoisie perceives him as a case for psychoanalysis. Hegel does not feel entirely comfortable with this perception, one of "valets" who on top of everything else give themselves airs as "schoolmasters." "No man is a hero to his valet." This proverb rings true for Hegel, with the valet becoming acquainted with the hero at close proximity and thus from his (all too) human side. He "takes off his boots, assists him to bed, knows that he prefers champagne etc." He sees him as a "private person," as a person who does what others do, he must "eat and drink," sustain "relations to friends and acquaintances," have "passing impulses." To the bourgeoisie, heroic deeds thus appear to be driven by private passions, the conquering of whole continents to be the effect of a desire to conquer, the victory over a powerful enemy to be the effect of a desire to be famous, and so on. Hegel appreciatively derides the reductionist logic of such "psychological valets."[11] His critical insight regarding myths and heroes remains untouched: myths and heroes are ruined by psychology. The deeper analysis goes, the more details are known about them, and the less fascinating they become.

The hero clutches to the law, is a man (or woman) of deeds (not only Hercules but also Electra; not only Achilles but also Antigone). The hero is not a man of words, which really means not of mere words, of words to no end. For what characterizes "the status of heroes in world history overall" can also be true of intellectuals: "through them new worlds open up." Socrates is proof of this. The new world that he opened up, the new "principle" that he introduced, was "subjective reflection," colliding with another, much older principle of the Greek world, namely, a close connection between religion and the state.[12]

A hero is not only someone who aids the breakthrough of a new world, a new form of living and thinking, but also someone who does so in irreconcilable and hopeless confrontation with the old world, prepared to defend his views to the death. The *art form* that corresponds to this characteristic is *tragedy*. It is geared toward precisely this form of confrontation. In addition to the epos, tragedy is therefore for Hegel the ideal place for heroism to unfold; notwithstanding the tragedies that occur in reality. Socrates's own fate was "genuinely tragic," according to Hegel. As a structural rather than an aesthetic principle, tragedy means that "one right emerges beside another," not so that "one is right and one is wrong, but so that both are right." For Hegel the solution lies in a dialectic of the victim, whereby the individual appearing for a new and universally valid principle does have to recompense this with his own death, it is true, but the principle, and thus the universal, becomes successfully established. Heroes "individually find their doom," but their principle "penetrates, albeit in another guise, undermining that which existed previously."[13]

The tragic aspect of this, however, is not only the bald truth that an individual sacrifices himself for the sake of the universal, but also that the universal does not reward him for his heroic deed. At the very moment at which the universal asserts itself, the individual who has fought for this all the way to his own sacrificial death ceases to be necessary. After he has achieved what he "had to achieve" out of subjective and objective, internal and historical philosophical necessity, "he has in the process rendered himself superfluous."[14] Heroes only seemingly die at the hands of their enemies; it is far truer to say that through their glorious deeds they do away with themselves. The progress they are serving, according to Hegel, ploughs on without them. They are secret agents of their own abolition.

For Hegel there are tragedies in real life because there are heroes in real life. Conspicuously there are not many of them in his opinion; in fact, there are essentially just four. Hegel is forever listing them: Socrates, Alexander the Great, Caesar, and Napoleon. This sparse number is an indication of his conviction that the ancestral home of heroes is tragedy, more generally art, and more specifically ancient Greek art.

This viewing of art, the Greek art of tragedy (and epos), as the ideal location for heroes consequently means that tragedy (and epos) becomes dislocated, the further it distances itself from the heroic-mythical age. Shakespeare, Cervantes, Goethe, and Schiller are all evidence of this in Hegel's eyes. In the bourgeois epoch tragedies are still possible, but, as Hegel demonstrates with *Iphigenia* and *Tasso*, they constitute more a reconciliation than an irreconcilable conflict. In particular, they focus on the modern "principle of subjectivity" to a much "higher degree" than their ancient Greek role models. In their ancient Greek form, and this means in their "most magnificent and satisfying" form—with *Antigone* a part representing the whole—tragedies cannot survive.[15]

Hegel further attributes the heroic independence, the autonomy directly and exemplarily embodying the universal, not only to a particular age, but also to a particular *social class*, namely, that of the aristocracy. In ancient Greek tragedy, the heroes and heroines always come from royal families, due to the fact that these elevated social circles are able to maintain their "independence" regarding the "restriction by existing circumstances" and thus also the autonomy necessary for the performance of outstanding actions. The "lower classes," by contrast, are better suited to comedies and comic interludes. "For, in comedy, individuals have the right to spread themselves however they wish and can." They are permitted to "claim an independence" that is then once again "annihilated by themselves and by their inner and outer dependence."[16] This is further clarification of why old-style tragedy can no longer be appropriate to our new, modern age. The economic surpassing and political disempowering of the nobility through the bourgeoisie has been concomitant in both areas, that is, economics and politics, with the establishment of that systematic mutual dependency that Hegel was the first to analyze in such detail. Caught up within this system, bourgeois civilians do not have the makings of heroes.

In nonmythical times and in the real life existing beyond art, in the "prosaic" conditions of bourgeois society dominated by a "father's care of his household, and his honesty, the ideals of decent men and good women,"[17] the hero can for Hegel still appear in three different guises, however: in conventional times as a philosopher, and in unconventional ones as a warrior or as a revolutionary.

Hegel celebrates Socrates and also Descartes as heroes of the spirit, as heroic intellectuals addressing the problem of a new beginning, a fundamentally new foundation of the world, opening it up, and therefore appearing to their contemporaries as violent, destructive, even hostile men. Heroes are men of deeds, but deeds can also be perpetrated from the desks of intellectuals, known somewhat disparagingly as "desk perpetrators."

Bellicose or revolutionary heroism is different. It tears the bourgeoisie out of its peaceful and complacent night-watchman existence in order to test its true strength. "The evil and the bad, war, battles, revenge," "barbarity and savagery," as well as the "security of life and property" may be primarily rooted in the epoch of myths, but they can reemerge in "historical" periods, that is when "bonds of law and order are relaxed or broken" and individuals "acquire again the required independence and self-reliance."[18] War gives heroism a fresh chance. The "laws" are different from those presiding in times of peace. War especially overcomes particular, self-involved, complacent, "ossified" individualism. According to a passage by Hegel, blatantly disrespectful and strong in metaphor, "in peace, the bounds of civil life are extended, all its spheres become firmly established, and in the long run people become stuck in their ways. Their particular characteristics become increasingly rigid and ossified." War, by contrast, "stirs up" the lethargic political community of the bourgeoisie by testing its ideals. It is then no longer a case of fighting for one's own property and one's own limited interests, but of relativizing them, of seeing them in relation to something else—namely, death—as what they really are: merely finite interests.[19]

Another opportunity for autonomous and arbitrary action in bourgeois times is presented by revolution, albeit in a self-exposing manner. In the famous chapter of his *Phenomenology of Spirit* "Absolute Freedom and Terror," in which he analyzes the French Revolution, Hegel provides evidence for his theory that individual insistence on social effectiveness may be in keeping with the modern and thus unstoppable consciousness of freedom demonstrated by the revolutions of 1688 in England, 1776 in the United States of America, and 1789 in France, but that this immediate, direct path does not lead to a unification of the individual with the general public. Far more, individual freedom that has become universal sweeps forth its terrorist horror. The horror of *terreur* is an admission that even in revolutionary times it is ultimately true that an individual can no longer be the law.

"I Am the Law": *Red River*

When Tom Dunson has made up his mind to do something, nothing can change it. He is a man who knows what he wants, and his will is his strength, although it will also be his downfall. In 1851 he heads west as part of a convoy of wagons. But he soon goes his own way with his old partner Groot, having noticed that there is good pastureland in the area on which to breed cattle. He makes this decision even though it makes him easy prey for the Indians who have been observing the convoy for days. And he makes it even though it means separation from the woman he loves. In order to bridge their time apart, he performs a symbolic act that will be of repeated significance in the further course of events and that will form a link between all the crucial characters. As a sign of their mutual bond he gives her a bangle that is all the more significant for having once belonged to his mother. That evening, having just arrived at Red River, Dunson and Groot see dark billows of smoke in the distance and know that the Indians have attacked the procession of wagons. Dunson can only be sure that the woman has died, however, when a little while later he himself is attacked by a small group of Indians and discovers that one of them is wearing the bangle on his arm. He kills him in a one-on-one fight, then takes back the bangle without a single word. What began so promisingly has ended all too suddenly. The circle of people who have worn the bangle has, at least temporarily, come to a close. It was supposed to signify future life, but it has brought only death.

This strand of the action has only just been completed when a new one starts. One way or another, future life has entered after all. Following a lost cow, a boy of about fourteen years has survived the attack, and this first encounter between him and Dunson establishes a basic pattern for what is to come. He is young and therefore inexperienced, but he is not afraid of facing the older man who is (still) his superior in both physical strength and cunning. This confidence is partly due to his skill at using a shotgun. When Dunson gives the confused boy a short, sharp slap to bring him back to his senses after the recent traumatic events, the boy is amazingly quick to pull his revolver from its holster. Dunson can only save the situation by pretending to surrender before knocking the boy over. "Don't trust anyone you don't know" is the first lesson that the boy, called Matthew, or Matt for short, learns from his new father.

Dunson is to become, as we learn later, an almost overpowering father figure to Matt. He is building up his cattle empire and takes the land spread out before him by force from a rich Mexican, just as the Mexican once took it by force from the Indians. Fourteen years of fighting for this land have made him hard and embittered. The Civil War is finally over; Matt, who now wears the bangle, is back home, but the South has become poor, and Tom Dunson will be bankrupt if he does not somehow manage to sell his herd. He decides to drive it to a place where there will be a demand for it, northward to Missouri. (The Western hero is usually from the South, a victim, through whom the United States attempts to find self-reconciliation, self-unification.[20]) Historically, in 1865 after the end of the Civil War, the large slaughterhouses in Chicago resumed their work in order to deliver meat to the cities in the East. Until the railway network had been extended west and south, Kansas City, with its major freight station, was the first port of call for cattle herds. In the same year, a rancher also drove his herd from Texas to Kansas City, on a route subsequently named after him: the "Chisholm Trail."[21] This cattle drive provides the real-life background for the story related by Howard Hawks and scriptwriter Bordon Chase in *Red River* (1948). Tom Dunson is played by John Wayne, the role providing him with a first chance to build up the figure of mythical dimensions with which he later came to be identified. Unlike John Ford, however, Hawks is a major realist and, in particular, a humorist. He even derives pleasure from repeatedly thwarting the myth before ultimately dismantling it just for fun.

Dunson rules over his people with dictatorial severity. During the cattle drive, as this despotic structure is increasingly reinforced, the characters face ever-larger tribulations, the hardworking cowboys complain more and more loudly, the danger that Dunson will fail becomes greater and greater. Hawks portrays the everyday reality of a cattle drive with almost as much attention to detail as a documentary. The first major incident occurs after thirty days, when one of the cowboys carelessly triggers a stampede. Like a little boy (with a highly symbolic sexual gesture, using a moistened and extended middle finger), he cannot refrain from trying the sugar kept in one of the food wagons. In the process he knocks over some tin cans, which in turn is enough to make the already nervous cattle herd panic. One of the cowboys and several hundred animals die. Dunson wishes to punish the culprit by whipping him, and as the latter reaches for his revolver to defend himself, it is clear that he would have had no chance against Dunson, the faster to the holster, were it not for Matt, who shoots the revolver out of Dunson's hand, thus averting certain death. With this form of punishment—whipping and, on resistance, shooting—Dunson has gone one step too far.

After sixty days, with the cowboys as tired as the cattle, their mood is bordering on mutinous. Three men attempt to rebel, block Dunson's path, and are shot. The "have a burial and read from the Bible" ritual repeats itself. When later three more men creep off, are brought back, and are to be punished by hanging on Dunson's orders, there is an altercation. By now Dunson has assumed the persona of a madman increasingly under the delusion of being surrounded by enemies in his own camp. It is clear from the outset that he wishes to make an example of the three cowboys, sweeping aside hesitant objections on legal grounds with the autocratic and telling comment: "I am the law." When he announces that he will not shoot the delinquents in line with the Westerners' code of honor, but hang them instead, this is the final straw. It is Matt who resists, calmly yet firmly, with a simple "no." (Foster) father and son turn to face each other, but before the crucial duel can begin another man intervenes. His name is Cherry, and throughout the proceedings he has been acknowledged as the third good and fast shot within the group. He shoots Dunson in the right hand, rendering him unable to fight. The transfer of power is perfect. Matt takes charge and drives the herd to Abilene, a closer and more easily reachable location that also has a freight station. But before Matt can depart, Dunson swears that he will pursue him relentlessly and kill him. His logic is that of a manic fixation: anybody destroying his life's work will in turn be destroyed. With his legs far apart and limping, his body and soul injured, he is left behind like an evil spirit. And now, if not before, another great monomaniac figure of the Western, and in particular American culture is called powerfully to mind. Just as Ethan Edwards from *The Searchers* is similar in his obsession and inner despair to Captain Ahab in Melville's famous novel, so too is Tom Dunson a "Captain Ahab of the billowing prairie," indeed this whole film of John Ford's has even been called "the *Moby Dick* of the Western genre": "Ahab has crossed the seas of the desert, the prairies, the mountain ranges, has killed his whale and goes down with it. He sinks into the land whose buffalo he has shot, whose people he has massacred, whose earth he has attacked with knives, with bullets, with his fists."[22] Ahab, Ethan Edwards, and Tom Dunson are all "American heroes" who know the difference brought about by the Declaration of Independence, who know that only those who say "No" are free, and who thus say, "Yes, we will go to Hell if we have to."[23]

The showdown takes place in Abilene. With the fear of revenge a constant companion, the cowboys feel unsettled by the evil spirit they have left behind, and now the time has come. Matt has sold his entire herd. When Dunson arrives a day later, things move fast. Cherry, who once again blocks his path, manages to injure him but in the process is seriously wounded. Matt does what everybody expects him to do: he refuses to react to Dunson's increasingly furious demands that he draw his gun, instead arousing the impression of being a "pushover." Dunson, however, is incapable of shooting him in cold blood. They do what unarmed men are wont to do; they attack each other with their bare fists. At this point it is already clear, as old Groot mumbles cheerfully, that "it will all be alright." The son finally proves himself to be the man he is supposed to be in the eyes of his father, one who is not "too soft-hearted." Only now does he really grow up. *Red River* is a prime example of the great socializational task continually celebrated in Westerns: furthering the law of masculinity or, in psychoanalytical terms, passing on the scepter of masculine connotation. The imperious exclamation 'I am the law' is taken by Hegelians to be expression of a mythical world of sociality, whereas the followers ("sons") of Freud, for example Lacan, see it as a brazen epigraph to the father figure. In the midst of their battle, father and son run into a wagon full of pots and pans that then come crashing to the ground, burying the two men. A shot is suddenly heard, and the showdown, which according to the principles of the genre really demands a death, transforms definitively into a reconciliation.

The woman has her ultimate performance. Faithful to the bourgeois tradition installed since the nineteenth century, it is she who represents a civilizing, that is, nonviolent (albeit asserted through the violence of her gun) and humorous power. Once again the clashing of pots and pans is a signal, this time not for a herd of cattle to stampede, but for the dawn of dominance by the head of the kitchen; not for an outburst of untamed wildness, but for the pacifying effect of communicative culture. This resolute and handsome example of the female sex became acquainted with Matt a few days previously when he and his men came to the aid of the group she was trekking with when they encountered some Indians. She is the latest to have received the bangle that Tom Dunson gave his sweetheart so many years earlier. And now she reads the riot act to these two men with all the charm of a fury. Verbally adept, she makes the two men aware of just how ridiculous their behavior is, and they sit in front of her on the ground like two tousled schoolboys who have been called to order for scrimmaging. Matt will marry this woman, and the brand mark borne by the cattle will be extended to include his initial. "You have earned it." With this utterance of bourgeois spirit the old patriarch gives his blessing to his foster son before exhilarating music brings the movie to its emphatic close.

The conciliatory conclusion to the story is thus brought about by the woman. But it is also alluded to more than once beforehand in minor gestures, for example, when father and son occasionally share a cigarette, thus smoking a little peace pipe of kinds, or when they give us to understand through the same (symbolically sexual) mannerism that they share the same roots: a brief and pensive rubbing of the nose with the index finger. Matt ultimately embodies the new generation, a new principle gradually acquiring validity. He counters a law arbitrarily enforced by Dunson with a law prohibitive of lynch-law; he counters patriarchal power with the morality of a human dignity that does not require the whip as a means of instruction; he counters a ceaseless conviction in the correctness of one's own deeds with an attitude that leaves room for problems, deliberates and understands, permits the existence of anxiety. With a woman by his side, Matt embodies a bourgeois society that is acquitting itself of the patriarchally influenced, American vestiges of European feudalism.

Hegel and the Western

When Hegel was giving his lectures on aesthetics in Berlin in the 1820s, the Western did not yet exist in its literary form, the dime-store novel. The early novels by James Fenimore Cooper, appearing at the same time, were the only herald of what was to emerge a hundred years later.

There were, of course, already adventure stories long before Hegel's time. They followed on from tales of knights being put to the test, like the saga of King Arthur, and developed their own style in works such as *Don Quixote* (1605, 1615), *Simplicius Simplicissimus* (1669), *Robinson Crusoe* (1719), and *Wilhelm Meister's Apprenticeship* (1795/96). Hegel analyzed "adventurousness" within the context of the "romantic form of art," an epochal arc spanning from the Middle Ages to his own day. Coincidence rules the world of adventurousness; in it nothing happens with the necessity that drives tragedy, for example, onward. Honor, love, and fidelity, the weighty duties of knighthood, are here completely profaned and for this reason appear in a comical light, through the contextual shift.

In one of the most beautiful passages from his *Lectures on Aesthetics*, Hegel provides a concentrated version of this view of the world. This passage requires citation in extenso in order to convey the way in which the vulgar form of "gay science" (a type of thinking that makes one laugh) is not reserved for nonidealists. It is the worldly wise bourgeois individual speaking, with a cheerful/humorous or derisive/cynical turn of phrase:

Young people especially are these modern knights who must force their way through the course of the world which realizes itself instead of their ideals, and they regard it as a misfortune that there is any family, civil society, state, laws, professional business, etc., . . . Now the thing is to breach this order of things, to change the world, to improve it, or at least in spite of it to carve out of it a heaven on earth: to seek for the ideal girl, find her, win her away from her wicked relations or other discordant ties, and carry her off in defiance. But in the modern world these fights are nothing more than the "apprenticeship," the education of the individual into the realities of the present. . . . For the end of such apprenticeship consists in this, that the subject sows his wild oats, builds himself with his wishes and opinions into harmony with subsisting relationships and their rationality. . . . However much he may have quarreled with the world, or been pushed about in it, in most cases at last he gets his girl and some sort of position, marries her, and becomes as good a Philistine as others. The woman takes charge of household management, children arrive, the adored wife, at first unique, an angel, behaves pretty much as all other wives do; the man's profession provides work and vexations, marriage brings domestic affiliation—so here we have all the headaches of the rest of married folk.[24]

Regarding the hero, adventure stories are obviously no match for Westerns. An individual cannot appear in an adventure story and say what he *has to* say in a Western: "I am the law." The Western delivers a genre in which the heroic figure as described by Hegel can celebrate its modern resurrection. If Hegel had had access to the Western, he probably would have been astonished to discover so much premodernity within modernity. By contrast, he probably would not have been astonished by the historical context in which the stories are set, a culture located at the frontier of civilization. The Western is thus a curious genre that transcends prominent timelines, a premodern-modern mixed bag that, in the opinion of modern theoreticists, especially those inspired by Hegel, is worthy of closer attention. It is, therefore, all the more perplexing that philosophy, and a theory of culture instructed by it, has closed its eyes to it to date. (The only notable German exception I am aware of is hidden within a commentary.[25]) There is, then, no time to waste: the Western must become a theme for philosophy.

The End of the Individual

Of Bourgeoisie and Heroism

Hegel was not alone in his insight that the bourgeois do not have what it takes to be heroes. It vexed the entire nineteenth century and is still virulent today, as can be clarified by an exposition of cultural, art, and ideological history.

Like Hegel, the conversational dictionaries of the early nineteenth century negate the compatibility of bourgeoisie and heroism. There is no entry to be found under *Held*, while the entry for "heroes" contains a reference to Homer and "men of ancient times." At the beginning of the nineteenth century (in 1807), in keeping with a romantic glorification of the Middle Ages, the *Nibelungen* saga was translated into New High German. One year after the defeat of Prussia on the battlefields of Jena and Auerstedt (Hegel had just managed to complete his *Phenomenology of the Spirit* under great pressure, both financial and regarding the deadline; he also came to admire Napoleon, the *Weltgeist*, riding past him on horseback, before French troops ransacked his Jena apartment) the medieval saga was well suited to dreams of resurrecting the German nation.[1]

First, though, was to come the Biedermeier period, it too drawing on the physically small but historically huge French emperor in order to establish a figure capable of opposing the new pervading mediocrity. In *Napoleon or the Hundred Days* (1831), Christian Grabbe, the most prominent dramatist of the clamorous young Germany alongside Georg Buechner, has his main figure say: "I am me, that is Napoleon Bonaparte, who created himself in two years." Napoleon figures here in his ambivalence, in his rise *and* his fall, as a representation of the historically insignificant ego of the Biedermeier period.[2] In the case of Julien Sorel, the "hero" in Stendhal's novel *The Red and the Black* (1830), his heart also races at the thought of Napoleon. No less hypocritical than the bourgeoisie he despises, yet driven by a strong will and passion, Sorel tries to become his idol's successor, consistently turning everything into a battle, even love. Bad news regarding the hero's chances of survival in the nineteenth century also reaches Europe from the "New World." Tocqueville, for example, a legally trained administrative specialist and moralistic analyst of society, wrote in his famous book *Democracy in America* (1835) of the small and conventional pleasures ("petits et vulgaires plaisirs") with which people in the democratic age seem to be satisfied.[3]

However, the most ardent manifestations of this phenomenon were in Great Britain. In 1840s Scotland, Thomas Carlyle gave incendiary speeches *On Heroes, Hero-Worship, and the Heroic in History* that were to appear in print in both British and American English throughout the century and to be translated into nearly all the European languages. Carlyle was a decided advocate of the historiographic maxim "history is made by great men." His line of great men spanned from the earliest historical origins—beginning with the Germanic god Odin—through the age of prophets (Mohammed), poets (Dante, Shakespeare), and priests (Luther, John Knox) to that of writers (Samuel Johnson, Rousseau, Robert Burns) and kings (Cromwell and Napoleon). The hero is only reactualizable in the shape of the royal ruler and writer, whom Carlyle imagines in line with the romantic conception of the genius or the Platonic conception of the philosopher king. As much as Carlyle eloquently bemoans the eighteenth-century assertion of *triviality, formulism,* and *commonplace,* on the one hand, so too, on the other, does he manage to reconcile the bourgeois with the heroic ideal, perceiving a *function* fulfilled in writing that is *ever the highest* and celebrating writing and printing as the equivalent of democracy ("invent writing, democracy is inevitable").[4]

In Marx, Carlyle is confronted with a no less eloquent theoretist, but one unequaled in his systematic thinking. History is so much a product in his eyes that he uses the sharp quill of the theater critic and interprets it as *theatrum mundi*, a concept familiar since Plato but only popular since early modernity. He backs it up with German idealism, employing the metaphor of stage management and thus discarding determination for the notion of freedom. His famous work *The Eighteenth Brumaire of Louis Bonaparte* from 1851/52 includes Hegel's comment that all great historic facts and personages appear twice, but adds bitingly: "the first time as tragedy, the second as farce." Marx has two coups d'état in mind, that of Napoleon on the eighteenth Brumaire of year VIII in the French Republican calendar, corresponding to November 9, 1799, in our calendar, and that of Louis Bonaparte on December 2, 1851. In both events the awakening of past times and dead heroes plays a key role, but the purpose is a different one in each case. In the one, something new is to be asserted; in the other, it is to be prevented. Therefore only one situation, the tragic one, sees heroes performing. They die for a better future, sacrificing themselves in the name of their ideals. But they do not execute their deeds without first securing support from the past. Danton, Robespierre, Napoleon, as well as other "bourgeois gladiators," found "in the austere classical traditions of the Roman Republic the ideals and the art forms, the self-deceptions, that they needed to conceal from themselves the bourgeois-limited content of their struggles." From the point of view of a radical critic of bourgeois society, the heroism of modernity is already a theatrical act. Not only is bourgeois society "unheroic," and not only did it "nevertheless need heroism, sacrifice, terror, civil war and national wars to bring it into being,"[5] but from the dramaturgic point of view of the socialist revolutionary of the future, the heroism itself amounts to pure theatricals.

For the bourgeoisie, so firmly allied to the present, an almost hysterical confirmation of the heroic image then becomes all the more necessary. The second half of the nineteenth century saw an increase in the need for heroes and a simultaneous change in their image. In his Basle lectures of the late 1860s, still influenced by Hegel, Jacob Burckhardt spoke of the "great man" as one who manages to bring about a coincidence of individuality and universality. Nietzsche, a member of the audience and only just appointed to the same university as a young academic, was impressed. Burckhardt's ideas were not just a continuation of the Hegelian conception, but also, like Carlyle inspired by Fichte, of the romantic concept of genius. The latter ultimately triumphed in the artist who led the apotheosis of art to its climax: Richard Wagner. Siegfried the invincible, forging a new sword from broken remnants, was for Wagner the ultimate incarnation of the artist or, turned on its head, the hero in keeping with the times. In the light of this identification it was easy for Adorno—far more practiced in Hegelian and Marxian theory than Benjamin, and also inspired by Nietzsche's later writing—to reveal the conservative bourgeois within the artist hero, and in addition to confront him with his overbearing need for redemption.[6]

Finally, a further contribution to this "popularization of the hero cult" was the Walhalla Hall of Fame and Honor for German heroes, built by Bavarian King Ludwig I in the years 1830–42, as well as "the immense increase in individual monuments on public ground." Whereas only eighteen such statues existed in Germany in 1800, by 1883 there were eight hundred. Following the death of Wilhelm I in 1888, this trend was further reinforced: "Three to four hundred monuments in honor of the first Emperor of Germany and King of Prussia were erected, initiated, and financed by political districts and municipalities, county and other associations before 1914. Since the mid-1890s—Bismarck died in 1898—more than seven hundred Bismarck monuments have been added to this number, posthumously honoring the Prussian statesman and founder of the Prussian Empire as a national hero."[7]

By the late 1800s the connection between hero and fatherland or nation was close to perfect, at least in Germany. Whereas at the beginning of the century, influenced by romanticism and culminating in Wagner, the artist was the chosen figuration of the hero, by the end of the century it was the warrior. In the 1920s, however, the figure of the hero gained its most perfect expression as a warrior, becoming self-referential despite the retained declamation of a national community or a community of class. In the words of Ernst Juenger, conflict and war appeared as an "internal experience," as a way of life that made sense in its own right. The warrior hero declared war definitively on the bourgeoisie. For, according to Juenger, the warrior amounted to one of the "genuine, true and unrelenting enemies of the bourgeoisie."[8] The former hated the latter's mercantilism, its materialism so fixated on possessions, its saturatedness, its averageness, its philistine attitude toward education, its sentimentalization of morality with its hollow humanism, its moderate comprehension of politics exhausting itself in endless discussions. But in so doing he hated the side of himself that had split away. Psychoanalysis, the root of this insight, is certainly not a universal method by which to interpret historically very different epochs. But for the nineteenth century, that "long century from Napoleon to the First World War" and that is almost universally identified with the bourgeois,[9] it nevertheless has validity as a valuable and fruitful, maybe even adequate, historical and sociopsychological method. It is the men and women of this century whom Freud subjected to analysis and then stylized as an anthropological, not a historic-psychological, type. Psychoanalysis can therefore provide at least an informative heuristic aid for exploring the nineteenth century. The fundamental conflict, indeed war, taking place between nature and nurture within every single individual, can then, as demonstrated by Peter Gay, be transported to a basic form of bourgeois experience, the strength and weakness of which lies not only in general terms but also in terms of psychoanalysis, in compromise, in the maintaining of a balance between extremes. Against this background it is therefore true to say that the bourgeoisie, with Ernst Juenger as its spokesman, instigated a rebellion against itself, the great rebellion of the twentieth century. The bourgeoisie waged war against itself, essentially a civil war, at the end of which it extinguished both itself and the hero in one fell swoop.

At the end of this process are the totalitarian forms of state and society. They carry to extremes a development that could ironically be termed the "democratization" of heroism. With military service, obligatory for all males since the beginning of the nineteenth century, and the consequent war of an entire people or nation, not only generals and famous commanders are considered worthy of remembrance, but so too is every single man who has sacrificed his life in the name of the fatherland. Anonymous heroes conquer the artistic battlefield, for example in paintings by Géricault or Delacroix, as well as in the frequently anonymous, but far more widespread, printed graphics. It is telling that the idea of erecting monuments to so-called unknown soldiers was born around 1800. After 1871 the war associations and their many members upheld this tradition, boasting countless war memorials listing by name all the so-called fallen. The number of these soldiers increased. Whereas in the Battle of Leipzig in 1813 approximately ninety thousand soldiers were killed, and in the Battle of Sedan in 1870 approximately twenty-four thousand soldiers, in 1918 Germany recorded a total of 1.8 million.[10] National Socialism and the Second World War surpassed this figure afresh, ultimately leading to the dissolution of the heroic status altogether. By awarding the aureole of the heroic to all *Wehrmacht,* or SS soldiers, as well as to all "soldiers of labor" and even to the entire "ethnic community," the heroic lost its status. If everybody is a hero, there are no heroes. This logical or dialectic consequence also suffused the international socialist workers' movement and the "real socialist" states within the Soviet model. According to its iconographic propaganda, millions of decent and energetic members of the party and trades unions were fighting hard to break down class barriers. When the "heroes of rebuilding" and the "heroes of labor" were proclaimed after the war, here too the award necessarily had to be lost in the potential mass of award winners. A democratized hero is fit only for satire. Stephen Frears's *Accidental Hero* (1992) is a wonderful example of this.

Bourgeois Society

The bourgeois battle with heroism has, then, to all intents and purposes been fought. The advance of one side, namely, bourgeois society, seems to have brought about the recession of the other side, namely, heroism. Incidentally, it should be noted that talk of bourgeois society, however firmly the term might have established itself, is precarious if exacting scientific standards are to be obeyed.[11] All sociologic and historiographic attempts to define the *bourgeoisie* have been less than satisfactory.

Taking class, social origins, income, and education alone, the nineteenth-century bourgeoisie was extremely heterogeneous, uniting the self-employed, civil servants, the privately employed, factory owners, bank managers, businessmen, physicians, and independent lawyers. The majority of them had no academic qualifications. In quantitative terms, the bourgeoisie in Europe around the middle of the nineteenth century only accounted for up to 13 percent of the population. Nevertheless, there was a definite internal cohesion and external distancing regarding cultural and social barriers. The first factor constituting the bourgeoisie was, accordingly, an early "upward" social barrier dividing it from the aristocracy and a later "downward" barrier dividing it from the "lowly people," the "simple folk," the "proletariat." The second constitutive factor was an ethos emphasizing values such as work and efficiency, family and privacy, education and virtuous behavior. These values have their roots in Christianity, early modernist tradition, and the Enlightenment, but in the western world were not to orbit the imaginary nucleus known as the "bourgeoisie" until the nineteenth century.

If what holds the bourgeoisie together is a common enemy, as well as a common culture, that is, a way of life, then all talk of a bourgeois society becomes increasingly unrealistic and unconvincing with the disappearance, or at least diminishing, of its social barriers and upheld values. *That* this is true is undisputed in the present sociologic and sociopsychologic discussion; the degree to which it is true is not.

Duel in Davos

Let us now return to the Hegelian perspective and look at the extent of its influence into the first half of the twentieth century.

After he has already related more than half the comings and goings in a sanatorium high above Davos, Thomas Mann introduces to the colorful selection of patients included in his novel *The Magic Mountain* an additional defining figure: "somebody else," as he is vaguely referred to in the title of the corresponding chapter. This somebody is Leo Naphta. He is never alone, always to be found in the company of Lodovico Settembrini, his indispensable debating partner. This inseparable duo is not, however, of one mind. Quite the opposite, in fact. In their philosophical, ethical, and political views the two men are diametrically opposed. Settembrini, a man of letters from Italy, is enthusiastic in his excitement at the ideals and optimism of the Enlightenment, excited by the mind, reason, science, truth, humanism, and republicanism. Naphta, by contrast, has converted to Catholicism from Judaism and become a Jesuit. He is full of contempt for Settembrini's ideals. In his opinion they are "nothing but useful and thus pitifully unheroic," characterizing a "shabby bourgeois existence."[12] In return, Settembrini accuses Naphta of presumptuous arrogance and a self-destructive orientation toward death as an ideal. These reproaches are, however, interchangeable. When Naphta negates the objectivity of truth, believing it instead to be dependent on personal interests, he himself advocates that notion of usefulness and subjectivity he is wont to castigate; Settembrini, like it or not, has his feet firmly on the objectivity side of the fence. Two characters thus come together who not only contradict each other, but who are also "in contradiction with themselves."[13] Together they represent a contradiction that is be found within every individual. It is the contradiction of modernism, fueled by the spirit of the Enlightenment and its progress.

The fact that Naphta and Settembrini seek a decision, a definitive clarification of their respective claims in a duel with pistols, is only right and proper in the existing historical circumstances. In the years directly prior to the First World War, the period in which Thomas Mann has these two men meet, the duel still possessed a strong attraction for male members of the so-called easily satisfiable noble and bourgeois societies. According to an hypothesis put forward by Ute Frevert, in the nineteenth and early twentieth centuries this was not "simply a remnant of the feudal epoch, a relict of old, pre-bourgeois conditions," but "adopted and embodied" by bourgeois society in its entirety, not only in Germany.[14] Historically and sociologically it is therefore the equivalent of the Wild West duel with revolvers, paralleling it chronologically, yet reserved for a different social type. Westerns often draw on this parallel, a notable example being William Wyler's *The Big Country*.

It has to come to a duel between Naphta and Settembrini. Their discussions are verbal arguments, heated debates, passionate battles. It is impossible to arrive at a synthesis from the contents of their fundamental antitheses. They stand for the irreconcilability, as well as the inextricability, of bourgeois ethical ideals and modernism. In this context the two protagonists attempt to make an internal contradiction external, like in John Ford's *The Searchers*, to divide between them a conflict raging within every individual. The solution of indulging in physical battle, a now-alien ideal, is marked by cowardice, however, as might be expected from intellectuals. The two duelists apparently have the courage to be shot at, but not to shoot each other; passive, not active courage. Settembrini shoots into the air, and then Naphta shoots himself.

As has often been noted by other authors, Thomas Mann lends mythical aspects to the figures in his novel, yet always with that familiar ironic edge. The last thing he intended was an epic narrative. The novel is actually closer to a fairy tale. It is particularly the circumstance of being past, as stated on the endpaper, that lends a story something of a fairy-tale aspect and gives its narrator the chance to "conjure it up in a murmuring." Even novels, provided they tell a story, have an unmistakeable "once upon a time" ring to them.

Incidentally, Leo Naphta, a sharp-tongued critic of the bourgeoisie, yet himself no less of an "unheroic hero" than Hans Castorp,[15] the simple main character in Thomas Mann's novel, has a role model. His name is Georg Lukács.

A Transcendental Lack of "*Heimat*"

Thomas Mann and Georg Lukács met in the year 1920. Lukács had been a member of the newly founded Hungarian Communist Party since December 1918 and People's Commissar for Education and Culture since March 1919, with the proclamation of the Hungarian Soviet Republic. But by the end of July, with Romanian-Czech troops occupying Budapest, the postwar communist experiment in Hungary was already at an end, and that autumn Lukács emigrated to Vienna, where he was immediately arrested. He was released at the end of the same year following a petition by Austrian and German writers that included the signature of Thomas Mann. Lukács's name and works had long been familiar to Mann, with his *The Theory of the Novel*, published in 1916, strongly influencing Mann's own narrative, especially in *The Magic Mountain*.[16]

The opening lines of *The Theory of the Novel* are now famous:

Happy are those ages when the starry sky is the map of all possible paths—ages whose paths are illuminated by the light of the stars. Everything in such ages is new and yet familiar, full of adventure and yet their own. The world is wide and yet it is like a home, for the fire that burns in the soul is of the same essential nature as the stars; the world and the self, the light and the fire, are sharply distinct, yet they never become permanent strangers to one another, for fire is the soul of all light and all fire clothes itself in light. Thus each action of the soul becomes meaningful and rounded in this duality: complete in meaning—in *sense*—and complete for the senses; rounded because the soul rests within itself even while it acts; rounded because its action separates itself from it and, having become itself, finds a centre of its own and draws a closed circumference round itself. "Phi-

losophy is really homesickness," says Novalis: "It is the urge to be at home every-
where." That is why philosophy, as a form of life or as that which determines the
form and supplies the content of literary creation, is always a symptom of the rift
between "inside" and "outside," a sign of the essential difference between the Self
and the world, the incongruence of soul and deed. That is why the happy ages
have no philosophy, or why (it comes to the same thing) all men in such ages are
philosophers.[17]

This passage echoes not only the basic tone but also the basic thesis of the
essay. It is a desperate tone and a plain thesis, both deeply romantic and
German-idealistic. What is romantic is its glorifying slant on the past, expressed in biblical language yet also emanating Friedrich Schlegel's essay
On the Study of Greek Poetry. Also romantic is the dramatic and sorrow-
ful undertone in its description of alienation, in particular its definition
of philosophy as homesickness, borrowed from Novalis, rather than the
Hegelian choice of *Heimat*. What Hegel accords practical activity is also
true of philosophy, the highest form of theoretical activity. It fulfills the
purpose of stripping "the external world of its inflexible foreignness" and
of enjoying "in the shape of things only an external realization" of the human being itself.[18] Whatever else it is to Hegel, philosophy is the field able
to give mankind a *Heimat*, albeit only a spiritual one, but nevertheless the
ultimate, true *Heimat*, for the absolute, that unity dispelling all contradiction between the Self and the non-Self (the other Self and the world), can
only be realized in the sphere of the "absolute spirit," in the sphere of art,
religion, and thought.

True to the pattern of historical philosophy, two forms of the "total culture" and correspondingly two forms of the "great epic" are contrasted here. At the level of the total culture, the contrasting opposites are
Homer's ancient Greece and the age of the "New World"; parallel to them,
at the level of the narrative, the opposites epic and novel are to be found.
The epoch that Homer epically passed down is a blissful one of complete
and rounded sense, philosophically characterized by Hegel's term "totality." Totality means completion in a quantitative as well as a qualitative
sense, completeness as well as perfection: everything is included within it,
nothing is excluded; each individual element achieves its own, appropriate purpose. The post-Homerian age, by contrast, oversteps the horizon
of a well-ordered and unquestionable way of life. The advantages and

disadvantages of this balance out well. The loss of a life carried by purpose, an existence in which the plausibility of things and facts is immediately evident, is countered by a gain in "spiritual productivity" and "shaping." The ancient Greek world is spared those (romantically dramatized) "bottomless depths" that plunge the subject into solitariness: "Kant's starry firmament now shines only in the dark night of pure cognition; it no longer lights any solitary wanderer's path (for to be a man in the new world is to be solitary)."[19] Kant's famous "resolution" at the end of his *Critique of Practical Reason*, in which he confesses "two things fill me with wonder, the starry sky above and the moral law within," is here the guiding image for Lukács's contrast between the great epochs of world history.

The aesthetic literary form of the epic is no longer suited to this new manner of experiencing the Self and the world; according to Lukács's specific hypothesis, only the novel is appropriate. In this, he once more fundamentally follows Hegel, who likewise categorized the novel as a literary form corresponding to "prosaic" modern bourgeois conditions. But now the novel becomes not only one, but *the* literary form appropriate to a new existential age lacking *Heimat*. "The novel form is, like no other, an expression of this transcendental homelessness."[20] In existential and metaphysical terms, human beings in the post-Homerian era culminating in modernity are all homeless. The starry sky of ethical values has cleared; it is no longer a firm and safe home from which to find orientation through life. Psychologically speaking, this fundamental historico-societal and metaphysical contradiction ultimately finds expression in the heroes of novels being "searchers." Searching suggests that "neither goals nor paths can be direct givens," that there can be no confidence in the truth being an unshakable certainty, in "contexts or ethical necessities being evidently cognizable as truly being." This also means that searchers are not immune to crime or madness. The "transition from crime to affirmed heroism, from madness to life-mastering wisdom, is fluid."[21]

Dialectic of Enlightenment

Lukács's conception of the epic in Hegelian and historical philosophical terms as the narration of a mythical world laden with meaning, and as the counterpart to the novel, gave rise nearly thirty years later, at the time of the Second World War, to a crucial contradiction: this interpretation was not Hegelian, not dialectic enough. The epic, once more referring predominantly to Homer's epic, especially his *Odyssey*, is the end product of organized reason, the result of an author's ability to order and shape, not the apparently self-organizing expression of a collective mentality known as *Volksgeist* (the spirit of a nation). But, on a renewed philosophical perusal of the epic, "novel-like features" emerge, especially in Odysseus, "the hero of adventures," whom Homer reports at the end of the eighth century BC as being the "archetypal" bourgeois individual. The very myth itself is Enlightenment, as is stated in correspondingly rough terms; the epic is like the novel, and vice versa, the novel is similar to the epic. The epic is testimony to the "Dialectic of Enlightenment."[22]

The book of the same name, written in American exile by Horkheimer and Adorno, was to become a constituent part of critical theory. By the end of the twentieth century it had almost become itself what it had declared the *Odyssey* to be: a fundamental text of European civilization. As stated at the beginning of its preface, the driving and tormenting motive behind it was no less than to find an answer to the question of why humanity—at the time more or less worldwide—was plunging into a new form of barbarism, most strikingly expressed in the brashness of fascism, yet hardly any less terrible in state socialism. As is also frankly admitted in the preface, this historic sociopolitical ascertainment is the background to a theory presenting itself in obstinate fragments as it increasingly calls into question the point of scientific theory. With a peculiarity that is unsurpassed, the *Dialectic of Enlightenment* thus combines philosophically befitting extensive theories with a style that is philosophically unbefitting, consciously attempting to balance out its deficits in deductive and analytical argumentation by employing rhetorical exaggeration. Yet this does not mean that it shies away from argumentation's obligations completely. Far more, it draws on major theories in order to condense them—in the colloquial, aesthetic, and psychoanalytical senses of the word—to their empirical material. The said theories are primarily those of Karl Marx, Max Weber, and Sigmund Freud: historical materialism in its politico-economic form, sociological theory of western rationalization and psychoanalysis, respectively. Only within their framework does the book's theory make justified sense, a theory that has captivated philosophers and social scientists ever since: the theory of the end of the individual.

Backing from Marx, Weber, and Freud

For Horkheimer and Adorno, "individual" or "individuality" is primarily a historic, and not a biological or an ontological category. It denotes something that has emerged over the course of history and that is thus capable of vanishing again. Accordingly, individuality is first and foremost an historically acquired characteristic and not, as in the case of organisms, and especially human beings, one created by a particular genetic combination, or, as dictated by ancient metaphysics, one conferred by an ideal being, form, or substance shaping matter into single things. This historic perspective is specified further within a philosophy of history that, being fundamentally traditional and speculative, can only present itself as suitable for discourse because it in turn is essentially supported by the above-mentioned major theories taken from the different sciences. Historical materialism and the critique of political economics merit a particular mention in this context.

According to Adorno, writing his *Minima Moralia* in aphoristic and condensed language, "the individual owes its crystallization to the forms of political economy, especially the urban marketplace." The transactions of market economy, crystallizing initially in the cities of Europe, historically necessitated the emergence of individuals. The latter are defined by "independence" and thus also by a "resistance" to the pressures of socialization, an independence that, however, is only to be gained *through* socialization, namely, through the preservation of "individual interests" and the forming of "character." The marketplace binds members of society to one another as economic participants, just as it sets them up against one another, through the exchange of wares and the particularity of interests. "This testifies however," so Adorno continues, "also to the fact that its decay in the contemporary phase must not be derived individualistically, but out of a social tendency, as something that succeeds by virtue of individuation and not as its mere enemy."[23] If the individual serves to mirror society, then the explanation for its decay, insofar as it can be registered at all, cannot be separated psychologically from social theory. Indeed, these two theories are inextricably linked. For, as Adorno stresses once more, social tendencies assert themselves at the very core of individuals, in the principle rendering them individuals at all and which can thus be termed the *principium individuationis*.

The question is therefore whether and how decay of the individual can be registered, and this is simultaneously the question of what, for Adorno and Horkheimer, constitutes the principle of individuation. Only when that much has been clarified, do we have at our disposal a yardstick for decay, and only then can decay be evaluated with regard to its causes. To this end, let us remain for now on the path of social theory as supported by Marx and endeavor to collect its key argumentative elements.

The first element is that of autonomy, understood in the economic, not the Kantian (critical and moral) sense: "The signature of the epoch is that no human being, without any exception, can determine their life in a somewhat transparent sense, as was earlier possible by gauging market relationships" and therefore has lost their "autonomy."[24] The fact that no human being is excepted from this spectacular lack of self-determination, not even those with economical and political clout, the fact that every person in fact is subject to the "logic" and the "practical constraints" of capital, is a theory that both Marx (in turn an erudite pupil of Hegel's) and Max Weber embraced in detail. Unlike Marx, however, Adorno and Horkheimer positively emphasized the achievement of capitalism in constituting individuality, albeit only while it deserved the attribute "liberalist," before it entered the monopolistic era. Only within the liberalist era was it possible for the individual, that is, the (small) individual entrepreneur, to assess the conditions of the marketplace. With monopolistic, and especially state capitalism, the theory of which was developed by Horkheimer and Friedrich Pollok within the context of the Frankfurt School, the economic basis of the bourgeois-patriarchal type of entrepreneur crumbled. The safeguarding and expansion of one's own property were no longer decided by individual plans, but by national and international financial strategies. "The possibility of becoming an economic subject, an entrepreneur, a proprietor, is entirely liquidated. Right down to the small grocery, the independent firm on the running and inheriting of which the bourgeois family and the position of its head were founded, has fallen into hopeless dependence. All have become employees."[25]

The argumentation most closely linked to the politico-economic one is *sociological*. To use the language of the corresponding branch of science, this argumentation belongs to the realms of organizational sociology. Here the theoretical tone is set not by Marx, but by *Max Weber*. In a lecture from 1953 entitled "The Individual and Organization," Adorno collected all the crucial relevant arguments. Weber was also present in another and far more important sense. Adorno's explanation of bourgeois anthropology in this lecture, in concepts such as the fulfillment of duty, moral constraints, and internalized authority, also unmistakably points in his direction. In this context Weber is perceived as a sociologist of religion, in particular as the author of the famous text entitled *The Protestant Ethic and the Spirit of Capitalism*. In this work, the style of which is equally complex and meticulous (with proliferate footnotes forming texts within the text), Weber develops the theory that a rational lifestyle on the basis of professional ethics is constitutive for modern capitalism, as well as for modern culture, and that this lifestyle in turn stems from the spirit of Christian, or more precisely Puritan asceticism. With the Reformation, asceticism—also familiar to cultures beyond Europe, to the ancients (the Cynics and the Stoics) and especially to the monks of the Middle Ages—lost its character of detachment from the world. In Weber's terms, it became an "inner-world asceticism" and consequently a phenomenon requiring clarification within a comparative analysis of world religions.

He locates the crucial starting point for an explanation in the Calvinist version of Protestantism and its teachings on the Election of Grace. Accordingly, the bestowal or withholding of grace is left up to God's infinite wisdom. Nobody knows for sure if he is one of the saved or one of the eternally damned. For Calvinists, the severe and autocratic God of the Old Testament maintains the upper hand. In its "extreme inhumanity," this predestination doctrine must, according to Weber, have one consequence above all others: "a feeling of unprecedented inner loneliness of the single individual." In what was, for an individual of the Reformation, "the most important thing in life, his eternal salvation," he "was forced to follow his path alone to meet a destiny that had been decreed for him from eternity." No one could help him, no priest, no sacrament, no church, not even God, for even Christ died only for the elect. It is eternally decreed whether one belongs to that elect, and it remains concealed from man.

With this helplessness, "that great historic process in the development of religions, the elimination of magic from the world" comes to an end, a process that, as Weber adds in a later edition of his study, "had begun with the old Hebrew prophets and, in conjunction with Hellenistic scientific thought, had repudiated all magical means to salvation as superstition and sin." The result of this inner isolation is ambivalent. On the one hand, it "contains the reason for the entirely negative attitude of Puritanism to all the sensuous and emotional elements in culture and in religion," and on the other, it "forms one of the roots of that disillusioned and pessimistically inclined individualism" to be found in Anglo-American peoples ever since.[26] Its correspondingly ambivalent solution is located in professional ethics. For the surest proof of genuine faith is "intense worldly activity."[27] Faith can only prove itself, however, if at all, in its objective impact. Not in single, good works that can be accumulated in the course of a life, but in a systematic and methodical gearing of one's whole life to the performance of such works, mercilessly faced as one is, in the most literal sense and at every moment, with the alternative of eternal salvation *versus* eternal damnation.

This ideal is not only ascetic in its original Greek sense of practice, training, and exercise, of constant self-reflection, but also in the specific sense of self-discipline with regard to affects. Asceticism turned "with all its force against one thing: the spontaneous enjoyment of life and all it had to offer." To this extent, as Weber tells us, "its significance for the development of capitalism is obvious." Asceticism demands that one does not give in to Hedonism, does not fall victim to excessiveness and splendor, that one instead postpones the satisfaction of one's material needs and dedicates oneself solely to work, or more precisely to work as the execution of the same: to laboring. Here, too, it is not the result, the work, that is crucial, but its function as a means to the true end of working per se; "labor came to be considered in itself the end of life."[28]

Horkheimer and Adorno pick up on this ambivalence, which according to Weber is a necessary accompaniment to the successful establishment of ascetic Protestantism, but choose to lend it added emphasis with Hegel's concept of the dialectic and to radicalize it with the help of Marxist theory. The resulting formula is "self-preservation through self-destruction." Those with a desire to preserve themselves at all costs will destroy themselves. Destruction in this context is primarily not physical, but mental. It refers to internalized sacrifice and self-constraint, in other words to that asceticism historically forced by Protestantism and described by Weber for the western world: "The history of civilization is the history of the introversion of sacrifice—in other words, the history of renunciation."[29]

The politico-economic and sociologic-historic lines of argumentation are ultimately paralleled by a *psychological* one. Psychoanalysis in particular is massively enlisted by Adorno and Horkheimer as a means of justifying their theory of the end of the individual. In this argumentational context, self-preservation through self-destruction is arrived at under a heading satirizing that of a book by Kierkegaard: "The Health Unto Death." Here, the fact "that contemporary sickness exists precisely in what is normal," that human beings are mentally deformed without noticing it, requires psychoanalytical explanation, or more precisely and is so often the case with Adorno's love of the conditional, would require such an explanation. In this respect Adorno has no more to offer than a "suspicion" or an "assumption." Leaving aside his subjective opinion and polemics, which he also exhibits openly in this context, his attempt at an etiology of neurosis—which could be heuristically stimulating, going beyond Freud's precepts—remains. A psychoanalysis of the "regular guy" and the "popular girl," the types of person Adorno primarily has in mind, thus drawing on the American cultural sphere, has to assume that their everlasting "cheerfulness, decisiveness, sociability," their "quicksilver liveliness and overpowering energy" is the result of a repression of repression, a second-order repression that is directed not only against the stirring of impulses, but also against the symptoms that "in bourgeois times" are generated by (first-order) repression. Symptoms indicate diseases, but if symptoms can also be repressed, diseases can no longer be diagnosed. To Adorno, the explanation for this seems to be an "innervation of castration," which extends far beyond the "old task of identification with the father" in the bourgeois family. And this innervation of the prohibitory body represented by the threat of castration is presumably located in "still earlier phases of childhood development" than in those that, according to Freud, are attributed as being the origin of neuroses. Under these scientifically uncertain conditions Adorno does, however, possess the decency to admit that his assertions lack a moral yardstick. The true sickness of those believing themselves to be healthy can only be diagnosed "in the disproportion between the rational way they lead their lives and the possibly reasonable determination of their lives."[30]

However, the identification of this yardstick is a problem to which the older critical theory offers no solution. In his *Minima Moralia*, as well as many years later in his *Negative Dialectics*, Adorno lists all the unsatisfactory aspects in each moral philosophical approach, whether that of universalism, particularism, social contract theory, ethics of compassion, or skepticism. None of these is unconditionally apt. The best possible solution can only be that which is least bad. But, at least for Adorno, it remains unclear what that solution might be. In his eyes, the identification of a moral philosophical yardstick ultimately remains a *desideratum*.

The central criterion here, namely, that of autonomy, which Kant bequeathed to the moral philosophical discussion and that Adorno initially interpreted within a Marxist framework, may also of course be interpreted within the context of Freud and his school of thought. The "strong ego" is a psychoanalytical synonym for Kant's autonomous subject, that is, one judging independently and acting in a manner that has universal validity. Only this strong ego has the power to devote itself to a matter or a person in such a manner as to perceive in this Other more than just its own horizons. It is thus capable of liberating itself from what in psychoanalytical literature is known by the (mythologically) neat and (scientifically) equally multifaceted term of narcissism. Such liberation is inconceivable so long as the yielding, or in other words the "mimetic" moment is suppressed and repressed.[31]

Additional psychoanalytical theorems can be drawn on to substantiate the theory of the end of the individual, for example, Anna Freud's "identification with the aggressor" or Sigmund Freud's hypothesis of individual pleasure being increased through identification with the majority, developed in his study *Mass Psychology*. Adorno addresses all these theorems, yet not without radicalizing them and, in so doing, once more consciously removes any claim they may have had to empirical certainty. The downside of orthodoxy is that it is "wont to reduce to . . . humdrum conventions," and that renders wary not only critics of society perceiving anything unconventional as under threat, but also and especially thinkers believing autonomy of thought—that effortful and painful "labor of self-constitution" and "self-experiencing"—to rank above all else.[32]

For our attempt to provide not only psychoanalytical but also politico-economic and sociologic substantiation for the theory of the end of the individual, this ultimately means that the theory needs to be consciously rooted in the area between science and spontaneous experience. There is no point in accusing it of lacking empirical controls, at least not if the intentions of Adorno and Horkheimer are to be respected. It is merely the formulation of a hypothesis for further research and independent contemplation, even if it does do this in such a way as to seem like a thesis desiring to draw a veil over the difference between a thesis and an argument.

Culture and Critical Theory

Adorno and Horkheimer explore the hypothesis, compacted to a thesis, of the end of the individual not only at the politico-economic, sociologic, and psychoanalytical levels, but also at the level of cultural theory. "Culture" here means that well-differentiated area in which members of society store their different knowledge in order to actualize it as an historical variable. The concept of culture thus has an epistemic or, in Cassirer's terms, symbolic significance. It covers all symbolic forms in which knowledge can express itself: myths, religion, art, theoretical cognition, language itself. Under the precursors of German idealism and bourgeois humanism it encompasses the much-cited triad of the true, the beautiful, and the good; of science, art, and morality.

With this concept of culture, Horkheimer and Adorno's critique of society and culture shares two key premises, namely, those of normativity and dichotomy. The first premise is based on a concept of true culture, the second on a division between a high and a low sphere. The first claims to know what culture truly is; the second draws from it the discriminating consequence. That expansive phenomenon that Horkheimer and Adorno successfully publicized as the "culture industry" is the object of massive criticism on their part precisely because culture, through its industrialization, threatens to lose those moments that used to provide the potential for resistance, at least during the bourgeois era. In the age of its industrial producibility, culture inevitably seems to lose that negativity that had previously formed the inseparable reverse face of its "affirmative character." The term "affirmative character of culture" (which achieved fame in Herbert Marcuse's essay of the same name in 1937, one year after Horkheimer had coined it in his essay on *Egoism and the Freedom Movement* with a strong orientation toward Max Weber's study of Protestantism) has since become an established component of critical theory.

This concept has a defining historic, geographic, sociologic, psychological, normative, functional, and ultimately idealistic element. For culture bears the label "affirmative" as a well-differentiated area of society within bourgeois, philosophical, and idealistic European epochs, an area which presses for internalization, which claims its values (the true, the beautiful, and the good) to be universally valid, and which affirms the contradictions of social reality precisely by restricting the general validity of its values to the spiritual education of the individual, in an internalized form. A culture is affirmative if it realizes its noble ideals solely within the sphere of the spiritual, and in particular in art, and if, in so doing, it on the one hand leaves social reality elementarily intact, yet on the other indirectly criticizes it for lending those needs that cannot be realized in everyday practice, especially the needs of happiness and individuality, a heterotopic and vicariously Utopian status. Culture as conceived in the bourgeois and idealistic sense thus contains both: affirmation of social order and its sublime negation. Against this background, the extinguishing of this ambivalence in sole favor of the affirmative element has acquired the name "culture industry."

In his essay *Culture Industry Reconsidered*, Adorno works with two definitions of culture, both of which can be used to test his criteria for criticizing the culture industry, beyond that of ambivalence. Culture, first in the sense of the ambivalence criterion, "always raised a protest against petrified relations," never serving only the further ideological petrification of relations. More interesting and more momentous is the second definition: "That which legitimately could be called culture attempted, as an expression of suffering and contradiction, to maintain a grasp on the idea of the good life."[33] The concept of culture is thus impregnated with morality, its justification in the hands of moral philosophy. Adorno consciously fails to provide this justification, however, as we have already seen in the context of psychological argumentation with regard to the theory of the end of the individual. Accordingly, the concept of culture, which is bound to the idea of correct life, and the corresponding concept of cultural criticism are not built on safe foundations.

Proposing a *formal* concept of cultural criticism does not get around the difficulty. Far more, it once again leads into the problem of the conception and critique of *reason*, prominently publicized in the universalism *versus* particularism argument (conflict). It is initially true that an "inner" structural connection can necessarily be claimed to exist between culture and criticism for all cultures that "imagine themselves as cultures and in this sense have become reflexive," as was historically the case with the ancient Sophists, who introduced this concept to Europe. This connection can then be specified historically and structurally by adhering to Habermas's thesis that cultures are, in addition, *modern* "when cultural criticism is no longer oriented toward mythical, religious, or transcendental authorities, but has become conscious of the fact that the criteria and standards it follows have to be justified within the culture critical discourse itself."[34] But that still does not solve the problem of how to justify the criticism. For criticism of culture, that is of culture in the socially well-differentiated and holistic senses, as a reservoir of knowledge and self-understanding, as a way of life, is accordingly only possible if, on the one hand, it also repeatedly takes reflexive looks at itself, perceiving not only culture as a creation, and thus as a phenomenon that is principally open to criticism, but also itself. On the other hand, it must be capable of justifying itself through itself, through standards that can only be justified through criticism, a justifying judging and condemning, in other words through self-reflection and reason in the formal sense of the word. In this context, reason means purely *logon didonai*, being accountable, giving reasons, finding arguments. Cultural criticism is reflexive in this double sense: by referring to itself *at all*, and by doing so *in detail* according to standards that can only be justified *through* it itself, through justifying, and to this extent reasonable, criticism.

This reflexive concept of culture and criticism in line with the theory of modernity may indeed be acceptable to advocates of different, even contrary positions concerning the theory of rationality, universalists as well as particularists, contextualists, relativists. The conflict begins with the theory that reason is forced, yet is still in a position to justify a valid standard for all cultures and ages. It is therefore both necessary and possible to identify a standard that transcends context and is, culturally speaking, invariant. Axel Honneth readdressed this problematic area in detail within the discussion on critical theory. His proposals reveal the

difficulty of finding a mediating level between the contrary positions regarding the rationality theory, and thus of being able to do justice to the
claims of the critical theory under changed conditions.

In his essay *The Possibility of a Disclosing Critique of Society*, Honneth
assumes an opposition between a criticism-transcending context and con-
textualist criticism. The critique offered by Horkheimer and Adorno is disclosing. It refers not to issues of justice, but to those of the good life. Those
wishing to judge the good life, or, like Adorno in his *Minima Moralia*,
its reverse image, the damaged life, cannot do so with "argumentative
conviction," but only with "rhetorical persuasion." What is required is a
"new description" of things and matters that forces everything to assume
a new significance "abruptly," that is, according to the epistemological
model of evidence.[35]

Honneth's proposal, however, fails to satisfy. For, to use Habermas's
terminology, as certainly as an evaluative or ethical discourse relies on
weaker contexts of justification, rather than on a justice-oriented moral discourse, it is equally not to be reduced to its ability to change our
perception of the world. With a dualism of argumentation and rhetoric,
validation and world disclosure, Honneth adheres much too unreservedly to the path predefined by Heidegger and Habermas. A strict division
between argumentation and rhetoric is also not appropriate in the case
of Horkheimer and Adorno. However closely they stick to the rhetorical
pattern of chiasm, narration, and exaggeration set out by Honneth, they
also follow the lines of argumentation proposed by Marx, Max Weber,
and Freud. It is precisely this specific, compact linking of the argumentative and rhetorical levels that allows a book such as the *Dialectic of
Enlightenment* to be so powerfully convincing.

Honneth proposes another solution in his essay *Reconstructive Social
Critique with a Genealogical Reservation*. Its point of departure is Michael
Walzer and his distinguishing of three approaches to social critique,
namely, "discovery," "invention," and "interpretation." The first of these
is based on (religious or cognitive) empirical evidence; the second creates
a procedure of general validity, from Kant to Rawls, for attaining norms
that are justified; the third, which Walzer himself favors, uncovers normative ideals in culturally predefined values, socially established institutions, and tried-and-tested practices, doing so hermeneutically, but also by

means of a critique of ideology. With recourse to Nietzsche and Foucault, Honneth complements these three paths with a fourth, that of "genealogy," demonstrating the transition from normative ideals to distorted practices. Honneth ultimately views critical theory, from Horkheimer to Habermas and beyond, as desiring to unite nearly all these models: genealogy, interpretation (which Honneth calls "reconstruction"), and invention (which he calls "construction").

What is irritating about this second proposal is that Honneth, with regard to critical theory, does not wish to take this "disclosing" model of social critique based on empirical evidence into any further account. The reason for this seems to be his estimation of it as a "profane version" of the religious-revelational critique cleft to empiricism, which he now regards as no longer relevant. A further reason would be the unclear distinction between the world-disclosing and the interpretative or reconstructive critiques, with the achievement of the latter also being described by Honneth as a "creative new disclosure" of culturally predefined standards.[36]

Against this background, another proposed solution seems to me to be generally more convincing. It achieved prominence through those theoretical positions collected under the pithy label of postmodernism. They revolve around a central position in which the will toward an antisystem and an antifoundation first decidedly took shape, the position occupied by Nietzsche. In his famous work *On the Use and Abuse of History for Life*, he predefined the basic methodical pattern.[37] The three types of historical observation that he distinguishes are based on different principles of thinking and acting, or, as Nietzsche summarizes, of life: "monumental" history, based on the principle of practical (if possible world historical) impact; "antiquarian" history, based on the principle of hermeneutic self-communication; and "critical" history, based on the principle of (biased) assessment. The type of historical observation depends on the purpose that an individual or collective sets. Those wishing to achieve "great things" have to appropriate history monumentally, as a gallery of monuments providing role models for one's own monument; those wishing to know how they came to be as they are, that is, wishing to verify themselves through history, have to adopt an antiquarian, sustaining relationship to it; and those who feel burdened by all things historic and present, need to adopt a critical, judgmental, and condemning stance toward history. Each of these attitudes has advantages and disadvantages; none is objectively preferable to the others. In each case the advantages result from the purpose in question. There is thus no comprehensive attitude, no principle as a synthesis of the other principles. What Nietzsche performs using the example of historic observation can therefore be valid as exemplary of the rationality theory, and especially for the methodology of a critical social theory.

According to what we have ascertained so far, it is impossible to subject the types of reason (scientific, moral, ethical-evaluative, aesthetic, instrumental) and the types of (social) critique convincingly to a systematically oriented program of justification. Yet this does not seem necessary. For it could certainly be sufficient to place the types of rationality and critique, themselves ambivalent, in a *difference-theoretical* or *agonal* relationship to one another. In some cases it may be appropriate to adhere to the interpretative or reconstructive model of criticism, in others to the inventing or constructive model, and in yet others to the genealogical or world-disclosing model. What is appropriate will be decided by the purpose pursued by the critic. A certain discursive or political situation can require the use of means other than the purely rational, of the eye-opening power of verbal images opening up new forms of argumentation. Another situation, predominantly negotiated in discourse, in mutual talk with an obligation to argumentation, can vice versa require that the normative background assumptions of the empirical and worldview-changing talk be accounted for and that a moral principle of critique be constructed, the best that is available in the sense of the *Minima Moralia*. From this construction, its patent, systematic primacy would not necessarily have to follow, however. To use Lyotard's terms, *le différend*, the conflict and obstinacy of the forms of rationality and critique would remain preserved within this context of justification, differently weighted in each case. Critical theory would be nothing other than a changing of the critical perspective to suit the situation.

Movies and Fairy Tales

This pragmatic and agonal take on critical theory also puts a different slant on the résumé of theories regarding the culture industry compared to that presented by Adorno and Horkheimer. On closer observation, a pluralism of theoretical approaches emerges, at least in part. Hypotheses about the culture industry only form a towering monolithic block if looked at from one single perspective. The fact that Adorno and Horkheimer had the privilege of this perspective does not justify systematic dismissal of the others, something that is truer today than ever before. An example of this new emphasis can be observed within the sector of the culture industry viewed by the authors themselves as drastic, central, and characteristic, namely, the sector of film.[38] True, it does not provide us with a veritable theory of film, but it does demonstrate the way in which film is able to stand up to one of its severest critics, namely, the critical theory of Horkheimer and Adorno's generation, including the critic himself, Adorno.[39]

In their critique of *The Theory of the Novel*, the authors of the *Dialectic of Enlightenment* point out the crossover between the epic and the novel, those two narrative forms that Lukács contrasted in epochal confrontation against a background of Hegelian social theory and the philosophy of history. Both perspectives, that of Lukács and that of Horkheimer and Adorno, could be the way into an attractive film theoretical hypothesis. Lending the spheres of art and the media an historical and sociological perspective could mean film being conceived of as the legitimate successor to the novel, as the most appropriate aesthetic expression of a postbourgeois, mass-democratic society, as the adequate aesthetic expression of a quasi-"agonal" and "hybrid" modernity. Then cinema would not only be once again and unequivocally the most successful mass medium of the twentieth century alongside radio and television, but it would also singularly be distinguished as the *aesthetic* medium exemplifying that century, as the instrument and, more specifically, the particularly symbolic form in which that century is aesthetically, that is, in a broader artistic sense, most recognizable. With the introduction of "new" digital media, cinema is consistently losing, or so one must presume, this twofold accolade. The impending close of the film era is additionally confirmed by its definitive inclusion in philosophical theory toward the end of the twentieth century. In Hegel's famous words in the preface to *Philosophy of Right*, this means that cinema has "grown old," that it is entering its twilight years, and that, as the symbol of philosophy itself, the owl of Minerva can "spread its wings with the falling of the dusk." Cinema as an entity has received a finite framework; it is now possible to be sufficiently clear about it. Removing the conditional formulations from the aesthetic-cultural theory that film is the legitimate successor to the novel would, of course, require both a detailed theory of modern society and a corresponding aesthetic theory, in particular a formal analysis of film. That is quite a lot for one project. If, as in the case of the present book, this is only realized in part, then everything else depends on how large this part is estimated to be. The author would in any case like at this point to state that in his opinion he feels he has done enough for now.

One of the elements connecting the epic and the novel is the initial narrative gesture in fairy tales: "Once upon a time." Horkheimer and Adorno also found it in Homer. "Hope," so concludes their excursus on Odysseus, "in the report of the infamous deed lies in the fact that it is long past. Over the raveled skein of prehistory, barbarism, and culture, Homer passes the soothing hand of remembrance, bringing the solace of 'once upon a time.' Only as the novel is the epic transmuted into fairy tale."[40] In elements of cinema, predominantly the Western, these three genres resurface: the expansive gestures of the epic, the novel, and the fairy tale. The epic with its world of typical events and characters and eternal order, of the myth and the hero, slowly progressing events and high-key narrative; the novel, with its central figure of individuality in infinite self-reassurance, its lonely form desperately searching and attempting to master life alone; and finally the fairy tale, compressed to its ritual beginning, its evocative initial formula that enables the narrative to come forth while at the same time keeping it at a distance, maintaining it to be true while at the same time retracting it as mere invention.

Once Upon a Time There Was: *The Man Who Shot Liberty Valance*

Ransom Stoddard returns to Shinbone a famous man, a legend. He is accompanied by his wife Hallie, whom he met in the same place many years before. They have come back to visit their old hometown, but for a sad reason. The trip is for a funeral, following the death of a man they were both close to in their own different ways. We do not learn much about this man at first. His house "out in the country" is a ruin; his body is lying in a simple coffin, more a wooden box than anything else; his burial is being paid for by the community; nobody knows him. Only the old folk exchange knowing and silent glances: the thin, short undertaker; the retired sheriff, waddling around bemusedly like a fat teddy bear; the dead man's laborer, a black man sitting silently beside the coffin with large work-worn hands and legs wide apart; and, of course, Mr. and Mrs. Stoddard. This last addition attracts the attention of the local press. Ransom Stoddard is no less than a Washington senator, casually yet elegantly dressed, with snow-white hair and generally respected. A person in the public eye traveling to a small town out West in order to pay his last respects to a man who was poor and unknown, a seeming failure during his lifetime, has the whiff of an interesting story, a story including all the basic elements: friends and enemies, success and failure, love found and lost, and other things besides. And all this surrounding a person with a political function, responsible for more than just his own private affairs. The editor-in-chief of the local newspaper therefore adopts an argument bound to appeal to a democratic audience, insisting: "The public have a right to hear this story." The senator is convinced, at least when his wife nods her agreement. It becomes immediately obvious that he would do nothing against her wishes. Her story is far too intertwined with that of the dead man who—that much is clear—went by the name of Tom Doniphon.

Ransom Stoddard begins to tell his story and, for the movie portraying the narrative, this means a flashback. The senator talks about "the old days" before Shinbone had a railway, that mode of transport that enabled the West to progress. Instead one had to travel by stagecoach, just like the one next to him as he begins to tell his tale, a discarded thing, dusty and covered in cobwebs, a relic from days gone by, relegated to the attic of history, possibly later to a museum, just like the main characters in the story about to be told. In retrospect the roles are clearly allocated: there is a winner, Senator Ransom Stoddard, and a loser, cowboy Tom Doniphon. The latter is even to be subjected to the ignominy of being buried without boots or spurs, without belt or gun, in other words without the insignia rightly belonging to a man of the West who has died an upright death, both literally and figuratively.

As a younger lawyer, his case full of legal books, Stoddard travels West, heading for the fame, happiness, and adventure said at the time to be awaiting him there. Adventure comes immediately, with bandits ambushing the stagecoach in order to rob its passengers. Defending a woman at the mercy of a violent bandit, the young gentleman from the East draws the attention of the leader, a swaggering man noticeably carrying a silver-tipped leather whip, a weapon he wastes no time in using. He demonstrates to the fearless but naive Stoddard that the place is governed by laws that are different than the ones in his books, namely, "Western laws." He spits out the words furiously before beginning to beat the defenseless man lying in the dirt, and not stopping until his men pull him off.

When Stoddard finally comes to, hours later, he is looking into Hallie's eyes. Tom Doniphon found him lying on the ground and has brought him to her. She runs a restaurant in Shinbone with her parents, feeding the cowboys and the sheriff (very round even then) with huge portions of steak, beans, and potatoes, followed by equally huge pieces of deep-dish apple pie. Here Stoddard is nursed back to health and then works in the kitchen washing dishes, a large white apron tied around his middle, in order to pay off his debt to the family. In these surroundings he is soon to meet his tormentor again, whom he now knows to be called Liberty Valence, "the most dangerous man in the area," so Doniphon stresses, not without adding meaningfully, "after myself." In the situation that unfolds Stoddard has to learn the hard way, the way of the West. For the first time in his life he is forced to realize that outlaws are not intimidated by laws, only by weapons, and that in lawless times the law is only accepted if backed up by weapons, by a strong executive force. Yet the sheriff of Shinbone, the embodiment of the executive force, is an anxious and obese clown (making the contrasting role of Ransom Stoddard perfect for James Stewart: a lanky actor with soft, youthful features, energetic, convincingly true to his principles and stubborn as a mule if necessary).

When Stoddard, who is helping Hallie with the serving, enters the room in which cowboys are noisily waiting for their food, he immediately recognizes the whip lying on one of the tables. Liberty Valence and two fellow bandits have appeared on the scene. On seeing this "new waitress" the three of them laugh out loud. Valence sticks out a leg to trip up Stoddard, who is still calmly going about his work. Stoddard falls, the steak and usual "fixin's" tumble to the floor. The ensuing laughter does not die down until Doniphon joins the scene. He has pushed back the right-hand side of his jacket and has his hand near his gun. It is his steak on the floor in the corner. Stoddard was bringing it to him, and the question now, the question of honor, is who should pick it up? This is a situation bordering on the grotesque: two grown-up men threatening to shoot each other—over a steak. They stand across the room from one another, Valance on one side, Doniphon on the other, like two fighting cocks in mutual appraisal, and in between them Stoddard, the man in the apron. He, of course, is the one who puts an end to this threatening and ridiculous situation. He picks up the steak because he cannot believe that two men could possibly kill each other over a piece of meat.

The Man Who Shot Liberty Valance deals with two major themes. One of them, the battle between civilization and wilderness, dramatically escalates in this situation. Here it is a battle between the law and lawlessness, between bourgeois order and anarchic freedom, between the democratic community and individual self-will. The three men embody three lifestyles.

As his name suggests, Liberty Valance stands for freedom, that unregulated, unleashed (autocratic) freedom resounding in the unbridled and debauched dominance of the Libertines. He is a loner, outside the community, proud, masterful, unpredictable, a figure as elegant as a Nietzschean aristocratic beast, representing the individual in its social and economic self-determination, its egotistic and separate interests, its hedonism.

In contrast, Tom Doniphon is a loner in the real sense of the word: homeless, roaming the border country between wilderness and civilization. Like Liberty Valance, he is convinced that "out here" in the West people have to solve their own problems. When he says this, he unequivocally fingers his gun. Like Ransom Stoddard, however, he is also a law-abiding man, not the written law but an internalized one, a man of morals. This is reflected in his willingness to help others, his honesty, a certain measure of public spirit, and his politeness toward women. He, too, comes across as a proud figure capable of giving orders, yet with a relaxed attitude that is ponderous, almost cozy, and therefore trustworthy. As it transpires, he is to be the tragic figure in this triangular constellation, the warrior not allowed to die in battle, but pushed carelessly aside by the epoch he has helped to succeed. He represents the individual in its thoroughly lonely and unrelenting guise.

Finally, Stoddard personifies the epoch that emerges victorious, surviving both his counterparts. He is the assertion of that bourgeois and constitutional order that has no place for either Valance or Doniphon. He brings not only the law to Shinbone, but also education. (Since Hallie cannot read or write, Stoddard proposes to teach her, an offer that is then taken up by others as well—children, women, a black man [Pompey, Doniphon's laborer], but also three cowboys, ridiculous lads as is only to be expected: cowboys in classrooms are always figures of fun.) Stoddard also instills in the hesitant locals an awareness of civilian democracy, of courage as a virtue in those democrats who exercise their right to vote and cease to be afraid of the big-shot cattle breeders, the stooges of those with economic power. "What are votes compared to guns?!" Doniphon smirks. And yet he is wrong. Sooner or later the weapons make way for the law. Stoddard therefore, on the one hand, represents the bourgeois constitutional state, and, on the other, he represents the heroism of anarchic times. In his character the individual surfaces for a last time before disappearing into the bourgeois constitutional cage. In line with the left-wing Hegelian tradition, John Ford once more portrays the obstinate and strong-willed subject, the individual who is not afraid to fight his corner alone, against majority opinion, and if necessary against brute force. Stoddard becomes a hero because he dares to fight a battle that could end in triumphant victory, but could also end in his own death. He does not want the battle to take this shape and, as the representative of a movement that recognizes the state as having the monopoly on power, he attempts to prevent it from doing so. Yet when he is forced to accept that the battle will be violent and potentially fatal, he does not run away.

This moment comes when the man outside the law publicly challenges the champion of the law to a duel that very same day. Maybe Stoddard's pragmatic intelligence could have triumphed, and he would have disappeared from town as everyone suggested. But when Valance attacks the newspaper editor, who is old, jovial, and fond of a drink, for repeatedly pillorying him with his journalism, Stoddard's mind is made up. "Eat your own words!" Valance cries out in fury as he stuffs the newspaperman's mouth with his own workmanship. He quite literally uses the written word to feed a hungry mouth. (In Peter Greenaway's *The Cook, the Thief, His Wife and Her Lover* the same thing happens to the lover, who is also a lover of books—a method of torture for intellectuals in the age of Gutenberg.) Stoddard, who a long time previously began to practice shooting in secret, gets out his gun, an old thing reminiscent of a toy, and goes out into the dark streets. Valance has been passing the time at the saloon with whiskey and poker. And now here they are, face to face: the thin man in the white apron, clumsily holding a gun in his right hand, and the gunslinger, his weapon dangling from his belt like a marksman. Valance is leaning provocatively against the veranda and he begins to play with his opponent, his victim, first with words and then with deeds, all too certain of victory. His first shot, which skims past Stoddard's forehead, is only supposed to scare him. The second wounds his right arm, however, and the third is also well aimed, again intended to scare and to demonstrate his own superiority. At this moment Stoddard tries for the first time to pick his own gun up off the ground, using his left hand. With his fourth shot Valance intends to put an end to his amusing game. "This time straight between the eyes," he threatens, calmly taking aim, his arm outstretched, and then a loud shot is fired. But it is Valance, and not Stoddard, who collapses like a massive and seriously maimed animal. It appears that the two men have shot each other more or less simultaneously. One is lying still in the dirt, the other returns to his kitchen, wounded, silent, and confused.

With the *shoot out* (which is not at the end, but two-thirds of the way through), the first major theme of this movie is basically concluded. What follows is merely an extension of what has gone before. Hallie can no longer conceal her love for Stoddard, not even from Doniphon, who has been wooing her both shyly—as men have been revealed to be in this respect by the difference theory—and charmingly. Now Doniphon's plans are in tatters, and in a fit of despair he burns down the extended part of his house intended for his future wife. The flames destroy that "home" where, as he knows, "the heart is." The only relationship remaining to him now is loneliness. Stoddard, by contrast, irrefutably gains not only the love of a woman but also fame and rocketing professional success. At a convention of lively democratic characters to pick the delegate to Washington, Stoddard is nominated. Shortly afterward, following brilliant rhetorical support from the recovered newspaper editor and second delegate at a no less lively democratic convention, Stoddard is elected to Congress and then later elected governor of the newly founded state three times. Happiness and fame have fallen into his lap. His incarnate adversary is dead, legislation is winning through, and his rival in matters of the heart has surrendered. A personal history in keeping with that esteemed American pattern: "from dishwasher to governor," from rags to riches.

He did have a bitter lesson to learn, however. Forced to accept that the law alone is powerless against the might of the lawless, that violent means are needed for law and order to achieve validity in the first place, Stoddard had to betray the very principle that he initially wanted to use as his sole backup. Whereas at the beginning of the story, in an attitude of "abstract negation," to put it in loose Hegelian terms, he opposes violence only with books and the law, in time he gradually adopts an attitude of "determinate negation." In the world of Westerns, this latter position is usually held in the Wild West by a capable sheriff, but in the absence of such a figure Doniphon filled the gap. In its determinate form, negation does not simply dismiss the negated *in toto*, but holds on to it in a different manner. The tyranny of violence cannot be broken without violence, but a violence that negates violence (as a monocracy) necessarily negates itself (as a monocracy), specifically imposing self-restriction. Unlike for a postmodern difference theoreticist, for a Hegelian the idea of civilization (partly) being founded on violence is by no means an insurmountable problem entangled in never-ending paradoxes.

This is where the second major theme of the movie comes into play. The focus is no longer on civilization triumphing over the barbaric, but on the myth triumphing over the truth. This theme unfolds as follows: at the convention the main reason why Stoddard is nominated as a congressional delegate is because, as everyone is aware by now, he is the man who shot Liberty Valance. But he experiences pangs of guilt, not wanting to base his career on a fame that is extremely dubious from the point of view of a state governed by law and order. Again it is Doniphon who intervenes. Stoddard chose not to run away from a dangerous bandit, and Doniphon now prevents him from running away from an election that will send the right man, a noncorruptible man, to Washington, opening the door to a major political career.

Doniphon achieves this by telling Stoddard the true story of the *shoot out* with Liberty Valance. At this point there is a second flashback. Once more we see the unequal duel, now at the conventional juncture in the movie, namely, at the end, yet this time through the eyes of Tom Doniphon. That night he was standing in the dark on the other side of the street, and it was him, as his black laborer can testify, who pulled the trigger at the crucial moment. This was a particularly difficult feat since he could not shoot before Stoddard and yet still had to precede Valance. In Hegelian terms, the constellation of the male triangle gains consciousness of itself. The relationship between the three men, a mesh of animosity, competition, and friendship, proximity and distance, familiarity and foreignness, compressed to one single point. In the shots that sounded like a single shot, all three protagonists become one just for a moment—a fatal moment. "It was murder, pure and simple, but I can live with it," Doniphon comments tersely. He saved Stoddard's life because Hallie begged him to. He did it, knowing that in so doing he would lose the woman he loved forever to his rival, her begging alone being proof of her love for Stoddard. It also meant forsaking his own happiness in order for her to be happy. The situation in which he tells Stoddard the truth is in keeping with his feelings of victimized desperation. Since it was Stoddard who taught Hallie to read and write, so Doniphon argues, it should be Stoddard who now gives her an opportunity to use her new skills, taking her to the place most likely to make that possible, to the East.

This is where the story of the man who shot Liberty Valance ends and the story related by the movie resumes its initial structure. As we now know, this is a twofold story, a legendary one and a true one, told by a man whom everybody perceives to be a hero, even though the *act* that made him a hero was *act*ually performed by someone else. In contrast, the person who *act*ually carried it out is now forgotten. And now that he has been rendered unforgotten by this narrative, nobody is interested in the truth. The deed is no longer heroic and its perpetrator has become a criminal, one who does not regret what he did for a second. "It was murder, pure and simple, but I can live with it." Those representing the interests of the public, in the movie the newspaper's owner, its editor, and a young journalist to whom Senator Stoddard tells his story, therefore have no wish to print it. Through an act of paternalism they deny the public at large its right to read about the story. The act is paternalistic because it aims to protect the public, while at the same time ignoring its wishes and diminishing its ability to decide for itself. Their decision has an ethical and political justification, with an anti-Enlightenment slant. Collective identity is at stake here, the question of that life one would collectively like to live, of how a community perceives itself. At the same time the theme of unconditional enlightenment is addressed, doubting the idea that the discharge of the myth through the truth could be conducive to collective identity. Here the first and second major themes of the movie come together. It is acceptable to the members of civilization for civilization to be constructed on violence, provided that the violence does not stretch to counterviolence. If it does, murder is admitted and a life lived in untruth is favored over a life lived in truth. The editor-in-chief utters the crucial sentence: "When the legend becomes fact, print the legend."

John Ford, the director of this masterful movie, reveals the truth. This brief statement requires elaboration, for Ford portrays not one simple truth, but a twofold one: not just the truth *about* the legend but that *of* the legend. And at several levels. He follows a contrary cinematographic procedure that philosophically adheres to both negative dialectics and deconstruction. He himself describes it simply thus: "But it's good for the country to have heroes to look up to. Like Custer—a great hero. . . . But you know damn well they weren't."[41] When heroes are needed, as well as when those celebrated as heroes are not heroes, then it is necessary to build heroes up before knocking them down.

At a first narrative level, Ford portrays the story of Ransom Stoddard, who goes down in (collective) history as the man who shot Liberty Valance. At a metalevel the movie destroys this legend, while simultaneously showing, at the object level within the story, that it cannot be destroyed. Revealing the truth behind the legend cannot impinge on the curious truth of the legend, consisting in nothing other than its factual strength. The fact that the legend has a real function makes it an element of cultural self-communication, a factor within the overall context of the collective question of who or what one really is and desires to be. (Removed from the phenomenon of myth creation, this is a theme addressed at a more general and existential level in the fiction of Max Frisch. His protagonists, whether they be Stiller or Don Juan, cannot free themselves from the images that others, "the others," already have of them.)

At a second narrative level, the movie portrays the story of Tom Doniphon, who has been forgotten by the collective memory at the object level and will never be acknowledged, for his story will never be printed. At the metalevel of the movie, however, he is imprinted onto the collective memory, thus enabling a legend to be created. The movie erects a monument to the tragic heroes of the West, those men who paved the way for civilization in the knowledge that this deed would be their ruin. This second narrative level is therefore a mirror image of the first one. Whereas in the first case a legend is destroyed at a formal, cinematographic level, in the second case, at that same level, a legend is conversely created.

The movie executes its deconstruction, namely, the dialectic of building up and then destroying a legend, not only against the double backdrop of object and metalevels, however, but also and ultimately at the metalevel alone, so to speak at a third narrative level. At this third level a Western is relating the story of the North American West, in other words *the story of the Western.* Ford unfurls it for public perusal in the age of cinema. However, when this movie was playing back in 1962, audiences were already looking back on the Western as a genre in its own right, and were already revering John Wayne as the icon of this genre. Yet John Wayne, no less, plays Tom Doniphon. This piece of casting throws a whole new and devastating light on Doniphon's admission of murder. It comes from the lips of not just anybody, but the embodiment of the Western himself. John Wayne as a murderer—this nearly amounts to the Western becoming a crime story (in the pre-urban context). This level thus realizes both deconstructive aspects at once: as a cinematographic tool, the Western successfully builds up the legend of the "Wild" West in the twentieth century, only to destroy it, or at least undermine it. In the words of the editor-in-chief, as the guardian of the public: Ford prints the fact, but in the same move the legend too.

It is this double and contrary characteristic that lends the movie *The Man Who Shot Liberty Valance* (and others besides) its aura, its glint of melancholy. The expression "aura," actualized for the field of cultural theory by Walter Benjamin, chiefly obtrudes, however, because, on the one hand, the movie is not characterized, as many Westerns are, especially Ford's, by "space, expansiveness, distant horizons," but by "the dimension of time, a game between the present and the past, between arrival and parting: recollection,"[42] and because for Benjamin, on the other hand, aura is located at the semantic level of memory or "commemoration"; it then amounts to a "cult of remembrance," with the connotations of a "fleeting expression of the human presence."[43] From its outset this movie is dressed in widow's weeds, so to speak. (This is effectively underlined by the fact that it was made in black and white.) It is a death that has brought the protagonists together, and those who are still alive are now old and gray. The time they reminisce about is another time, a wild time, but certainly not all bad compared to the one they are living in now.

At the end of the movie the senator is pained to realize that he has to continue living with a fundamental untruth. His attempt to uncover the truth at last has failed. He is therefore thoughtful and resigned, staring into space when on his return train journey the guard attends solicitously to his famous passenger, commenting loudly that nothing is too good for the man who shot Liberty Valance.

Thus ends the tale that John Ford conveys through film using two leading actors in their early fifties at a time when he himself was aged sixty-seven. In the late 1960s Sergio Leone was to take up this wistful narrative gesture in *Once Upon a Time in the West*, triumphantly, as if it were definitively to be the last time. "Once upon a time" refers the narrated to a time gone past, from which the present has distanced itself. This distancing in the mere act of narrating, of speaking about something (past), serves the purpose of self-reflection, as Horkheimer and Adorno also emphasize using the example of Homer's *Odyssey*. This alone helps to escape the myth, albeit not in abstract negation, even for them. The only path beyond the myth, which deviating from Horkheimer and Adorno also means beyond pictorial, elementarily dualistic thinking, providing relief and establishing common ground while overcoming contingency, is that of a thinking that itself draws on these abilities. The movie's novel-like narration by the man who shot Liberty Valance demonstrates, no differently from the Homerian epic, the well-understood dialectic of enlightenment. For this reason the narrative also enters the realms of the fairy tale.

The End of the Subject

Communicative Reason

"Happy are those ages when the starry sky is the map of all possible paths." Thus begins, in his *Theory of the Novel*, Lukács's eulogy of the mythical ages aesthetically illuminated by the literature of Homer. "For this age everything is adventurous and yet about belongings, the world is wide and yet like home, for the World and the Self are not yet alienated." Horkheimer and Adorno do not subscribe to this dualistic pattern of a mythical *versus* a new age, preferring to view alienation as rooted in the oldest epoch, long gone and thus suited to glorification.

In the classical Western, exemplified by the movies of John Ford, the superposition of these perspectives constitutes material predestined for culture theory. As protagonists, the heroes have an inner sense of calm and know what they have to do. At the same time, however, they are uncertain, they are searchers, no longer at home in a world of superordinate values, even hopelessly lost regarding the good life. Despair is gouged into their faces; their characters display criminal and manic traits. The Western thus feeds on both elements: that brazen starry sky of values, and existential loneliness, transcendental shelter, and homelessness. This double perspective is most aptly expressed in the bipolarity between wilderness and civilization. The starry sky, into which the Western hero gazes up as he settles down for the night "in his natural surroundings," and which protects him like an expansive metaphysical tent, is losing its illuminatory powers through precisely that law which civilization is introducing and precisely that bourgeois convention the hero himself is promoting, albeit with uncivilized or dishonest means. These means include violence extending to murder, as well as a fundamental lie that Ibsen termed the "life-lie." Through this abolition of Self he enters a tragedy heightened by the fact that he is adrift within this transient bipolarity and floundering accordingly. *Heimat* harbors the promise not only of wilderness but also of civilization. Deep down he therefore has to remain homeless, thus lending himself as a mythical figure of the modern age, as a collective (psychological and cinematographic) projection, creating a seemingly insoluble conceptual conflict while at the same time seeming to reconcile it. In this way, for this and other reasons, he creates existential familiarity and social integration, while proving himself resistant to discursive-argumentative resolution. In an initial, mildly hybrid form, modernity sees ("realizes") itself symbolized in the Western hero. Myth and modernity are therefore not to be separated with a simple cut from this perspective either.

The "entwinement,"[1] the difficult, insoluble, and mutually devouring relationship between myth and enlightenment pursued by Horkheimer and Adorno in their absurd (in Beckett's sense of the word), hopelessly hoping, skeptical yet confident work on this concept, is far less dramatic from the point of view of Jürgen Habermas, the second-generation representative of critical theory. Whereas in his early study on *The Structural Transformation of the Public Sphere* he was still heavily influenced by the idea of a culture industry, diagnosing a "unilinear development" between the mid-eighteenth and mid-twentieth centuries "from a politically active public to one withdrawn into a bad privacy, from a 'culture-debating to a culture-consuming public,'" he later admitted that this diagnosis was "too simplistic." This revision stemmed from media research with increased empirical accentuation, taking into account the cultural context of the reception in question in line with the new discipline *Cultural Studies*. In the background, however, the theoretical framework had also altered, as Habermas explains in his *Theory of Communicative Action*. He intended this theory to compensate for the normative deficit in the critical theory of his predecessors, resulting from an ambiguous equating of reason with control and domination. It is still reason that is behind a critique of reason, meaning that reason must extend beyond mere control. By revealing the potential of reason invested in communication-oriented everyday practice, Habermas deduces that the normative criterion for critique no longer has to be seen only in a public specific to one epoch, namely, the Enlightenment.[2] Habermas's starting point is thus deeper, not only historically and sociologically, but especially philosophically: according to him, it is not the individual, as the principle of the bourgeois world, which is at an end, but the subject, as the principle of modernity.

Habermas has taken Hegel's declaration of subjectivity as the principle of modernity and made it the point of departure for a new theory of modernity. Subjectivity means a superior form of existence that is capable of referring to itself "contemplatively" or "reflexively." In the self-reflective relationship, the Self as the subject refers back to itself as the object in an act of cognition. As the subject and object rolled into one, it becomes the foundation of all knowing and acting perceived as relationships to objects. It accordingly becomes the foundation of science, morality, law, religion, art, politics, and all other rational, as well as social dimensions. Thus, in a more accurate light, the Self reveals more than a cognitive dimension bearing the label self-awareness. In fact, following Kant's three *Critiques*, there also emerge a moral-practical dimension bearing the label self-determination and an aesthetic-expressive dimension bearing the label self-fulfillment. Habermas links this philosophical division of the Self to a number of other triads, with prominent status attributed to the differentiation made by sociology between science, morality (closely linked to law), and art, as well as the differentiation made by rationality theory between cognitive-instrumental, moral-practical, and aesthetic-expressive rationality. It is only such differentiation and linking that ultimately make it possible to offset modernity against early modernity. Since Descartes, more recent philosophers may have concentrated on subjectivity in the sense of theoretical self-awareness, but the first written evidence of extending subjectivity to include the notions of self-determination and self-fulfillment was Kant's *Critiques*, differentiating between theoretical and moral-practical reason, as well as an (aesthetically) reflective faculty of judgment. It was not until Hegel that the reverse side of this gain through differentiation could be highlighted as the "division" of a whole, and only with Marx did social theory finally begin to implement the philosophical precept using its own methods from the social sciences.

Passing through these four stations of theory—Descartes, Kant, Hegel, and Marx—Habermas, however, presents subjectivity as a one-sided principle. It may have the power to cultivate reflection and subjective freedom, but it is not strong enough to bring back to life that unifying power formerly constituted by the authority of religion. Not being a sufficient resource for normative orientation and social ties, it has to be replaced by another principle, namely, the overriding principle of inter-subjectivity. The former principle is certainly overridden in the Hegelian sense. Unlike postmodern attempts at "discharging," "transcending," and "overcoming," Habermas is concerned with "reshaping" the principle of subjectivity and the linked "classic" concept (as he puts it) of "ambiguous modernity," developed by Hegel via Marx, Max Weber, early Lukács, and the older Frankfurt School.[3] Habermas claims to be the spokesman of ambiguity, the advocate of ambivalence. The classic concept of modernity, just like the current concept of postmodernity, is based on an "abstract contrast between a disciplining society and the vulnerable subjectivity of the individual," set since Nietzsche in the "leveling image of a totalitarian modernity." The intersubjectivistic "neoclassic" concept of modernity transformed by the communication theory, by contrast, compels one to take a "stereoscopic view" of the ambivalences of modernity, the increasing social complexity of which does not "per se bring about alienating effects, just as easily (potentially) expanding the scope for further options and capacities for learning."

This hypothesis regarding the ambivalence of modernity is based in part on the diagnosis put forward by social theory that there is no commanding or "colonializing" encroachment of the economic and administrative system on the key ideological areas of culture, society, and socialization; in other words, the relationship between system and ideology is largely intact. It is also based in part on the philosophical concept of rationality with its threefold differentiations. A particular point of discussion is the status of so-called aesthetic-expressive rationality, which corresponds to the aspect of self-fulfillment within the subjectivity concept.

Here it is Max Weber who provides the classificatory and conceptual precept, for according to him it is the area of aesthetic-expressive rationality, the area of art and erotic love, that is, love beyond the everyday and marital, in which the subject takes his self-fulfillment in hand under the modern conditions of lost universal values. In art and eroticism the modern subject is thrown back on itself in its moral concepts and attempts to express itself as Self. These two private areas are what essentially remain to him if he is to safeguard his identity, and they are areas, as should be mentioned with no further ado, which acquired their significance through romanticism. More profoundly than Max Weber, however, it is Hegel who consciously addresses the ambiguity resulting from the philosophical and cultural differentiation of reason. This ambiguity refers not only to a positive, namely, a gain in subjective freedom, being countered by a negative, namely, a loss of social ties, but also to a kind of working division, a complementary relationship between the different types of reason and culture. A possible objectification of the cognitive and moral-legal area, on the one hand, and an emotionalization of the subjective area, on the other, now also stand mutually opposed. In addition, one side, namely, the culture of feelings, necessarily presupposes the other side, namely, the culture of the mind and legal institutionalization. To put it another way, only this prerequisite enables a romantic discourse to emerge which for precisely this reason proves to be a modern discourse; the subjective dimension highlighted by this discourse follows the differentiation between autonomous areas of action.[4]

The term "esthetic-expressive rationality" is certainly an apt makeshift title, following on from Habermas's triadic compulsion and in line with Max Weber's precept linking the two areas of art and eroticism under the sign of self-manifestation. Here it is interesting to question whether there indeed exists a complementary relationship between the various forms of rationality, in particular between cognitive-instrumental and moral-practical rationality, on the one hand, and aesthetic-expressive rationality, on the other. If one exists, what kind of complementary relationship is it? For there are several kinds. The relationship between two or more elements is complementary (or even compensatory) if one provides what the other or others cannot. They balance each other out. The *balancing* does not have to mean a *balanced* relationship, however. It is still possible for one of the elements to assume primacy in relation to the other(s). If we take a look at the relationship between philosophy and art as Hegel conceived of it, for example, art is recognized as having been an initially indispensable part of the human self-knowledge process, but as having been ultimately superseded by philosophy in the course of this process. However well each of them fulfills its independent function, ultimately they are weighted differently. In contrast, a balanced relationship is a complementary one lacking primacy, one that is reciprocal or equal.

The concept of communicative rationality with a threefold differentiation is undoubtedly of this latter kind. It can only function as a yardstick for social critique because it is like this. Critique of the "incomplete character" of rationality brings to mind a "complementary relation" between cognitive-instrumental, moral-practical, and aesthetic-expressive rationality that is already established, according to Habermas, in everyday practical actions geared toward communication. He also describes this complementary relationship as a "balance," as an "equilibrated interplay," and employs the fitting metaphor of a "mobile" that has become entangled as a result of the imperatives of rationalized society and that needs to be set in motion again.[5] It is thus inappropriate to charge Habermas with creating a primacy of the moral-practical dimension under the guise of a reason oriented toward communication and reconciliation. Habermas does not echo the one-sidedness of Max Weber from a different perspective; he does not replace a precedence of cognitive-instrumental reason with that of moral-practical reason.[6]

One could make the critical point, however, that the attention he pays to the intellectual tradition historically linked with differentiating the aesthetic-expressive dimension, namely, romanticism, is inattentive. In his theory of modernity influenced by the spirit of the Enlightenment, romanticism seems to be particularly underexposed. That is more than just a minor criticism because it harbors a problem to which Habermas is unable to provide a satisfactory solution, namely, that of a contradiction that arises in the differentiation of reason and its principle of subjectivity, a contradiction between self-determination and self-fulfillment, autonomy and authenticity, a contradiction that in the Hegelian sense cannot be eliminated even by its transformation in a theory of intersubjectivity, instead coming to a standstill due to the primacy of one side, self-determination. This is a romantic contradiction in that structural sense which grasps romanticism not as an epoch, but as a notion.

Habermas's conception of reason is unable to sustain its complementaristic approach, or at least not in its initial triadic form. He differentiates his conception of reason even further; the various areas are split again. Whereas he originally attempted to assign self-fulfillment to the aesthetic-expressive type of rationality as an aspect of subjectivity, he later firmly grasped it as belonging to the moral-practical type of rationality. From now on it is viewed as part of the "ethical" use of practical reason, which is distinguished from "pragmatic" and "moral" uses and which is internally subdivided into "ethical-existential" and "ethical-political" dimensions, into the dimensions of individual and collective "self-perception."[7] What Habermas originally envisaged as a compacted conceptuality has broken apart. It has now become accepted that an ethical rationality exists, but not an aesthetic-expressive rationality. The hidden contradiction within the complementaristic conception of reason accordingly shifts in its relationship to morality from aesthetics to ethics. In this context Habermas leaves us in no doubt that, in a conflict between ethical and moral uses of practical reason, between issues of the good life and those of unbiased morality, self-perception and justice, authenticity and autonomy, it is always the *ethical* perspective that has to take a back seat. In a conflict situation, the model of reason structured around mobility and complementarity comes up against a boundary, in this case the primacy of morality.

Against this background it is also possible to rediscover a dimension in Hegel's theory of modernity that deserves the label tragic. Modernity proves to be tragic when the power to "break in two" proves irrevocable and then takes hold of the principle of subjectivity. Then the two underlying aspects of subjective freedom, namely, self-determination or autonomy on the one hand, and self-fulfillment or authenticity on the other, both have to be on a fundamentally equal footing and inevitably have to collide. Hegel thus not only proves all those theoreticists to be wrong who claim that one of the two sides takes precedence, especially Kantians regarding the one side and individualistic Liberalists regarding the other, but also proves himself wrong, in that we no longer take him to be a philosopher of history guided by the teleology of reconciliation, but to be a theoreticist of tragedy. Classical tragedy, like the *Odyssey* for Horkheimer and Adorno, then also delivers the "original scene" for modernity (in particular).[8]

This interpretation of Hegel is clearly inspired by postmodernism, stimulated by that conflict which Lyotard revealed to be the flawed basis of all speech, not at all cheerfully postmodern, but tragic, from the inflection to the thesis. This description would not be at all apt for Habermas. Tragedy is not his element. But neither is comedy as its simple counterpart. Habermas's intellectual attitude is more that of a thinker with set principles, yet undogmatic; a German idealist, yet an American pragmatist. For him the subject has ceased to be the hero of modernity. It has grown old with scrapes and scars, but also with dignity, and from now on will only be found in the plural. In its glorified individuality it has outlived itself; its further survival may only be in a union with others. But then there can be no more mention of heroism. And there should be no regrets on that score. "It seems to me that whenever 'heroes' are honored the question arises as to who needs them and why. Even in this looser sense of the term one can understand Bertolt Brecht's warning: 'Pity the land that needs heroes.'"[9]

Dignity, Friendship, and Comedy: *Rio Bravo*

The Man Who Shot Liberty Valance is a Western in which the person who wins (for now) is the one who talks the most, a professional lawyer. Dominance of the law goes hand in hand with an emerging dominance of words, and when battles are transported to the level of argumentation or rhetoric, the raison d'être of the hands-on, violent, crowing hero falls by the wayside. In his first Western in 1939, *Destry Rides Again*, James Stewart plays a role of this kind. In this movie words alone are not yet sufficient to rid the world of a certain evil. When the going gets tough, the hero still has to master the art of shooting better than his opponent. But he is a gentleman in the West, the incarnation of male reconciliation between the civilized East Coast and the Wild West. More notably, however, this movie marks the start of the "classic Western comedy." Joe Hembus pointed out in this context that the mythology underlying the Western is "essentially a comic mythology." "With its ludicrous humor," the Western literature of the nineteenth and early twentieth centuries "understood this consistently better than movies did," and the folk ballads of the West were always familiar with it. He quotes Max Eastman as saying, "All mythological heroes have been exaggerations, but they have been serious ones— America came along too late for that. Her demigods were born in laughter; they are consciously preposterous. They are cockalorum demigods."[10]

Destry, the hero of the movie by the same name, is at ease within this tradition of ballads and tall tales. With feigned naivety he loves to tell little warning tales, always beginning with the same words: "I once knew a man who . . ." There then follows one of those many stories, hard to believe and yet readily believed, with which cowboys in the West used to love to brag, or so the historians tell us.

Howard Hawks takes up the tradition of tall tales in *Red River* (1948), specifically in the figure of a dotty old narrator, played by Walter Brennan. As the movie documents, this story has been written down, thus giving it a brazen claim to validity, just like everything else that has been written down in the last two thousand years, following the "book of all books." With this cheerfully chatty narrator, however, one can never be completely sure whether everything really corresponds to the sober truth. In *Rio Bravo* (1958) Brennan is also in the cast, once again playing an old, toothless, mumbling, endearing, complaining comrade-in-arms of the hero, this time not as the narrator, yet certainly as one of the characters who talks the most. In Westerns talking is for politicians and women; this old man, both a cook and a guard at the sheriff's house, always slightly out of sorts and usually suffering from a withdrawal of love and affection, is reminiscent of the typical nagging housewife, a figure well known from comedies, also in its male version. In *Rio Bravo* and particularly in *El Dorado* (1966), the comedy stems from genre-typical figures and situations, but also at the most basic level, from playing around with the genre itself.

A man enters a saloon—in Westerns a standard scene driving events forward, for besides the sheriff's office the saloon is the main room where action takes place. (These two rooms also depict a fundamental civilian dichotomy, with one of them representing the law and the other representing everything that undermines the law: alcohol, gambling, and scantily clad women.) This time, however, the man does not enter the saloon through the swinging doors at the front. Instead, he sneaks in through the back door. He looks ragged and wipes his hand across his mouth in an agitated movement, obviously a drinker. A man at the bar notices him and, grinning, throws a coin into a spittoon. The drinker, who knows which game is being played with him, bends forward hesitantly and shamefacedly. Yet before he can grab the coin, the spittoon is kicked away from him.

The drinker looks up. In front of him is not the man intent on playing this humiliating game, but the sheriff. From down below he (we) looks up into the face of a man, played by John Wayne, who has planted himself there like a threatening father made of solid rock and who at this moment has nothing but contempt for the man (and us) on his knees.

With this introductory scene *Rio Bravo* constructs its first major message: it is not worthy of a man to enter a house by the back door, and especially not to kneel down, as this puts him on the same level as the trash. Later on, the same man will come through the front door of the saloon and confidently confront a murderer. This enables him to regain his self-respect and gain the respect of the others for the first time. The man, called Dude and played by Dean Martin, is the covert main character of *Rio Bravo*. The movie really focuses on his problem. The plot might seemingly once again be about the victory of justice over arbitrary violence and economic power, but the true victory here is that of the humiliated individual over himself. This is a victory, however, that he can only achieve with the help of his friends. And this is the second major, wider message of *Rio Bravo*: friendship, male friendship, is the highest good. Not only do friends support each other, especially the one most in need of it at any one time, but together, as a sworn group, they can also prevail in a battle against a supreme power. The hero no longer goes it alone. He now needs reinforcement, but will only accept it from those he deems to be his equals. The elite is no longer singular, but egalitarian.

This elitist pluralization of the hero not only contrasts with the lone wolf of the singular hero concept; it also attempts to dissolve an opposition characterizing the hero as a mythical figure, in particular the Western hero, namely, the contradiction between the individual and the community. This is not simply a contradiction between strength and weakness, but one that comes to a head when a weak community does not want to help a strong individual, even though it could, at least to a certain extent. This happens, for example, when the hero is prepared to give his life for a society that, in his hour of need, then pitifully lets him down. The Western demonstrating this better than any other is, of course, *High Noon*, that disharmonious song of songs to lonesome masculinity. In *Rio Bravo* and *El Dorado* Howard Hawks and John Wayne make a point of assuming the opposite position.[11] An increasingly nervous and bitter sheriff running through town looking for help nobody is prepared to give him goes against the rules of the genre. The culture that gave birth to this genre, namely, the American culture, recognizes itself and reinvents itself time and again. The solution is apparently simple: either the hero goes it alone in the time-honored tradition, or he joins forces with equals. But he does not seek help from people who are not his equals, who cannot handle a weapon, or who lack the courage to enter a seemingly unequal fight.

Joining forces is the solution Hawks favors. The group takes the place of the individual and single hero. This is a first step toward democratization of the hero concept, even if Hawks does remain bound by the limitations posed by the different sexes, and even if within the Western genre he does more or less mark out the extremity of what this genre permits. (Heroism distributed not only among a large group, but among a group of women, thus overstepping not one, but simultaneously two genre boundaries, can be observed with wonder and amusement in the 1951 movie *Westward the Women*.) It was not until crime and war movies that a crucial step further was taken; only then could anybody (albeit still within limits) become a hero. Hawks thus opened up a traditional direction for Westerns, which shortly afterward was to take an independent turn in John Sturges's *The Magnificent Seven* (1960), before coming to a disillusioned end in Sam Peckinpah's *The Wild Bunch* (1969). *The Professionals* entered the movie theater, as in the 1966 Richard Brooks's movie of the same name, and they were to dominate it throughout the 1960s, a group of professional fighters, gunmen, each displaying additional special skills: as weapons experts, horse experts, tracking experts, explosives experts, and so on.[12]

The friendships that Hawks presents in his Westerns come across as exquisitely human, bathed in a Utopian, conciliatory, Aristotelian as well as Hegelian light. For here friendship is based on equality, on the unity of independence and relatedness to others, on the interdependence of autonomous individuals. "Hawks' universe is the happy Utopia of a friendship under the sign of emancipation for all, mutually defended and mutually created; everyone has the right to try to maintain or gain equal status." The clue is in the name of *Rio Bravo*'s sheriff, Chance: "Nobody has the right to tell another how he should behave."[13] Colorado, for example, in *Rio Bravo* is the youngest in the gang of men, and he does not like the fact that his boss has to speak up for him in front of the sheriff, when he, who is also present, could speak up for himself. Understandingly, he resents being degraded from a subject to an object. Stumpy, the old, limping, toothless, and pugnacious deputy sheriff, has had enough of the sheriff's constant commanding and criticizing and, from time to time, does exactly the opposite of what he has been told to do. He stands flagrantly in the doorway to the sheriff's office, for example, simply because Chance ordered him not to, that to do so would be too risky. The owner of the hotel, a Mexican (thus a member of an ethnic group, which in Westerns is seldom taken seriously), does not permit others, not even the imperious sheriff, to tell him what to do or what not to do.

Then, of course, there is the female sex. Its representative in *Rio Bravo* answers to the soft and lascivious name of "Feathers." She no doubt got her name from the feather boa she chooses to wear when sitting at the saloon gambling table by night. She thus belongs to the genre subgroup known euphemistically as a saloon lady, which might be a gambler, a singer, a dancer, a hostess, the owner's mistress, or the owner of the saloon herself, and who does not have a good reputation in terms of bourgeois categories. Some of her performances in Westerns are no less than splendid: Marlene Dietrich in *Destry Rides Again* (inspiring one enthusiast to float the suggestion that Dietrich, standing on the bar in her black stockings and belting out the song "See what the boys in the backroom will have" may even be a greater work of art than the Venus de Milo[14]), Joan Crawford in *Johnny Guitar* (1953), and indeed Angie Dickinson in *Rio Bravo* as Feathers.

It is immediately clear that the "mighty" John Wayne is no match for this woman. He is speechless; she is the speaker. She twists the man she has fallen in love with playfully and deviously around her little finger. She takes the initiative, kisses him, tells him what he should do next, which is to go—and he goes, as helpless and taken aback as ever in his dealings with her. When, late at night, a woman of this caliber says to a man, "Sleep tight!" in sultry, soft, seductive and ironic tones, he can only answer truthfully: "You're not exactly helping," before giving in to restless dreams. Faced with this conundrum of a woman, the sheriff has no better idea than to use the vocabulary he is most at home with. Ultimately he says not "I love you," but "I arrest you." For him the two things are the same. He would like to lock her up in the prison of housewifery, but she will undoubtedly know how to put a stop to this. His friends, at least, have great fun picturing his future married bliss.

Battered Heroes: *El Dorado*

Hawks never made a sequel to *Rio Bravo*, otherwise we would know more, but in 1966, with *El Dorado*, he did present a variation on the same theme. By now the Western was in the midst of an age-related crisis. Once again, "for old times' sake," the two main figures endure an adventure. In the process they are quite demolished. The sheriff (Robert Mitchum) turns to drink and only regains his "self-confidence" with the help of his friends; the gunman at his side (John Wayne) suffers from numbness in his shooting hand and can no longer "deliver the goods." They have to travel to their last battle, battered as they are, on a bumpy wagon, and at the end the two invalids hobble sedately through the town on crutches. They have only won this fight due to cunning, which even extends to ignoring the rules of fairness. The heroes in this film are so beleaguered that it would not take much for them to be no longer any good to young women other than as "hot water bottles." That, anyhow, is the humorous comment uttered by the hero at the end of *Rio Lobo* (1970), played once again by John Wayne. (And there is not much else positive to be said about this, the last part of Hawks's trilogy following *Rio Bravo* and *El Dorado* and incidentally also his last movie.)

Two means remain to the aged heroes in order to cope with the scratches that are actually more effacing to their self-image than to their bodies: laughter and violence. Sometimes the violence erupts from them ruthlessly, for example, when the sheriff brutally slams the butt of his gun into the face of his rich adversary, who is certainly a rogue but who in this scene is also defenseless, and would even shoot him down if his friends did not intervene at the last minute. Or when Thornton, alias John Wayne, forces two men from the enemy gang to run into the very trap they had actually set for him. He knows he is sending them to their death, and that in so doing he is morally no better than they are, yet he shows no mercy: they are to be torn apart by the very bullets intended for him.

Brutality contrasts with humor. The heroes also see the funny side of getting older, just as they no longer take the insignia of the Western all that seriously. Only the spaghetti Western is able to unite these two elements, comedy and violence, in a forced synthesis. In Hawks's movies they are curbed by the element of humanity. Overall, he maintains the middle ground between the extremes with *Rio Bravo* and *El Dorado*. Here the heroes are neither mythical, superhuman figures (as in the style of the spaghetti Western, also emerging from the mid-1960s onward, in which the characters are reduced to roles and as such to perfection), nor is the myth dismantled (as in the style of the psychological Western, which draws a complex picture of its heroes). The heroes are neither pioneers nor anachronistic relics; neither flawless, brilliant, noble knights of the modern age who allow good to prevail, nor are they laconic, "terse" in their statements and actions. They are familiar with neither boisterous slapstick comedy nor tragedy. With their steadfast principles they are also pragmatic and human, even prone to human weakness, in other words not really any different from their dutiful fellow men. As old warriors they are simply better at handling a gun; that is all.

ROMANTICISM, CRIME,
AND AGONAL MODERNITY

The Return of Tragedy in Modernity

Let's reinvent the gods, all the myths
of the ages
Celebrate symbols from deep elder forests
(Have you forgotten the lessons of the ancient war)

—JIM MORRISON, "AN AMERICAN PRAYER"

The Agonal Principle

According to the theory to follow, romanticism harbors an irresolvable contradiction. It finds expression in both a yearning submission to the Other and an emphasis on the willful Self. The romantic idea of infinite and free individuality is linked to an all-encompassing totality, which is different from and larger than the Self, and which is based (or based more) on dependence rather than reciprocity. Yet romanticism views creative capacity as an absolute, in turn awarding a higher rank to human individuality as an instance of this creativity in posttheological times than to a canopy-like totality. Autonomy and submission together form a contradiction that is not only to be found in the theoretical works of romanticists, but that is actually and glorifyingly sought. Infinite freedom, an uncontainable urge toward experimental self-expansion, stands opposed to finite unity, a total integration of the Self into a cosmic community, producing a state of mutual challenge. "And yet this paradox, or more accurately, this contradiction, is the heart of European Romanticism."[1] At the heart of romanticism, and not only its German variation, there is a pursuit of diverging directions that threatens to tear it apart. It is unclear whether, in the language of Adorno, these two directions challenge each other as opposites negative-dialectically, or whether one of the two, namely, the quest for unity, far more proves to be the "flip-side and product" of the other, namely, the quest for individual freedom. Maybe this longing for unity is that well-known "hangover" (appreciatively broadcast by romanticism critic Hegel) that inevitably follows in the wake of modern age effusions of individuality (for Hegel this especially refers to the adventurous battles of youthful hearts in love).[2]

Aesthetically, too, the unity of romanticism can be grasped as a consequence of that fundamentally conceptual paradox that in turn represents an answer to the transcendental philosophy established by Kant and continued, as well as radicalized, by Fichte. For just as philosophy, as an analysis of the conditions facilitating cognition, can no longer just issue direct material statements without having first explained their formal conditions, in other words can only *be* philosophy by always also being a philosophy of philosophy, so too does romantic poetry—"transcendental poetry," as Friedrich Schlegel called it—comprehend itself as a reflective refraction of perception, as a description of an object or a matter whereby the manner of this description is also a central theme. The fundamental poetologic elements that (literary) romanticism has pushed to the fore: irony, fragmentation, a blending of genres to create an overall work of art, imagination, fantastication, and so on, are a poetic-aesthetic expression of the fundamental paradoxical element that, to the romantics, appears to be the consequence of a duplication of reflection motivated by transcendental philosophy, of a knowledge that knows about itself.[3]

Accordingly, it is not Hegel's dialectic, but the aesthetics of the paradoxical that lead out of the circular and dangerous nature of transcendental philosophy, not forgetting Christian religion of course, which from the start emerged as a redemptive authority in the writings of Novalis and Schleiermacher. Yet, to stress the point once again, this aesthetics is a consequence of transcendental philosophy as purported by Fichte. The danger of this philosophy is, first, the "nihilism" issue, as Jacobi chose to summarize it in his early critique of Fichte. A philosophy that transforms reality into mere edifices of ideas, which reduces objective reality to the ego and its constructional principles, in so doing not only nullifies the essence of certain things, but ultimately the ego itself. The ego is disintegrated by this "reflection" as well, assuming that the latter divides what is being reflected and keeps the two things irreconcilably separate, pivotally subject and object, and thus the subject and that special object which itself is the subject.[4] This self-destruction, in both senses of the word, is highly ambivalent, however. Nihilism does not *have* to have the last word by any means. It is true that nothingness, that is, objectlessness par excellence, can claim to be the true object of romantic yearning. But objectless yearning equally aims at another, maybe higher form of objectivity. Longing is "a painful, self-feeding desire which finds no peace, not because it cannot attain the desired object, nor because the object remains hidden, but simply because it cannot be objectified. What cannot be objectified is nothingness."[5] By contrast, the same is true for the ego, which "is" nothing other than endless movement, execution of the equation I=I, a separating and at the same time connecting act of referring to oneself. If the movement were to be halted, the sides of the equation held fast, the ego would be just as objective as all the objects for which it is supposedly the constitutive basis. The constituting element cannot, however, be of the same kind as the constituted element; it cannot simply be objective, a mere object, opposed to the subject. The nature of the ego is neither that of the objective being, nor is it nothingness. By pursuing this concept so central to German idealism, romanticism, not unlike German idealism itself, is faced with the alternatives of drifting toward nihilism or giving itself over to a logic that is hard to conceptualize, paradoxical, possibly even dialectic.

Second, this logic attempts to circumvent the danger known as the circular structure of self-reflection. If the Self or self-awareness is perceived in accordance with the reflection, imagination, or representation model, then it is subject to a circular structure that Fichte recognizes, but is unable to solve satisfactorily. This central critical aspect has been the focus of in-depth analyses by, first, Dieter Henrich and, later, Manfred Frank.[6] Independent of this research, Foucault examined the same aspect in his *Archaeology of Knowledge*, according to which the restless desire for knowledge springs from the fundamental aporia surrounding knowledge. If, accordingly, conception is usually the conception of something, something other than the conception itself, then in the special case of self-awareness this is precisely what can usually be excluded: conception of the conception, conception of itself. In order to execute such conception, that is, in order as the subject to refer to oneself as the object, a knowledge of oneself must already exist, and thus be presupposed, so the objection reads. Otherwise the subject could never know that what it is conceptually referring to is itself. It has to possess knowledge about itself in order to refer reflexively to itself. This "self" can only be identified, however, under the precondition of a *pre*reflexive consciousness, as precisely that Self assumed by the act of identification, under the precondition of a consciousness in which subject and object cannot be separated, but which, in the words of German idealism, are "absolutely" one. Self-reflection can only render explicit what it is implicitly already familiar with: with itself as the Self.

The philosophical discovery of both German idealism and romanticism is that subjectivity, as the principle underlying modernity, amounts to a principle which is self-contradictory, tense to the point of breaking, even self-destructive. The groundwork leading to this discovery was completed by Fichte and later elaborated by Schelling—first the young Schelling, with his enthronement of art as the cognitive form of the absolute, and later as an older man, with his defense of the immemorial prerequisites of thought, of proximate being in the light of imparting concepts—as well as by the young Friedrich Schlegel, Novalis, and Schopenhauer. In accordance with its underlying principle, modernity sees a renewed outburst of *the tragic*. In Hegelian terms, a conflict is tragic if it comes across as inevitable, irresolvable, or, as is often said, fateful, precisely because it involves a clash between two claims that prove to be equally justified. For the equally rationalistic and optimistic self-conception of the Enlightenment, which facilitated the breakthrough of this modern principle, namely, critically reflective and autonomous subjectivity, the tragic is not a topic of interest, however, standing as it does for a limitation to reason that the age of reason refuses to grasp. For Hegel and his antipode Nietzsche, as well as their successors Horkheimer and Adorno, the abolition of tragedy (and of tragedy as an art form) is constitutive for a modernity characterized by the mediating—in this case that also means mediatizing—level of a bourgeois, prosaic society guided by its own interests. To use the barbed language of Nietzsche, Horkheimer, and Adorno, this is especially true for a modernity that eliminates that opposition between the individual and the socially universal under the sign of mass culture and political totalitarianism.[7] For its part, romanticism has not cultivated the tragic one-sidedly, but rather has cushioned it in its fundamental aesthetic element of irony. Thus it is more correct to say that tragedy returns in a less tragic guise: in *agony*, in battle and competition between equally strong elements. This may be serious and even fatal, but it can also be playful; it may be existential to the point of despair, but it can also be aesthetically stylized. If, in accordance with its philosophical principle, modernity chooses to focus these battles on the subject, this means that its internal battles are feuds between general, historically successful "powers," especially the modern right to individuality versus the right to equality, the singularity of the ego versus the unity of the community, autonomy of the Self versus self-abandonment, independence versus devotion, but also traditional powers, such as good versus evil, the role of victim versus that of perpetrator, or powers as gender categories, male versus female.

The Silence of the Lambs and the
Two Faces of its Heroine

A woman in the woods. Holding onto a rope, she pulls herself uphill. She is young, her hair in a ponytail, dressed in sneakers, tracksuit pants, and a sweater. She draws breath, gets her bearings, and carries on. Fallen leaves, fog, a cool blue misty and murky atmosphere. The camera stays with the woman. Is she being followed? The camera jumps ahead. Now we see her face, sweaty and agitated. The camera moves along beside her, faster, trees rush past. The music, until now rather dark and ponderous, becomes more vigorous, vibrant, trenchant, hounding. The camera now focuses on her feet, moves to her side, then behind her again. The woman scales a netted obstacle made out of ropes and skillfully rolls down the other side. It is obvious now: this woman is not being followed by an unknown threatening entity, but rather by us viewers. She is tackling an obstacle course soon to be revealed as belonging to an FBI training camp. Having just been forced into the role of pursuer, we at least need not worry about this woman, who would quite clearly be capable of defending herself. Then we hear a voice, a man's voice, dispelling any previous feelings of unease and clarifying the situation once and for all: "Starling" is the elucidatory word, the name of the young woman. The boss wants to see her in his office.

This opening scene from the movie *The Silence of the Lambs* plays with preconceptions, building up a stereotype only to dash it to pieces again moments later: a deconstruction of the weak woman. "A victim," or so we think, "running away from a murderer." In a minute she will stumble, and it will all be over. A fairy-tale princess alone in the dark woods. Our associations take us a step further. "But in a minute a prince will appear and save her." Yet out of the fog appears a coach, and the woman we thought was running away is really just keeping fit. She is preparing herself for the horror that we as viewers thought was already upon us and that we shall encounter later on. This woman, played by Jodie Foster, has "two faces," starting with her physiognomy. Her face is "small and pale," but with "wide cheeks, a visible forehead, a chiseled nose and a narrow mouth," as well as blue, "clear, challengingly large eyes." With her "open countenance" she conveys to equal extents two characteristics elementarily opposed, namely, defenselessness and fearlessness. The psychiatrist/psychopath whom she later visits in jail sees through her immediately. When they have only just met, he tells her straight out that she is inwardly torn. On the one hand, she knows how to make him cooperate, by paying him attention and building up his trust. On the other hand, he can also see that she is almost consumed by ambition and puts her career above all else. When she leaves the jail, she starts to cry. She remembers how as little Clarice, a child, she threw her arms around her policeman daddy's neck. The camera cuts abruptly to shooting practice, where she fires a revolver over and over. We see a close-up of her eyes and of the end of the gun. She fires at us, the viewers, the voyeurs who saw what was supposed to be private, although we were only doing what the heroine herself does throughout the movie: we looked. This constitutes a first identification between us the viewers and the heroine. "In Jodie Foster, the ambivalence of weakness and power, of vulnerability and emancipatory impulse, begins to take shape. She combines the classic clichéd female and male roles: unprotected beauty and bodyguard, victim and savior."[8] A victim, to be more precise, who saves herself by saving others; a savior who is willing to sacrifice herself, and who, through this willingness, attains the defined status of a hero(ine).

The two faces of the heroine (and of the viewers who identify with her) are not limited to the binary codes of (mental and physical) strength and weakness, savior and victim, fearlessness and defenselessness, however. This is most obvious, even penetratingly so, when she comes face to face with Dr. Hannibal Lecter, known as "Hannibal the Cannibal." In psychoanalytical terms he has a related double role, appearing as both psychiatrist and psychopath. He is highly intelligent, with the eloquence of the educated middle class and exquisite manners. This intellectuality is reflected in his name, reminding us of both *lector* and *lecture*. The flipside of Dr. Lecter, as the young FBI agent respectfully refers to him, is that he is also a serial killer with cannibalistic tendencies. However tactful and educated he appears, he proves to be just as primitive and brutal. One of his preferred delicacies is human liver with a glass of Chianti. This highly socialized product of civilization breaks one of the greatest taboos of our civilization, namely, the eating of human flesh. According to civilizatory standards he is thus at the lowest level. As the jail director puts it (himself an ill-concealed sadistic sexual offender), Lecter may be termed "a monster." (Anthony Hopkins portrays the ambiguity of this character so perfectly that ever since the role he has been in danger of suffering a similarly ambiguous fate, namely, of being identified with it forever.)

When the FBI agent visits him for the first time in his high-security wing, with its numerous barred gates and heavy metal doors, shimmering in diffuse red light and with condensation dripping from the walls like in an underground vault, the prisoner asks her in a gentle and charming, yet dangerous tone to show him her ID and step closer. She is protected by a pane of glass, yet she is still aware that she must not come too close or touch the glass. The camera shows us a close-up of his face, then cuts to hers, then cuts back to his. From the point of view of the camera, and thus us the viewers, the two people move closer and closer to each other until they are literally *face to face*, as we are with them. They gaze unwaveringly into each others' eyes and thus always also bore into ours. We are the third party, invisibly present, an entity involved maybe not physically, but certainly emotionally. This bond, already starting to emerge, is a connection that will prove to be tight, almost intimate, and lasting. At one meeting Lecter takes pleasure in saying, "People will say we are in love."

Later on, when the FBI appears to be prepared to make a deal, a "quid pro quo" with the prisoner in order to save a young woman, the kidnapped daughter of a senator, from the clutches of another serial killer known as "Buffalo Bill," Clarice, as Dr. Lecter now familiarly calls her, sits once again before the pane of glass in the jail cell, and once again the camera brings them closer by cutting from one face in close-up to the other. (The same thing is repeated at their last meeting, when the bars are no longer in the picture, the separating element has disappeared, and the two characters appear in the roles of doctor and patient, him in dazzling white, her framed by darkness, that is, by her suppressed story that she now finally tells.) In a pressurizing and conspiratorial gesture (she wants the crucial clue regarding the hunted killer), Clarice eventually bends toward Lecter and he toward her. The movie renders this an almost mystical movement, with Lecter's face suddenly appearing on the right, behind Clarice's back. Our initial shock at perceiving the danger behind the heroine's back ebbs with relief at our realization that we have fallen for a trick of the light, a reflection on the glass. For one terrible second we as viewers are dispelled from our privileged position of being in the know and even of knowing the most, and we are tricked, just like at the beginning of the movie. For a moment, an irritatingly long while in fact, the viewers, the subjects of the observation, become the playthings of the director, become objects, a manipulative element in a game that turns the sadistic and aggressive sexual impulses of the murderous figures within the movie inside out, in the direction of us viewers. Not even a second look helps us to regain our comforting distance, for now it seems as if, with the help of the camera, we ourselves are standing inside the cell and looking not only into Clarice's face but also into Lecter's, which also means: into our own. We are now where Lecter otherwise is. We are no longer the threatened victim, but the threatening offender. This second glance catapults us into the position of the murderer, where we are held fast until the perspective changes again and we are back on the same side as Clarice. The movie portrays this changing perspective, this adoption and readoption of roles, with impressively perfidious perfection, following the rules of the horror movie genre in their clearest crystallization since Hitchcock's *Psycho* in 1960: the linking of sexuality and violence, especially in their sadomasochistic ambivalence, turns the viewers into victims and perpetrators simultaneously.[9]

In this scene the viewers are not released from their enforced self-reflection, here literally a glass reflection, until the movie returns to the psychological interpretation of its protagonists. The man's face that appears above the shoulder of the young woman is a reference to her dead father, who was shot while chasing a criminal and who now appears to her like a ghost in the form of Lecter. The latter is a serious offender who nevertheless clearly assumes a fatherly function for the inexperienced agent, helping her not only directly to solve a crime, but also indirectly via her own psychological self-enlightenment. He thus becomes a father figure not only at a criminological level but also and primarily at a therapeutic level. He is a successful maieutic, at least in Clarice's case, a "midwife" who uses the Socratic method of skillful questioning and indirect reference to induce his pupil to arrive at the solution to her problem. It is also Lecter who gives the butterfly cocoon (hidden by "Buffalo Bill" in the throat of one of his victims) symbolic status, telling us that "the great significance of the butterfly lies in its metamorphosis."

Clarice, whose name is reminiscent not only of enlightenment and reformation (*to clarify*), but also of the "Poor Clares" convent of nuns founded by Francis of Assisi, bows to the first instruction she receives from Lecter: "You have to look deep inside yourself!" Ignoring orders from the police never to tell him anything about her personal life for her own protection, she relates her worst childhood memory: not, as she had first claimed, the premature and violent death of her father, but the screaming of the lambs prior to the spring cullings. By then an orphan, she had been forced to listen to their scream "akin to a child's" on her uncle's farm. In the western world the lamb's image is that of an innocent creature swathed in mystical significance as an inevitable consequence of its associations with the figure of Christ, his suffering, death, and Easter resurrection. As has now become obvious to us, Clarice is following "the impulse of a missionary."[10] Her profession is revealed to be part of a subconscious basic survival strategy. As a policewoman she is following in her father's footsteps, resurrecting him as a woman while at the same time attempting to act like a man. (She has to assert herself accordingly in the male-dominated world of the police.) Inextricably linked with this path, however, is her pursuit of a broader, moral goal: no innocent victims! It will hardly come as a surprise that the movie's title, *The Silence of the Lambs*, is as ambiguous as its central characters. When lambs are silent, they are either being left in peace or dead. In the case of the senator's kidnapped daughter, the "lamb" escapes death. Yet the movie leaves us with no doubt that this constitutes an exception, shown by the endeavors of its heroine in single combat.

Clarice's metamorphosis, in which she becomes aware of what is actually driving her, is a path leading metaphorically down to her own inner depths, mirrored by the depths of the vaulted jail holding the dregs of civilization and the underground chamber where the serial killer keeps his victims imprisoned. Clarice has to take the plunge into the legendary and much alluded-to dark side of civilization. This use and visualization of metaphor draw on images that have long been floating around our collective cultural head, especially since black romanticism and horror stories. They are employed to make us enjoy feeling scared. *The Silence of the Lambs* employs these images too, at least for those watching the movie from a distanced vantage point. Yet it is the analytical aspect that constitutes the most interesting level of this movie.

At its most superficial level, *The Silence of the Lambs* is no more than an exciting crime story centering on the chase to find an offender and solve a case. Its second level is psychological, concentrating on the heroine's dangerous quest to find herself. The crucial question here is not "Who did it, and can we catch him?," but "Who am I, who is Clarice Starling?" And also "Who or what is Hannibal Lecter?" As well as "Who or what is behind the sobriquet Buffalo Bill?" The pivotal issue here is "identity" and in particular "self-identity." One could even call it the "key category" of the movie.[11] (Yet its most interesting case study is not Clarice Starling, but Hannibal Lecter, for he not only has a double identity, psychiatrist and psychopath, but also and ultimately no identity at all. No categorization system known to us applies. "There is no name for what he is," Clarice has to admit.)

At a third level the identity issue is repeated, but this time for the viewers. From the outset, changing camera angles place us in the shoes of the protagonists. We are victims and then offenders; we chase the young woman and inexperienced FBI agent, then we are hunted ourselves; we are Hannibal Lecter, then Clarice Starling; we see events (albeit very briefly) through the eyes of the senator's kidnapped daughter imprisoned in an underground shaft and then (repeatedly) through those of her kidnapper.

We, the viewers, catch sight of the kidnapped victim through the night-vision goggles worn by the kidnapper, and in the showdown, it is also us who come face to face with the brave-yet-terrified agent after she has worked her way from door to door, room to room, through the underground vault, until the light is suddenly extinguished. The kidnapper has turned it off, and now, in the greenish light provided by his special goggles, we see Clarice, with her eyes wide open and struggling to breathe, helplessly feeling her way along the wall in the dark, touching junk, reaching a door. Then the camera cuts to the opposing vantage point, and we see from some distance the outline of the kidnapper's head. Then another cut, and we see once more through his eyes. We are closer to Clarice now, who is fiddling around in the darkness with her pistol. We approach, he does, mortal danger stepping ever closer. Clarice stumbles and rights herself. The camera cuts to the other side once more; the killer is moving slowly forward, toward Clarice, toward us. Then back again and with his next step he is so close to her, we are so close to her, that we can almost touch her. She walks in front of us. The camera switches back again and once more we see the kidnapper following Clarice in the dark, coming closer to us, before we quickly reassume his perspective. The tension, the stimulus (with the sexual connotations) is nearly at its climax when his hand, our hand, reaches out ever so gently for Clarice's head, first her hair from behind and then, as she turns around in her confusion, her face. The camera cuts ever so briefly to the other perspective. Then, back in night-vision mode, the killer's hand is seen for the second time, this time holding a gun. He points it, we point it, at Clarice, just one step behind her now. The camera zooms, our sights change once again, this time to the gun. The music, which until this point has been underscoring the events in deep tones like a dark, rolling wave, now swells; we hear the trigger being released, echoing loudly through the underground vault, then we see and hear from the standpoint of the killer how Clarice spins around, pointing her gun at us, at the murderer. As she pulls the trigger, his shape flashes in the fire, as does hers in his: we the viewers are now on the outside, as we come to realize when the camera shows us both protagonists in a clear light. In reply to the question "Who am I?" we the viewers, both male and female, have to say: "We are like the movie's protagonists: hunters and hunted, victims and offenders, normal and perverse, the personification of ambivalence. In us there is morality in the shape of the police, and civilization in the shape of the spiritual aristocrat, but also a small, scared girl, a cannibal and a woman-skinner, in other words: a creature in need of therapy and a serial killer."

Closely interwoven with the above is a fourth level. The identity being scrutinized at this level is that of film in general. *The Silence of the Lambs* is a reflection on the connection between visuality and identity, and beyond that on film as a genre of visuality and changing perspectives. With regard to this first aspect—visuality and identity—Demme's movie picks up on philosophical thought regarding the primacy of vision, which has dominated western culture at least since Plato and his "look at" or "contemplation of" the "idea" in *theoria*, for which—in the seventh book of his *Politeia* (Republic)—he created the effective allegory of the cave: human beings sit still in the dark, observing artificial (shadowy) images created by light, which they believe to be reality and the truth. It is an allegory still held true in the twentieth century, especially and most obviously for the situation experienced by a movie-theater audience. Vision facilitates knowledge ("insight") more than anything, lending objects contours and rendering them physically tangible, and thus also mentally graspable. Above all else, by cementing them firmly in place, vision endows things and persons with an identity.

Sartre's analysis of the gaze in his *Being and Nothingness* made this hypothesis famous. His ontology attributes identity only to the area of existing objects, of Being-in-itself; in the area of conscious Being-for-itself, identity therefore literally amounts to reification. For Sartre it is not a mutual Hegelian sighting that leads to self-consciousness, but being sighted by an Other. When one subject meets another subject and perceives his gaze, only then is it possible, so to speak, for him to gaze at himself. Accepting the prerequisite of Sartre's ontology, which essentially attributes "transcendence" to the Being-for-itself subject, a Being-beyond-itself, an "horizon of possibilities," a "draft character," this of course means that being sighted by another subject restricts the sighted subject in his options and limits him to the identity of an object by making reductions, in accordance with the categories of space and time, to objectivity and the present. "I am seen, therefore I am" is Sartre's formula for self-identity. Later on, in his book *Discipline and Punish*, Foucault adapts this to the context of social theory: "I am seen by an invisible power, therefore I am."

Being made to feel like an object is a prerequisite for being made to feel like a subject, for making oneself a subject. This duplication, a "dialectic" especially true for Sartre, can also be seen in *The Silence of the Lambs*, for example in the final scene. Clarice becomes the object of an intention (by the murderer) to kill. She is seen, and thus the object of a (murderous) force, yet at the same time she clearly makes herself an autonomous subject. "I am seen (by an invisible power), therefore I am" here implies two things: a "horror trip,"[12] and an act of liberation. Yet the movie does not, in the manner of Sartre or Foucault, carry the burden of ontological or social theoretical premises required to explain this duplication. The final showdown concludes with a critique of the primacy of visuality. Since Clarice cannot see in the dark, she has to rely on her other senses, crucially on her hearing. She hears the killer release the safety catch on his gun, thus not only revealing his location to her but also giving her the signal to act immediately, to shoot faster and more accurately than him. Her auditory sense saves her life.

This is the second aspect of film theory incorporated within *The Silence of the Lambs*: reflection on film as a genre of visuality and changing perspectives. For the recipients, that is the viewers fading into the darkness of the movie theater, this situation carries the familiar psychological tag of voyeurism. "Can't you feel eyes wandering all over your body?" Lecter the psychologist asks the young FBI agent, who is all too aware of the gazes on her in the male world in which she has chosen to immerse herself. The eyes are a quasi-tactile organ that lay the (coveted) person or object bare to savagery by the imagination, thus opening the floodgates to amorality. Clarice herself voices the ambivalence of the situation with reference to the screaming lambs: "I didn't want to look, but I had to look." What she sees is terrible, in moral terms, but for inner reasons she cannot avoid looking. A psychologist would even have reason to surmise that she enjoyed the terror. Hearing the screams was not sufficiently specific or exact. Looking brought certainty. A major interest in the movie is therefore Clarice's visual perspective. We repeatedly see what she sees, glancing over photos and newspaper cuttings, looking with her colleagues at an awfully butchered body undergoing autopsy. (From a feminist point of view, it is of course also relevant that it is a woman *into* whose eyes we, the viewers, see in order to see *through* them. "As the subject of the observation, Clarice is acting somewhat scandalously. Such curiosity is unbecoming in a woman." She is nearly punished for it, as the dramatic closing scene holds her tightly within the "classic female role, the object of our observations."[13])

The ambivalence shown by the heroine of the movie toward the visual perspective also applies to us, the viewers, however. We, too, oscillate between fear and enjoyment, the elementary characteristic of all thrillers and horror movies: seeking the thrill, then fleeing from it, the ambiguous stimulus, arousal through waves of feeling and states of tension in accordance with a (sexual, also varied) pattern of calm, intensity, climax, then calm again.[14] A "paranoid horror" takes hold of us here. In contrast to "secure horror," the danger no longer emanates from an alien creature beyond normality and usually externally identifiable as abnormal, for example, in the early pioneering movies *Frankenstein, Dracula, Dr. Jekyll and Mr. Hyde*, all made in 1931, or in *King Kong* two years later. Since Hitchcock's *Psycho*, but also since the concluding phase of the film noir era in the early 1950s (and *The Silence of the Lambs* follows in the tradition of film noir in many respects), horror is far more likely to originate from a psychopath and to defy ultimate explanation. Danger no longer looms from without, but from within, from a human being who is externally no different from a normal member of the species. This opens the mental door to a paranoid philosophy dictating that sheer terror lurks behind all normality and a monster behind all human beings. This is the crucial aspect of paranoid horror, the fact that it blurs the dividing line between the normal and the pathological, the familiar and the strange, thus allowing a profound mistrust to permeate our social order, or at least lend expression to it in a medium such as film.[15] The basic pattern of the horror movie, whereby normality is threatened by a monster, by an extreme case of abnormality, is still in force here, as is the genre's use of affect, expressed in a threatening atmosphere, moments of horror and often disgust. Horror movies aim to terrify their viewers; if they fail to do this, then they hardly merit the label horror movie.[16] Analyzed in psychological terms, it is also true that here the fear is directed toward the other area of human nature, toward what is referred to in literature as humanity's "dark side," its evil or more specifically animal, wildly sensual side.[17] But that other side has ceased to be localized cleanly and absolutely within a different creature or another human being. Just like God or his devilish adversary, it can be anywhere, even and especially inside ourselves.

As a medium of visuality, film is therefore an excellent vehicle for experiencing that ambivalence linked with visuality: horror-provoking desire and desire-provoking horror. Of course, further criteria are required to shed light on this insatiable desire for images. Against a psychological background and expressed in strong metaphor, *The Silence of the Lambs* offers the following explanation: "In each and every one of us lurks Hannibal the Cannibal and Gumb the woman-skinner. We gobble up the cinematic images greedily and are more than happy to assume the persona of the screen heroine,"[18] but also of the woman-skinner and of the cannibal. Following the dictates of *The Silence of the Lambs*, we as moviegoers are nothing but sublime serial killers, mass murderers who make ersatz objects pay for our urges.

Yet what is the explanation behind the *film*-aesthetic reception of the serial killer mentality? Why do we as *moviegoers* repeatedly gaze at the screen even if we do not, as in the case of horror movies, (always) want to look? Why does film basically "not allow" us not to look?

The answer is that, in accordance with its form, it actually does not allow it. Whereas in a museum or a theater we always have a wider range of things in view (in a museum our eyes drift, sometimes to this corner, sometimes to that, either within an observed exhibit or outside it, a cursory glance at another exhibit or a look at the other people looking at the exhibits; in a theater our eyes follow the main actor on the stage or choose to pay attention to the supporting actors for a while), movies do not allow us such freedom. The montage technique guides our gaze; the technical presentation forces us to follow the course of events as if recording them. The only exception to this is when we as viewers regain control over the narrative course by watching a recording of the movie on video or DVD. As a temporal art dominated by composition, film is dirigistic in a manner second only to music. The only choice we have is to stay with it (the movie or the piece of music) or to abandon it and leave. But if we do stay with it, we also have to (as with music) "follow" it, move with it, or rather rush after it and accede to it. In this respect, the desire for images is also the desire to be drawn into a maelstrom, that is, to have our vision guided and controlled by an anonymous, invisible power. The desire to experience fear and terror that is instilled by horror movies and thrillers is a simple step from this power-guided desire to receive. Put another way, the desire for cinematic images then becomes a desire to submit oneself to a power greater than oneself. In contrast to music, this is especially a desire to expose one's own visual perception and thus identification and (self-)identity, the medium of assurance central to the western world, to another, guiding power. It is therefore, in political terms, also expression of an ambivalent tendency equally (positively) devoted and (negatively) submissive, requiring a second, analytical look to achieve balance. For an (aesthetic) experience, however, as Adorno repeatedly demonstrates with Hegel, both the "immediate" and the "mediated" ways of looking are constitutive. From this, film theory deduces the genre of thrillers and horror movies. This genre is inherent to film as a temporal art, just as other genres, like the action movie with its elements of violence, are inherent to it if we define the constitutive element differently, for example, as movement.

Buffalo Bill as a Serial Killer

The Silence of the Lambs employs the "telling-names" technique. This is particularly noticeable in the names of the main characters, Clarice Starling and Hannibal Lecter, but the nickname of the man who murders women is also carefully chosen. We find out from policemen who nickname him "Buffalo Bill" that "he removes their skins." They thus choose to give him the name of an archetypal American hero. Now, as far as we know (the truth is difficult to ascertain), the historic Buffalo Bill did not kill women and certainly did not skin them. He was awarded his sobriquet by an author of adventure stories in the late 1860s, due to the fact, glorified by legend, that he was an army scout and a brave (some say, though others prefer obsessed) hunter of buffalo.[19] So he did skin (male) buffalo, and he also scalped Native Indians, or "redskins." At the heart of his legend he is portrayed as the man who, to avenge General Custer, defeated so disastrously at Little Big Horn, held in his hand the very first scalp in the war against the Sioux and the Cheyenne in 1876. "The Red Right Hand; or, The First Scalp for Custer" was the title of a melodrama in which he was to perform that same year. (Previously, from 1873 onward, he appeared in his own show, the "Buffalo Bill Combination," replaced by "The Wild West" in 1882. Until 1916, the latter was to become one of the largest, most popular, and financially most successful undertakings of commercial entertainment for more than thirty years, a mammoth circus that toured North America and Europe with hundreds of animals, actors, musicians, staff, and loaded trucks.) "The First Scalp for Custer" was also the title of one of the many dime-store novels since 1871 starring Buffalo Bill as the hero, some of which he wrote himself. The image of Buffalo Bill waving a scalp to and fro in his outstretched right hand will forever remain an established part of his iconography.

The Buffalo Bill in *The Silence of the Lambs* has exchanged buffalo and Indians for women. It is they who now have their skin removed. The psychological explanation for this, given by Dr. Lecter, is that Billy hates his own identity—male, homosexual—and would like to disown it in favor of a female one. He attempts this literally, and thus pathologically, by sewing himself a dress, a second skin, from the skins of women. He literally and physically slips into the skin of others in order to become another mentally. In so doing he illustrates a universal truth. In a perverse way he performs physically what we do mentally, for example, in the movie theater, and what in moral terms we actually should do, namely, put ourselves in the position of others. But if we take his sobriquet and related background seriously, Billy also illustrates a universal truth in a very specific sense, and this time it is not as easy to separate the perversion from the norm. Seen in terms of his individual psychosis, Billy is nothing more than a perverse gay by the name of Jame Gumb. (Incidentally, the movie refuses to extend its toying with ambivalences to this character. Here, with an astonishing perfidiousness and lack of reflection, it upholds not only a crude contrast between men and women but also a resentment toward homosexuality, stigmatizing both the female identity and homosexuality as sick.[20]) Yet, as "Buffalo Bill," Jame Gumb is elevated to the symbolic level. Now his perversion is no longer an individual fate but a collective one. Now he is being linked to a figure central to collective American nostalgia, and because this figure has a mythical aura, *The Silence of the Lambs* amounts to blasphemy. The movie puts forward a theory that is hard to swallow, namely, that through this serial killer the Western hero (Buffalo Bill) is exposed for what he really has been all along: a man who hates himself, a man who really wants to be a woman, but who is not allowed to be and thus kills again and again. The *frontier* located in the expanse, the vastness of the prairies, the forests, and the world at large, has disappeared; what remains are the alternatives of pursuing it in outer space and the future (a function aesthetically assumed by the science-fiction genre), or of relocating it in time conceived of mathematically quantitatively, in a succession of episodes, in series, and to make its corresponding psychological location internal. Since this shift in perspective, horror from the inside has been a perpetual threat. Buffalo Bill no longer has to fight buffalo and Indians; the wild animals and wild natives now lurk within him. As a serial killer, the path he chooses out of this plight is one of desperation. But in his hard, male core he has always been both a serial killer and desperate.

The historic Buffalo Bill became a star of the entertainment world. Among the various men of the West he was the most successful at creating and preserving his own image. The movie theater had a hand in this from the outset. Since the history of film dates back to the recording of fairground attractions, it is easy to understand why thirty-second circus acts from the 1894 Wild West Show might have been included.[21] What is astonishing, however, considering his early and successful media presence, is that movie directors later showed little interest in Buffalo Bill as potential for the big screen. The only movie adaptations worth mentioning are those by William A. Wellman (1944) and, particularly, Robert Altman (1976). But the character embodied by Buffalo Bill in *The Silence of the Lambs*, namely, the man who hates himself, or rather hates being a man and thus kills, has been unforgettably represented in Westerns, especially in some of the genre's (qualitatively as well as commercially) outstanding productions.

Will Kane in Fred Zinneman's *High Noon* is one of these men, unable to escape a masculinity founded on violence. Another striking example can be found in *The Wild Bunch*, Sam Peckinpah's ruthless, brutal, and depressing reckoning with the ideals of the Western, culminating in a showdown of blind, elementary, virile destruction. The movie demonstrates the dialectic of the myth "regeneration through violence."[22] It demystifies the myth by surpassing all that the genre previously stood for. Acts of violence are not the necessary and satisfactory solution to every problem that emerges and mounts up; all they leave behind are desolate, depressed characters who have gone to seed. Richard Slotkin, who in his book *Gunfighter Nation* examines the racist theory of Anglo-Saxon superiority and its influence on popular culture and American politics, believes this theory to be especially well outlined in Theodore Roosevelt's seven-volume work *The Winning of the West* (1885–94). Slotkin views *The Wild Bunch* as the "*Moby-Dick* of Westerns" (for Joe Hembus, it is *The Searchers*) and draws a parallel to Vietnam.[23] Then there is the male figure created by Clint Eastwood.

The Angel of History: *Unforgiven*

A few names have been so closely linked to the figure of the cowboy as to become icons of the Western genre. John Wayne is the most obvious; Henry Fonda is another. Then there is Clint Eastwood. In *Unforgiven* (1992) his Western persona makes a comeback. The icon is long since soiled and flawed, haphazardly patched together in places, yet still capable of making an impact. And its flaws are from within, that safe aura of the mythical crumbling just like that image of a masculinity believing itself under control.

Like *The Wild Bunch* before it, *Unforgiven* is a Beckettian finale, an ultimate and yet never-ending toying with conclusion. It has had a place within the Western genre for a long time, ever since the "adult Western" came into being in the early 1950s, with *High Noon* being its most prominent example. *Unforgiven* can be seen as a continuation of the story of Will Kane, after beginning a new life with his wife. She "straightened him up," stopped him shooting (and drinking), gave him two children, and then died. He loved her, so he has no regrets, but the work he is currently doing has sent him plummeting down the social ladder. He runs a small pig farm, a paltry homestead in the middle of nowhere. He is quite literally in the dirt, in the pig dirt, when one day a young man seeks him out in order to persuade him to come to a little town called Big Whiskey. There a cowboy has knifed a prostitute for laughing at his small penis. The sheriff has had the cowboy and his friend whipped and ordered them to give the woman in question, or rather the owner of the brothel, seven horses in order to atone for what they have done. The prostitutes, however, are not satisfied. ("Maybe we ain't nothing but whores but we, by god, we ain't horses!") They have made an offer of head money. William (Will) Munny, the man who used to be an evil gunman and who now holds his head above water as a shabby pig farmer, initially refuses, having closed that chapter of his life and not wanting to have any more to do with shooting and killing. But the humiliating misery surrounding him causes him to change his mind. His children should have a better life than one in a warped old hut in a deserted prairie with cackling hens and a dilapidated backhouse. This is a reasonable, even morally acceptable justification for his decision, yet the more often Munny repeats it to himself, the more he knows he is just trying to calm his nerves. His violent alter ego is reemerging, and that is what he is afraid of.

And so an aged gunslinger once more mounts his no less aged horse, struggling as his body has grown stiff. The horse is likewise no longer used to being ridden and protests. Nor is Munny still a good shot, unable to hit a tin can until he swaps his revolver for a shotgun. His children watch him practicing, and the spectacle is embarrassing. Killing for money is no easier, as he discovers when he arrives at the scene. He grits his teeth, takes hold of his gun, and fires. Thinking of the reward, he shoots one of the two cowboys in the stomach. He has to wait several tortuous minutes until the young man, writhing around in terrible pain, is finally dead. He says that he used to "kill out of pure meanness." Now that he has taken up arms once again for the sake of his children, for the future, killing has become a miserable business. A third variation is still ahead of him: killing for revenge.

His old friend, who could not bring himself to shoot the cowboy and set off for home instead, is arrested and whipped to death by the town sheriff for not revealing the name of his partner. In other words, the man who refrains from killing for money and is the only person in this movie to perform an heroic act, namely, to favor an undignified and cruel death over the betrayal of his friend and partner, suffers an immensely unjust fate, executed personally by the representative of law and order. The division between good and evil is as unsuccessful in this movie as Munny's attempts to separate out the healthy pigs on his farm from the sick ones. The "fatal consequences" of justice are a major theme in *Unforgiven*.[24] The prostitutes are right not to accept being treated like pieces of meat, yet in so doing not only cause the deaths of the two cowboys (albeit impetuous, yet also awkward, conciliatory, and ultimately scared young men), but also trigger the whole ensuing chain of catastrophic events. The sheriff wants his town to remain a peaceful one, yet asserts this wish by brutally beating troublemakers, or those he believes to be disruptive elements, half to death, sometimes even killing them. Without wanting to, the protagonists bring shame on themselves as a result of their good intentions, bringing about the very opposite of their justified desires. Will Munny, too, wanted to take up his gun just one very last time, for the sake of his children's future, yet at the end, like in a Shakespearean tragedy, the bodies are piled up high. In the light of the crime committed against his friend, of an injustice that stinks to high heaven, so to speak, all that remains to him is revenge.

His revenge is the showdown in the movie, orchestrated like the Last Judgment. It is nighttime, and a thunderstorm breaks over the town. Will Munny canters down the main street. All we hear is the dull clatter of his horse's hooves, the thunder, and the rain (not to forget deep and ominously wavering music). The camera moves slowly through the darkness. We are Will Munny. In front of the saloon we see the body of Will's friend laid out in an open coffin, a warning to all murderers. Inside we hear the voice of the sheriff. He is buying whiskey for his helpers and issuing instructions concerning the hunt for the other two bounty hunters the next morning. In the middle of his speech he stops, suddenly aware of what others have already registered and what we too, from Munny's perspective, also know. A man is standing at the entrance to the saloon, hardly recognizable in the dimness. In his right hand he is holding a rifle, his intentions ominously clear. He raises it slowly from his hip, bringing it into position. He asks who the owner of "this shithole" is, takes aim steadily, and shoots him. The owner of the saloon was unarmed, the killing a cowardly act. It is revenge for the saloon being "decorated with his friend." Next it is the sheriff's turn. But instead of a loud bang all we hear is a soft click. "A dud!" The sheriff's surprised cry triggers a final barrage of shots. It is over in seconds. Munny has shot down all the sheriff's helpers bar one, plus the sheriff himself. The rest of the people in the saloon scatter as fast they can.

Munny pours himself a whiskey. He is back on the drink, the past having now totally caught up with him. Then he notices that the sheriff is still alive. Like an executioner he stands over him, the sheriff lying defenselessly on his back and mumbling his last words like a grotesque commentary: "I don't deserve this . . . to die like this. I was building a house." When he realizes that his murderer is not impressed, he changes tack: "I'll see you in Hell, William Munny." The latter's answer, long before he squeezes the trigger, is simply a hoarse and illusion-free "Yeah." Munny leaves on horseback as slowly as he came, through the boggy ground. He calls back to the people, reminding them that breaking the commandment leads to the sanctions they have just witnessed: "Better not go cuttin' up, nor otherwise harm no whores." (From below we gaze up at William Munny, a figure with a bitter face, black as the night surrounding him, with the American flag in the background.) "Or I'll come back and kill every one of you sons-o-bitches." And then he and his white horse disappear into the darkness and never-ending rain.

This is a finale in total keeping with the rules of the Western genre and the style of Clint Eastwood. Here he reappears in the role that he made famous and that in turn made him famous, that of the taciturn, unscrupulous, shrewd, and remorseless Lonesome Rider, the dusty gunman with screwed-up eyes, cynical and coarse in a poncho, with a chewed cigarillo and a hardened poker-face, or apocalyptic, dressed in a long dark coat, the Western version of the Grim Reaper. He is the Devil and the messenger of God rolled into one, with that fixed expression, impassion etched on his face, always with a nimbus of untouchability. Together with Sergio Leone, to whom *Unforgiven* is dedicated (alongside Don Siegel), Eastwood created the cynical and coarse variation of this figure in the 1960s Dollars trilogy, later giving it an apocalyptic rewrite in his own Westerns. The "man with no name" from *High Plains Drifter* (1972) and *Pale Rider* (1985), who one day suddenly appears in some place or other, carries out a retaliation campaign or straightens out a lawless world and then rides off into the sunset, has dispensed with the traditions of the picaresque novel and slapstick—which the spaghetti Western has consistently merged with the theme of violence since Leone—as well as with the figure of the simple adventurer or bounty hunter. Instead he has regained something of the classic Western hero—a certain dignity, even virtue.

What sets *Unforgiven* apart from Eastwood's earlier Westerns is an existential hopelessness, a refusal to accept redemption even during the redeeming act. The finale provides no—literal or figurative—ray of light. The avenger himself looks like a dead man, with his scraped, pale, pinched face, like a corpse made out of tanned leather, a gaunt and stiffly awkward spook from the past. *Nomen est omen* here, for the name Munny sounds not only like *money*, but also a bit like *mummy*.[25]

In this Western, the catalytic function of the female once again achieves prominence. (Young) women repeatedly appear, especially to Eastwood's characters, as defenseless or innocent creatures whom men need to protect from rape by their own kind, by others like themselves. This protection comes across as penitence for their own disgraceful deeds performed against women in the past. In *Unforgiven* Munny is cured of killing and drinking, is delivered from his previous wrongful existence by a woman, the mother of his children. Her curative powers slowly diminish with her death, and the battle between the new man and his old self starts afresh. He begins to struggle when confronted with an act of violence against a woman (the fact that she is a whore does nothing to diminish her female right to protection), and he finally loses the battle completely with the news of the cruel death of his friend (for, as illustrated by *Rio Bravo*, in the lonely male world of the Western friendship is a lofty good). It should not be forgotten, however, that the real reason for the ensuing chain of violence is female derision of the male sex, or more specifically, in accordance with crude male self-comprehension, of the male genitalia: the prostitute laughing at the cowboy's small penis. From a psychological perspective, as well as that of cultural anthropology, Munny's battle represents man's battle against himself, against what in the occidental culture is defined as the "male self." This identity amounts to a fateful curse. "I am no longer the same person, no longer the person I used to be." This is the self-adjuratory formula—for the man, and thus also for the "hero." The male hero no longer wishes to be a hero, yet he has to be.

The showdown is also the point in the movie where fictional and real heroism converge. *Unforgiven* is an "adult Western," a Western that reflects on itself as a genre by visualizing its aging heroes. It links this retrospection with a look at narration and its ambiguous value as truth. It tells of both the old Western heroes and the tales these heroes give rise to, tales in two senses: the hero takes shape through narrated tales; and the tales are shaped (told) by heroes. This movie is about the origins of heroic tales, the origins of heroes through tales, in fact the tales they tell themselves. Accordingly, heroic self-creation has a dubious side. The hero creates himself not only through an outstanding deed that sets him apart from the rest but also through narration of this deed, sometimes even through the narration more than through the deed. A hero is someone who, one way or another, produces his own myth.

The movie, the narration visualizing this, also remains ambiguous. *Unforgiven* tells the truth while uncovering the alleged truth as boasting, exaggeration, and falsehood. The story of the cowboy who cuts the young prostitute's face, for example, grows each time it is told, until it is said that the woman's eyes were gouged out and even her breasts cut off. A classic example of this narrative toying with the truth is provided by another aging gunslinger, called English Bob, who dictates his past experiences to his biographer, a dime-store novelist. The biographer does not know what to make of all these grandiloquent and outrageous tales, published under the noble and sensationalist title "The Duke of Death," until he meets the sheriff of Big Whiskey, who brutally brings the self-proclaimed hero down to size. Having received a clobbering and been deprived of all his mystique, he is finally driven out of town. As the sheriff sardonically notes, the proud "duke" has become a lame "duck." Exchanging just one letter in his title is enough to rewrite the tale of this gunman. Yet *Unforgiven* does not only (plainly and simply) tell the truth. Since the movie is itself no more than an act of narration, this gesture, this showing act of revelation is also true of the movie itself. Its manner of showing can be distinguished from (mere) display, but not separated from it.

The entire final sequence provides a last proof of this. The writer is witness to the shooting in the saloon. He can hardly believe what he has just seen and wants his new hero, avenger William Munny, a resurrection of the former murderer, to give him some details: How did he know whom to shoot first, and in what order to proceed? The taciturn hero does not have an answer capable of satisfying a writer, this fearful and reverent child of the bourgeoisie. All he can say is that he was lucky, all along. The readers of (dime-store) novels, sociopsychologically of the same ilk as the writer, will not (wish to) believe this unheroic answer, however, and will thus be given more material to read than the writer actually witnessed. This is symbolized by the latter's glasses. When Munny rides out into the night in the pouring rain, the young writer watches him go. He puts on his glasses in order to see better, but that which is before him, the reality, blurs. In the end he follows in English Bob's footsteps, a con artist of the Wild West, the hero of a narrated tale, of an imaginary deed.

This legacy also connects *Unforgiven* to another major theme in Westerns: that of fathers and sons, of the initiation of boys as they become men. The young man, called Schofield Kid, who searches out Munny on his farm in order to tempt him with the prostitute's head money, proves to be a braggart. He could do with the writer's glasses, being too short-sighted to aim accurately, and after he has shot one of the cowboys close up (once again hardly befittingly, for the poor boy was sitting in the rest room) he is so overcome with guilt that, in tears, he renounces his life as a gunman and hands over, *quasi* hands back, his revolver to Munny, gunman senior. The son ("Kid") does not wish to become like the father. The writer, the intellectual, now advances to become the son. Also repeatedly called "son" by the sheriff in an imperious, indulgent manner, he "here proves himself to be the heir to the Western hero, and the ideal community created by the heroic deeds has shifted to the reading public," later the theater-goers, "to the fictions the Western has always owed its lifeblood to."[26] The hero is nothing without those who narrate his tale. They are his mirror image, in which he reproduces and expands himself. The narrators (the intellectuals) are vice versa nothing without their heroes. They need them in order to write (for example, about the impertinent Self as the hero of modernity), and since there is never enough information available they invent it, aspects of it or all of it. When the hero looks into the mirror he sees a fiction; when an intellectual looks into the mirror he sees a minor hero capable of development.

Just as the sheriff in *Unforgiven* is building his own house, so the heroes are building their own legends, and the results are equally warped. In this movie the Western is as likely to fall down as the self-built house, as dilapidated as the pig farm of the come-good gunman, and as fabricated as the tales of "English" marksmen.

Like John Ford, Eastwood maintains the *tension* between *demythologization* and *remythologization*. Like Ford, he deprives the myth of its mystique by simultaneously exploiting it. On the one hand, Eastwood deconstructs the myth by describing the conditions giving rise to it, while, on the other hand, he employs precisely those conditions to perpetuate the myth. He neither destroys the myth, nor does he restore it. Heroism is not reinstated with a vengeance, but neither does it dissolve in thin air as a mere figment of the imagination. Yet Eastwood's myth, even the deconstructed myth, has ceased to be the symbolic homeland it was for Ford. It is not melancholy that envelops his work, but a refusal to accept redemption following violence. When Munny appears in the saloon for the showdown, he is the image of Clint Eastwood we have from his time as the *Pale Rider*. But all that is left of that image is a silhouette, an empty shape. The hero has become a mere shadow of his former self, a dark shadow in search of its owner. The "hero returned" enters the world like a ghost emerging from an old picture, and the movie portrays this final return rather like a ghost story for adults. From a technical point of view, its only requirements are a great deal of darkness and very little light. Its message is sufficiently obvious: violence has no redeeming qualities. The myth of regeneration through violence, which Slotkin exemplified using the Western, and which Peckinpah sent to a mass grave in *The Wild Bunch*, regains its dark Old Testament coloring through Eastwood, only now without a vanishing point. "*Unforgiven* deals with the absence of God in that Paradise which human beings have made their living Hell. It is a penitential sermon set in grim times. And it is a snide attack on heroes."[27] *Unforgiven* is a movie that would surely have pleased Adorno, for it is a movie offering no less than a negative theology in the guise of a Western, only capable of circling laconically and in eternal damnation around its dissolved absolute, the hero.

"There is a Klee painting named 'Angelus Novus.'" Walter Benjamin, the owner of this picture, interpreted it in his thesis *On the Concept of History*.[28] "It shows an angel who seems about to move away from something he stares at. His eyes are wide, his mouth is open, his wings are spread. This is how the angel of history must look." But there is also another, more secular, albeit no less "inspired" image. It portrays Clint Eastwood. His eyes are narrowed and his mouth closed, a thin line on dry skin. He is wearing a dirty black coat that reaches almost to the ground and a hat that covers his thin, shrunken face. He stands silently, legs apart, the saloon doors squeaking behind him. It is the moment of apocalyptic horror and the final blow. An avenging angel has entered the world. "His face is turned toward the past," the corpses littering his path, "one single catastrophe which keeps piling wreckage upon wreckage and hurls it at his feet. The angel would like to stay, awaken the dead, and make whole what has been smashed." The disfigured and pale face of the young prostitute nursing the ill-treated bounty hunter back to health after he was beaten half to death by the long arm of the law briefly signalizes a potentially different ending to the story, a conciliatory one. "But a storm is blowing from Paradise," a dark, insistent, impervious power. He calls it "meanness," "caring," or "revenge," this thing driving him to pile up the corpses. "What we call progress," we the children of modernity socialized by America and the West, "is *this* storm," which always means the same thing regardless of the name it is given: deliverance from violence through violence. Its most faithful enforcer is the serial killer.

The Revolution of Romanticism

Better than any other author in the current philosophical discussion, Charles Taylor expresses the way in which the subject has become the "venue" for an agonal battle between the different principles of modernity, thus reinstating the element of tragedy. He began to uncover the romantic streak within the historically sedimented layers of modernity in a book about Hegel. In this comprehensive monography, written as a commentary intended to update the reader, he also refers to Isaiah Berlin, his teacher and friend from their shared time in Oxford. It was Berlin who, with his extensive research into the European history of ideas, expressly emphasized the romantic tradition. On the one hand, this makes it seem strange that Berlin is not cited in the relevant part of Taylor's book *Sources of the Self: The Making of Modern Identity*; on the other hand, this is understandable considering the extent to which Berlin's concept of romanticism extends beyond Taylor's. For the agony that Taylor perceives in the great moral sources of the Self under modern conditions is, according to Berlin, a consequence of the romantic perspective.

For Berlin, the romanticism that broke fresh ground at the end of the eighteenth century signified a "turning point," a "radical change in the entire conceptual framework," as had only occurred as radically within the history of western thought, especially political philosophy, on two previous occasions: the first time during the "puzzling" two-decade period between the death of Aristotle and the rise of Stoicism, when the individual was removed from the context of sociopolitical existence and viewed as determined by his personal salvation; and the second time in the early modern age, when Machiavelli confronted the entire previous tradition with the trenchant idea that political moral concepts are not only different from those of Christian ethics, but maybe even ultimately incompatible with them, as well as that religion is to be perceived as utilitarian, and that the concept of an ideal state is to be rejected. With romanticism, the eudemonism of the Stoics (which from an aretological standpoint did not, however, lose sight of virtue as the measure of private happiness) and the Machiavellian value-pluralism ultimately acquired a new quality. For Berlin, romanticism represents the "most important turning point to date," the significance of which he believes "still not to have been realized to its full extent." He sees this significance in the simple truth that "the essential premise" behind the previously valid system of thought has now been annulled, a premise that, as he believes, connected even recalcitrant skeptics with self-assured dogmatists, namely, that "a fundamentally unanswerable question is not a real question, that somewhere there is a solution to every problem," in other words that a correct answer is principally possible, that the truth of a thing or state of affairs can always be discovered.[29] This is the rationalistic fundamental premise underlying western culture.

Berlin commences his depiction of the emergence of romanticism with Rousseau and Kant. According to these two philosophers, we all know that in order to act correctly and to live well, we have to listen to the voice within. They enabled the idea to assert itself slowly but surely that creatures endowed with reason make their own laws, totally in keeping with the notion of "autonomy." Since Rousseau we have been familiar with the formula "I am free if I subject myself to a law that I have made for myself." The Self as the sole determining author of its own moral concepts enters the stage of world history. In Rousseau and Kant this still occurs in its "harmless" variation, however, both being philosophers of the Enlightenment and believing that everything that the inner voice is capable of commanding is objectively and universally valid, the latter going by the simple name of "reason."[30] The conclusions that romanticism draws from this are different, however. It sees art as the role model for moral and cognitive-critical autonomy. The fact that humans, as knowing and acting beings, are not dependent on a transcendental, divine power, nor a terrestrial one, nor that of nature and the epistemologically "given" (the objects to which they refer as knowing beings), the fact that they are not subject to third-party determination is interpreted by post-Kantians and critics of objective idealism thus: that the objective world and the realm of values is not something that one discovers, but that one creates. One example of this is artistic practice. Alexander Herzen, one of several Russian thinkers who exerted a great influence on Berlin, growing up in St. Petersburg and experiencing the Russian revolution there as a boy, asks, "Where is the song before it enters the composer's mind? Where is the dance before it is danced? Where is the poem before it passes the lips of the poet? They are not there in some external sphere waiting to be discovered by someone," a poet, a dancer or a composer. Each creation is far more "somehow always a creation from nothing. It is the only completely self-determined human activity."

This romantic version of artistic productivity following on from the theological *creatio ex nihilo* is certainly a myth, a self-deception that is productive in itself, functioning both as a substitute for recognition denied in the real world and as a way of overcoming contingency, an attempt to counteract, more or less successfully, the dissolution of the Self rooted in transcendental philosophy. Alongside dialecticians, deconstructivists, and genealogists trained in psychology or sociology, we have to evaluate the idea that there is one single thing that owes its existence entirely to self-determination, something entirely positive, untouched by negative, detrimental conditions as an illusion—albeit an heuristic and pragmatic one, but nevertheless an illusion.

The "radical break" initiated by romanticism is clearly visible: an end to the attempt "to adapt one's own self to something which obeys its own laws," to a cosmic order, natural right, or cognizable reality. In this sense, Berlin is more convincing in his talk of a premise consistent within western thinking. The concept of truth being linked to "agreement," to adequation, extends from ancient Greece via the specific formulations of Thomas Aquinas, to the late eighteenth century. The romantics were the first to break with a realistic or representationalistic theory of truth, and among them Berlin lists the poets Wackenroder, Tieck, Novalis, and the

Schlegels, but also Schiller, as well as the philosophers Schelling, Jacobi (who categorizes reason as an ability to perceive that holistically exceeds beyond common sense, but who does contradict Kant and Fichte by advocating a realism based on feeling) and Fichte, who views the Self as deed and will, as that body creatively subjugating the "repulsively" resistant not-Self to its own designs.

This break with the previous theory of truth is not reflected in all the authors mentioned, particularly the philosophers, however, or at least not in the same way. Jacobi, for example, categorizes reason as an ability to perceive that holistically exceeds beyond common sense, as has been familiar since Plato's analogy of the divided line in his *Republic*, and prominent (similar to the "recently prominent tone of superiority in philosophy" deplored by Kant in a late 1796 essay) since German idealism. Unlike Kant and Fichte, however, he advocates a realism founded on (Kantian "prominent") feeling. What makes him a romanticist is his orientation of reason toward holistic "perception." As is well known, Fichte continually revised his *Science of Knowledge*, permanently searching for a solution to the modern Cartesian problem of truth, to finding a basis on which being and Self, reality and conception, can be united, that of the (absolute) Self or, in later versions, the absolute (appearing only as an "image" in the finite Self). Between 1794 and 1809, in a frequently admired gesture of genius, Schelling no less productively bombarded the world, year for year, with one new system after another. In actual fact, his romantic phase was limited to the years 1800 to 1802/03. He is the only one of the aforementioned philosophers to grant art that exemplary status. He is also the one to fulfill most unreservedly the criterion that Berlin maintains is true of romantics in general, namely, that for them art most purely fulfills the antirealist conception of truth by being "not an imitation or a copy, but an *expression*," an expression of the Self in its *post*divine creativity, in both senses of the word.[31]

A Relationship of Conflict

Taylor may not make *expressis verbis* use of Berlin's research into the expressivistic tradition within the history of the arts in modern Europe, but he does pay this tradition equally detailed attention. Self-realization, the realization of internal, mental states in expressive forms, becomes a central idea. Within the distinction made by Berlin between "negative" and "positive" freedom, in which the accent is actually on the former, the "negative" side, despite a weighting that is principally balanced, within this distinction, then, between a freedom that means, on the one hand, the absence of external obstacles and, on the other, authentic realization through elimination of internal, motivational obstacles, Taylor chooses to place his accent clearly on the latter, the "positive" side. In his representation, Hegel's philosophy can claim to have achieved a synthesis between this romantic-expressivistic tradition and the Kantian-moralistic tradition. Despite his failures, Hegel will always remain a stimulating intellectual figure as a result of his attempt to unite self-determination and self-realization, autonomy and authenticity.

By the time of his book *Sources of the Self: The Making of the Modern Identity*, Taylor has departed from this emphatic appreciation, however. At least so far as the power of synthesis is concerned, he no longer believes any philosophy capable of it. Instead, he expands upon what he outlined in his presentation of Hegel, already written with the theory of modernity in mind. Accordingly, nature as an internal source, together with that of expressivism, form the basis for a new concept of individuation and a new interpretation of art. Of course, this concept of individuation is not completely new. Taylor uses much of his book to underline parity and disparity in existing concepts of subjectivity, internalism, and individuality. Psychiatrist Dr. Lecter in *The Silence of the Lambs*, who as a psychopath turns himself inside out without warning, issues the command, "Look deep within yourself!" which is one of the key instructions of western culture. St. Augustine was the first to refer to it and, according to him, by turning to one's own Self one gains access to a state beyond reason yet at the same time essential to it, a yardstick existing for all human beings and called "God." By experiencing its own thought process, the finite Self is able to recognize infinity and perfection as the condition governing that process. Descartes radicalized this move toward internalism, postulating that ultimately the sources of certainty and morality that the Self is subjectively searching for are no longer localized outside the Self, in a higher entity, the transcendental, in Plato's ideas or the Christian God. "Disengagement" of the world and corporeality, as well as an instrumental, rational, controlling stance toward them, now became a major characteristic, self-creation driven onward methodically and with discipline. Locke brought this tradition to a close with his conception of an atomistic, "punctual" Self, disallowing any communal ties. Romanticism contradicts both Descartes and Locke, just as it equally follows on from them. The general tie is in an internalized subjectivism, whereas the contradiction is in the emphasis of expressivism, of the ego—no longer exploring itself *more geometrico*, but expressing itself in its inexpressibility, forever circling itself in its individuality, fleeing the community while at the same time constantly searching. Through romanticism "expressive individuation" becomes one of the "cornerstones of modern culture," and with it, due to the "awe" we have reserved for artistic originality and creativity ever since, art "has come to take a central place in our spiritual life, in some respects replacing religion."[32]

This new conception of nature and expression is also the basis for a final detachment from the old doctrine of mimesis and its ontological restrictions. As Berlin never tires of emphasizing, whereas this detachment likewise leads to a removal of art from the old conception of truth oriented toward the theory of adequation, Taylor, by contrast, who is eager not to throw the baby out with the bathwater, makes a monumental effort—using art and theoretical history—to argue his case that removing the old conception of truth from art, by now antimimetic, need not mean detaching *every* conception of truth from it. According to his representation, in art it is far more the case that, via the conception of creative genius, expressive individualism joins up with a truth-revealing function, which for him bears the Joycean name "epiphany." In this respect, one of Taylor's foremost intentions is to demonstrate a continuity extending from romanticism, as an art historical and philosophical epoch, to the present day. From Taylor's persistent standpoint, what could appear as a break, such as Courbet or Zola's nature-despiritualizing realism, Baudelaire's antinaturalism, or Schopenhauer and Nietzsche's amoral metaphysical naturalism, is simply a transformation. Thus he actually does manage to provide the type of enlightenment he fundamentally prescribed for himself in his book, namely, to reveal those historical "sources" that are motivating for contemporary self-comprehension without a conscious awareness of the same. Romantic-expressive individualism is able to remain undiscovered for a simple, pertinent, and philosophically transparent reason: it characterizes modern culture to such a degree that it is almost taken for granted. The children of modernity are blissfully unaware of the extent to which they are romantics.[33]

But this is not the only source from which modern man derives his self-comprehension. Far more characteristic of modernity is the relationship of conflict and tension existing between the various sources, for Taylor being not only romanticism and rationalistic disengagement but also Jewish-Christian theism. This is a conflict that is particularly prevalent between rationalistic-disengaged reason and romantic-expressivistic reason. Taylor's concept of modernity does occasionally waver, and he does not rule out the possibility of a "conciliatory balance," as if in ancient obligation to Hegel, but deep down he maintains his view that the fundamental sources of western morality and modern identity are also the sources of equally fundamental conflicts.[34]

Individuality: Quantitative and Qualitative

With this, the fundamental conflict existing between the three sources of the modern Self, we are, in Hegelian terms, confronted with an irreconcilable contradiction residing within the principle of subjectivity. As Taylor has noted, this conflict is especially evident between the rationalistic-disengaged and romantic-expressivistic self-comprehensions; yet this contradiction is also, and especially, a product of romanticism. Astonishingly, Taylor pays this detail no attention whatsoever. For him, "romanticism" essentially means "self-realization." In this point he once again does not echo Berlin's representation, the latter explicitly describing this contradiction between the two poles of expressivism and rationalistic universalism, between individual expression and general norms, as an element fundamentally characteristic of romanticism.

The development of this contradiction has been memorably described by Georg Simmel. A century earlier, his book *Philosophy of Money* appearing in the year 1900, Simmel made a distinction between two forms of individualism thrown together by the French Revolution and its ideals of liberty and equality, with no heed paid to any existing "internal contradiction." The first form of individualism established itself with Christianity, especially the Reformation, thereafter with eighteenth-century Enlightenment, exemplified in the philosophy of Rousseau and Kant, and finally with nineteenth-century ethical socialism; the second form emerged as "specifically modern," from Goethe via romanticism to Nietzsche, although it is also partly characteristic of aristocratic antiquity, especially ancient Athens, as well as found in representations of various personalities by Shakespeare and Rembrandt.[35] Whereas the first form of individualism emphasizes the ways in which all human beings are equal, the second emphasizes the ways in which all human beings are different. The former focuses on the human being in its universality, its "dignity" and its "human rights," the latter on its particularity and uniqueness. In the first form the individual asserts itself as a single being standing apart from, and providing a contrast to the forms of collectivity organized by the state, the church, and guilds, whereas in the second form the individual asserts itself as standing apart from all other individuals, in a long line of independents. "Quantitative" or "abstract" individualism in the first case, and "qualitative" individualism in the second constitute a contrast within the conception of individualism, a contradiction that involves an inherent interdependency, or at least to the extent that qualitative individualism only emerges as an inevitable problem following a complete historical, that is, modern realization of quantitative individualism. Qualitative individualism does not presuppose quantitative individualism, neither historically nor systematically, for it is also an element featuring in societies of aristocrats and slave owners, in which the higher echelons attach significance to their special status. But once quantitative individualism has been realized, qualitative individualism is automatic.

As in Nietzsche's day, under modern egalitarian conditions the aristocratic idea of prominence once again claims its due, albeit a new and socially defused due of merely symbolic significance. Individualism, be it quantitative or qualitative, is therefore not an invention of modernity, and thus also not of romanticism, yet its significance during this epoch was new and revolutionary. Simmel's position with regard to this ambiguous concept of individualism is not transparent. On the one hand, he clearly favors the idea of qualitative individualism. In registering a "preponderance" of what in the Hegelian tradition is termed "objective spirit" over "the subjective"—a preponderance of a human spirit that finds expression in societal and state institutions, language and technology, reinforcing itself through convention and expanding through history—over individual subjects, in other words a "hypertrophy" of objective "culture" over the subjective ("culture" is Simmel's term descending from Hegel's term "spirit"), and in evaluating this overgrowth "in essence" as the result of a "growing division of labor," he not only resorts to the Hegelian model of relinquishment and alienation, as well as the literary and philosophical critiques of alienation in Schiller's *Esthetic Education*, Hoelderlin's *Hyperion* and the works of Marx, but also and at the same time, in the cultural critical tradition stemming from Nietzsche, perceives the individual as reduced to "a negligible quantity . . . , a single cog . . . against the vast overwhelming organization of things and forces."[36] Simmel's inclination is toward an individual capable of asserting itself as an individual. In agreement with Max Weber's (Protestant) taking of sides for the heroic-tragic individual, yet with a clearly Nietzschean tone, he sees in the "great and creative human being" the incarnation of an "individual law," for which art provides the blueprint. In each work of art, all the individual parts join together in line with the will of the artist to make a whole, just as in life individual phases and actions join together. In contrast, all those "lesser beings" who are "not strong enough," that is, the masses, must "adhere to a universal law," to a "style adopted from the outside."[37] The strength and greatness of a human being is reflected in his ability to subject himself not only to a law, but to his very own law. This is his formal affinity to aesthetics.

On the other hand, Simmel does not believe quantitative individualism to be inferior. Simmel's ambiguity even escalates to the following alternative: viewing both forms of individualism as equally valid or uniting them in a synthesis. He describes the first half of this alternative within an essay on the metropolis, viewing it as the function of the metropolis to "make a place for the conflict and for the attempts at unification" of these two concepts of individuality since here not only all manner of people, classes, and ranks, but also "conflicting life-embracing currents find themselves with equal legitimacy."[38] Simmel describes the other half of the alternative when addressing the task of creating a "positive synthesis." This can, of course, in turn be viewed in two different ways, in a harmonistic or in an agonal, even dialectic sense. The contradiction between the two forms of individualism is reshaped at a higher level until, in the first case, the contradiction disappears; in the second case it remains. The first realizes an ideal of the harmonious-integral personality; the second characterizes a person as *being* this contradiction. Ultimately Simmel seems to come down on the antiharmonistic side, and thus overall on the first half of the alternative between agony ("struggle") and synthesis. At least this is suggested by repeated formulations such as a "two-sided spiritual need," an "eternal struggle," the fact that it is crucial for the "momentum" of the human being "to keep that contradiction alive," and lastly that it is "a completely philistine prejudice" to think that all conflicts and problems are there to be solved.[39] Consequently, taking into consideration the lifestyle models deduced from this double concept of individualism and dismissing that of the methodic lifestyle developed by Max Weber, Simmel cannot be clearly allocated to the model recently discussed as a "patchwork biography" or a "hybrid" existence.

As a result of this contradiction within the principle of subjectivity, which for Simmel is "quantitative" *versus* "qualitative" individualism and for Taylor is "autonomy" *versus* "authenticity," "self-determination" *versus* "self-realization," the ambiguous front presented to the theorists by modernity accordingly becomes even more pronounced as soon as romanticism not only favors one side of the contradiction, namely, the latter, but also aggravates Berlin's contradiction afresh, pushing it to the point of irreconcilability and tragedy or, slightly less dramatically, agony. Viewing Simmel and Taylor from this perspective, they both—Simmel, for whom dualisms are fundamentally constitutive to his theory, and Taylor, provided he does not choose to pursue the Hegelian conciliatory model—argue their cases as romantics.

The Weakness in Taylor's Uneasiness with Modernity

In his *Sources of the Self,* Taylor provides a historical justification for key goods possessing a factual validity within modern culture. His answer to the ancient question regarding the good life is an indirect one, opting to enlighten us about the modern identity conflict that no longer permits identity to be located between the good and the just, self-realization and self-determination, authenticity and autonomy. This is precisely where he sees the ethics of modernity at the end of the twentieth century. There is no simple answer and no uniform answer to the question: "How should I live? What is it that I really want?"

As contingency research, research into historical sources with moral intent is at least in a position to reveal the reason for this calamity. However—and here comes the weakness—it does so in half measures. For there is no equally nominalistic orientation corresponding to its historic orientation. Goods—or as Taylor calls them, "hypergoods"—specify the relevance of all moral norms in the narrow sense of the word and are for him, on the one hand, inseparably furnished with a subjective viewpoint, unable to elicit the value of things neutrally, while, on the other hand, also having an objective element projecting beyond subjective evaluations. Taylor's ontological explanation concerns "articulation" of the "deepest" moral institutions of occidental human beings. This is why Habermas's triad of reason also fails to satisfy him, for it only concedes the possibilities of scientific objectification, moral formalization, and subjective expression. Moral-ontological statements have no place within this pattern. Their claim to validity is neither that of objectivity and neutrality, nor that of mere subjective expression.

Vice versa, however, Taylor finds himself unable to prove the motivational power of the highest goods using scientific argumentation, and of having to give his philosophy an artistic slant, at least to the extent of needing an equally expressive and metaphor-laden language if it is to have an "epiphanic," truth-inferring, horizon-opening, and motivating effect. If Taylor's philosophical theories are to be truly convincing, they need to be persuasive. Their argumentational logic fails to stand up without rhetoric. This only becomes problematic, however, due to the fact that giving philosophical, and in particular moral philosophical, argumentation an artistic slant harbors a far more profound intention. Art's epiphanic strength has enabled it to emerge not only as a medium for interpreting the world that constitutes meaning and argumentation in itself, but also as a medium for metaphysics.[40] In art, to use Hegel's words, because semblance points to a spiritual element, subjectivity to an objective element, it opens up not just a new and different semantic context in each case, but a context that is objectively meaningful, and it is this additional, overrunning claim that really puts Taylor on the spot, tying him to an aesthetics of truth containing premises that have become extremely doubtful.

Heidegger, Gadamer, and Adorno are the last twentieth-century philosophers of standing who have conceived of art in the tradition of romanticism, as a venue for a "higher" metaphysical truth. For them the premise is that an almost universal context of decline or blindness brought about by technical instruments and scientific methods leaves no room for the "other," unless it is art, as well as the philosophy that is reflected in it and that—ambiguously—finds self-reassurance in it. The notion that only art provides access to the privilege of truth is, for Heidegger, Gadamer, and Adorno (as well as the young Schelling, Schopenhauer, and the young Nietzsche), based specifically on the metaphysical premise, the premise of the theories of rationality and truth, that, first, the objectifying stance of (natural) science prevents us from viewing the essence of the being; second, that this essence exists at all; and third, that this view is disclosed in (aesthetically specific) evidence. Whereas there are good reasons to justify a theory of truth based on evidence and, even more so, to justify a critique of the comprehensive claim to truth made by the sciences, in the post-Hegelian age metaphysical or ontological theory no longer has such a claim.

For Taylor, the affinity between aesthetics and the romantic morality of authenticity possesses a special quality. Reassurance through art is essential for morality in general, but also and especially for the morality of authenticity. Yet it is precisely in this special case that an irreconcilable tension is revealed. In his letters *On the Esthetic Education of Man*, Schiller trenchantly shows off the close connections between art and the morality of authenticity, putting forward the theory that only beauty grants man his integrity, that is, authenticity, a playful state beyond economically conditioned specialization ("fragmentation") and the Kantian separation of (moral) reason and sensuality, obligation and inclination. Since Nietzsche the aesthetic has appeared to counter the moral as a positive entity, and to the same extent the authentic thus also has to appear to oppose the moral. However, Taylor's criticism is that with aestheticization the morality of authenticity remains behind its "ideal." In every case, from the hermeneutic perspective underlying Taylor's criticism, authenticity demands, first, a "horizon of significance" that, as a given "background," enables the foreground, that is, the authentic Self, to distinguish itself; second, it demands a "dialogic" definition of the Self. Differences only emerge against a common background or horizon of significances and values, the latter enabling us to become familiar with others through linguistic exchange, whereby "language" amounts to "expressive language," the language not only of words but also of gestures, feelings, art, and much more.

Authenticity, formally defined as "being true to oneself," as a temporarily constant expressive reference of the moral Self to itself, thus unavoidably requires a relationship to others. This is also true when, predominantly in the aesthetic tradition, authenticity is defined as "originality," and thus also as "opposition to the rules of society." It is necessary to comment here that, at this level of definition, Taylor fuses authenticity with individuality, for one can, at least temporarily, lead an authentic life without differing significantly from others (for example, as a happy gardener). By contrast, one can take shape as an individual without being authentic (for example, as a highly neurotic artist). At the practical and moral level, authenticity does not imply individuality, nor vice versa does individuality imply authenticity. Here authenticity is not an intersubjective relation like individuality, but an intrasubjective one; it refers to the realization of a notion, of an internal image. If authenticity is comprehended as an assignation of originality, however, according to which an original (for example, a text, a signature, or a manuscript) can be distinguished from a copy, then authenticity certainly does imply individuality; the authentic manuscript is the genuine one, the unique one. One can agree with Taylor, however, that the requirements of moral authenticity captured aesthetically and of intersubjectivity established linguistically and culturally, together with morality in the conventional sense, "may be in tension," indeed must be.[41] Individual morality and collective morality do not have to stand in mutual opposition, whereas originality and sociocultural rule observance do.

The connection between authenticity, understood in the sense of originality, and art is ultimately not only an historical one. With some caution, with a "perhaps" and a "maybe," yet nevertheless with systematic force, Taylor formulates: "If authenticity is being true to ourselves, is recovering our own 'sentiment de l'existence,' then perhaps we can only achieve it integrally if we recognize that this sentiment connects us to a wider whole. It was perhaps not an accident that in the Romantic period the self-feeling and the feeling of belonging to nature were linked."[42] The case in which we achieve the "whole" which is authenticity, an individual feeling of being, is that of art. "Authenticity" here amounts to individual feeling of being, to a feeling of idiosyncrasy, emotional self-assuredness, and not in an epistemic, but in an existential context. In line with Heidegger's actuality, for Taylor authenticity is an existential, moral-practical quality possessed by human beings, but also by human products, for example art. A human being is a person, yet in a figurative sense also a work of art if what he claims ("I am the one who . . . ") and what is really true for him are in agreement. Yet this presupposes that one has not made a mistake with regard to this claim. In Taylor's "positive" conception of freedom, which he places alongside Isaiah Berlin's "negative" conception, authenticity thus also requires a freedom from internal compulsions, from anxiety and the internalized norms that obey it. By linking authenticity to the dimension of feeling, Taylor does not simply respect philosophical cognitions as given but also shows reverence for that epoch extending from Enlightenment, in part characterized by sensibility and pietism, to romanticism. By including, with reference to Rousseau, the "comprehensive whole," the dimension of nature and the cosmos, he decidedly outs himself as a romantic, which in this context means: as a metaphysicist of feelings, as a supporter of a metaphysics necessarily insecure in post-Hegelian terms, yet emotionally secure in anti-Hegelian ones.

The Gangster as a Tragic Hero

The Westerner is the figure that best illustrates the self-grounding of modernity, the grounding of modernity in itself and in the Self. This figure displays blatantly tragic, as well as romantic, characteristics. Through his own actions, the hero of the Western film puts an end to the wild, libertarian prehistory of the West, of which he himself has been a part; he thus puts an end to himself. Once he has achieved the feat of implementing civilization, that very same civilization declares him superfluous. He is without *Heimat* and without peace, an involuntary romantic, condemned to roam forever or else find his destiny, find his death in the showdown. What is tragic is the underlying contradiction, the irreconcilable negative connection between individuality and community, liberty and order. What is tragic is the assertion of law and order with violence, with the aid of something that law and order is trying to eliminate. What is also tragic is the ritual of revenge commanding the world of the Western hero almost as hopelessly as once it did the mythical world.

The tragic element increases, however, with the Westerner's successor, the gangster. He is the embodiment of the modern (urban) romantic, but also of the modern (capitalist) entrepreneur, and is therefore the unity of a contradiction resolved within the modern environment in his person. As American movie critic Robert Warshow explains, there are some characteristic similarities between the gangster and the Westerner, as well as some pronounced differences. Most worthy of note, "The two most successful creations of American movies" (at the time of writing, in the early 1950s) "are the gangster and the Westerner: men with guns."[43] Like the Westerner, the gangster has no choice but to pursue his violent and murderous activities until he himself is killed. Yet, unlike the Westerner, the gangster, unscrupulous murderer that he is, does not radiate an "inner invulnerability." This is also reflected in other aspects of the gangster's character. The (classic) Western maintains a hold on the violence it involves through the self-composure of the hero. Self-composure is depicted as an ambivalent virtue, oscillating between (rigid) self-control and (relaxed) self-mastering, as followed through occidental history by Taylor in his *Sources of the Self,* between an ascetic dominance over one's inner nature and being mindful of its cultivation, as described by Horkheimer and Adorno, but in both variations it does largely exclude cruelty toward others.

This is not the case with the gangster, who welcomes cruelty, either feeling nothing or experiencing a sadistic pleasure. This is aptly demonstrated in *Scarface,* the 1930 or 1932 movie by Howard Hawks (Hollywood's self-censorship under Will H. Hays demanded that changes be made), the movie Warshow particularly had in mind. The gangster boss, based of course on Al Capone, the unofficial ruler of 1920s Chicago who was sent to jail in 1931, has eyes that sparkle at the pure joy of torture. This morally reprehensible yet socioculturally attractive hero is a neurotic. The Westerner's successor loses his personal invulnerability because he breaks with that specific code of honor or rank that states that one never draws one's gun first (unless, like for the battered heroes at the end of *El Dorado,* there is no other choice). However, the gangster boss, called Scarface due to a scar on his face (like Capone had), lives by the following motto: "Do it first, do it yourself, and keep on doing it!" Whereas the Westerner presupposes fairness and trusts in his ability, in his superior technique, the gangster relies on his own unscrupulous ability to circumnavigate fairness, as well as on his own unpredictability: the fact that at any moment he might lose his self-control is elementary to his success, based as it is on the fear of others.

"Do it first, do it yourself, and keep on doing it!" is a motto that not only holds true for gangsters but also for entrepreneurs and egocentric eudemonists. They all have in common an uninhibited striving for success, and they link their happiness to that success. This explains the gangster's impatience and nervous activity. James Cagney awarded this trait a lasting pithiness in the genre-typical movie *Public Enemy* (1931), as did Edward G. Robinson in *Little Caesar* (1930). These two actors defined our image of the violent criminal in the same way as more recently only Al Pacino, Robert de Niro, and—standing apart from the rest in the *Godfather* trilogy—Marlon Brando have managed to do.

As soon as the gangster believes he can rest on his laurels, he starts to fall, just like the entrepreneur driven on by the marketplace. Vice versa the rise of the gangster, like that of resourceful and unscrupulous entrepreneurs, takes place at breakneck speed. In this respect he is another version of the *American dream*, its evil incarnation, free from all moral restrictions that might hinder his success. "The World Is Yours"—a neon sign bearing this message appears in *Scarface* on several occasions. The gangster is not only attractive as a man with a gun, but as one who uses this weapon exclusively to serve his own social success and happiness. He is thus attractive as someone who does not believe in the "normal" routes to happiness. "The gangster is the 'no' to that great American 'yes,'" and this is precisely why he has to die. He is abandoned to death not so much because he disregards legality and morality, but because he does not uphold appearances in a culture that obliges one to have "a cheerful view of life" and that, as an egalitarian society, views a sense of tragedy as a luxury reserved for aristocratic societies.[44]

Gangsters remind the culture of optimism that it has a dark side. The gangster is the "tragic hero" of modernity, trying to assert himself as an individual within the conditions of modernity—bourgeoisie, capitalism, and states ruled by law—and doing so by making some of these conditions—success, happiness, restlessness—absolutes, thus demonstrating in loyal fulfillment of their own logic that they are incompatible with the others. It is not necessary to follow on from Nietzsche in his early works and construct an analogy to ancient Greece, suggesting that "at the bottom" of American and ancient Greek optimism smolders the pessimism of tragedy. But it does seem reasonable to ask nonmetaphysically and nonfundamentalistically whether and why modernity (so influenced by America), like ancient Greece before it, should *require* a tragic element. The gangster movie can provide us with some answers. As Warshow stresses, it is the movie, the symbolic, or in Hegelian terms the "spiritual" area of culture that is responsible for our picture, for our image of the gangster. The gangster is "primarily a creature of the imagination." "The real city, one might say, produces only criminals; the imaginary city produces the gangster: he is what we want to be and what we are afraid we may become."[45]

Here Warshow not only provides a short (and simple) psychological explanation for the creational connection between the gangster and the imagination, for the ambivalence, the twofold fear and desire that revolve around the figure of the criminal; he also names its social habitat. Just as the Westerner belongs in the open landscape, the gangster clearly belongs in the cramped and hectic environment of the city. Their environments also color their differing maverick styles. The Westerner is a loner because of the principle he lives by, singled out as the only upright within an anxious or corrupt community, or at least one of few, like a tree in the landscape, whereas the gangster is a loner because of his will for power and his egoistic conception of happiness. The gangster's loneliness is forced on him by his hard-fought success, the aggressive assertion of his own predominance, whereas the Westerner accepts his loneliness with certain Stoicism. The loneliness of the gangster is that of the tyrant who can trust nobody. For him being alone, even in a room, signifies danger. The moment a movie shows the gangster boss or one of his cronies alone—in the bathroom, in the sauna, at the barber's, in a corridor—we know he is about to be killed. ("No convention of the gangster movie is more strongly established than this: it is dangerous to be alone."[46]) The Westerner, by contrast, thrives on this type of danger; his inner and outer calm are strengthened by it. The nervous activism of the gangster indicates his precise lack of calm, pro-pelled by fear. The gangster is permanently fleeing, whereas the Westerner wanders aimlessly. The latter is therefore "a man of leisure" par excellence, giving the constant impression of being "unemployed" and having noth-ing to do.[47]

However tragic the hero of the Western or the gangster movie might be, he does have a younger, funnier, and more self-deprecating brother. In the wake of all the swan songs at the end of the 1960s, from John Ford to Sam Peckinpah, the Western genre witnessed the outwardly tragic and aging hero being joined by a fun-loving and youthful one. Peckinpah brought to the screen in turn Butch Cassidy, the Sundance Kid, and Billy the Kid, and with them the impertinent Self entered the Western scene. The story of Butch and Sundance shows us two outlaws at the turn of the twentieth century who understand each other extremely well. One of them, Sundance, alias Robert Redford, likes to appear expressionless, as if eager to honor his nimbus as a poker player and gunslinger on all accounts. To make up for this, the other one, Butch, alias Paul Newman, pertinently finds life all the more fun. When he is not busy trying to find a way out of a permanently tricky situation that has arisen because he and his friend carried out a double raid on the Union Pacific Railway and are now being tenaciously pursued, he is making new plans ("I have vision, and the rest of the world wears bifocals"). He dreams of other countries and their many badly guarded banks, of having a good time, all the while doing handstands on his bicycle ("the future's all yours") to the dreamy bouncing rhythm of "Raindrops Keep Fallin' on My Head" playing in the background. At the end of the movie, in Bolivia and still pursued by the military, they can no longer escape death, a fact that for them is no longer worth addressing. They ignore it like two little boys who want to carry on playing their game.

Billy the Kid also has to die. He does not give in to the urging of sheriff Pat Garrett for him to leave the country and escape the impending danger of being hanged or simply shot. Ultimately he is shot by Garrett himself, his old friend. There is too much wild vim and vigor about him ("Billy, they don't like you to be so free," Bob Dylan sings in a rough and whiny voice), too much untamed pride. His youthful face (that of actor Kris Kristofferson) is far too relaxed, far too resigned to its fate, smiles far too sweetly. He knows that his decision not to run off means his own death. But he is not prepared, for the sake of survival and the principle of reality, to pay the price that Garrett has to pay, namely, that of compromise and being bought by those with enough money. He is not prepared to commit the inner suicide that Garrett has to commit. When the latter kills Billy "the Kid," he also kills the kid, the child within himself, or, to put it in psychoanalytic terms, he kills the principle of desire oriented toward the fulfillment of desires. In one respect, however, many of the youthful, playful heroes resemble their older, tragic rivals—namely, in their coolness. The figure in which they can most easily see themselves is, for good reason, the gambler or poker player.

6

Heroes of Coolness and the Ironist

Nothing is more witty and grotesque than ancient mythology.
—FRIEDRICH SCHLEGEL

Indefinability and Self-reference

Cool is cool. This is not just a tautology. Far more, it means that those who are cool are—to put it uncoolly—good. Cool is a positive attribute, a distinction within the system of values held by a culture, *our* culture, our *current* culture, or even more accurately: our current adolescent subculture. When the *kids*—another slang word difficult to define precisely—say that artificial fur is cool, that George Clooney is cool ("he makes 'cool' cool again"), that the new bar on the corner, the titanium Apple Macintosh PowerBook, this, that, or the next thing is cool (anything can be cool in principle, even the truth), then they primarily and quite simply mean that all these things are approved of and deemed good. And yet "approval" is a broad concept permitting a whole list of specific terms: "great," "fab," "in" (that is, "in fashion"), and so forth. In this variation "cool is cool" therefore means: being "in" is good. Yet not one of these meanings is exactly the same as "cool," nor all of them taken together, even though each of them is linked to it in some way. It is far more accurate to say that "cool" has a semantic arena all of its own.

Tautology does put us on the right methodical track, however. The formulation at the beginning of this section was not selected by chance.

Cool is cool is cool . . . And "a rose is a rose is a rose. . . . " Endless loops such as these indicate many things, including the issues of *indefinability* and *self-reference*. So far as the problem of definition is concerned, coolness is no easier to define than time was for St. Augustine, or pornography was for Justice Potter Stewart: "I'll know it when I see it," the Justice declared for the record (naturally with no legal import).[1] To the ancient philosophical question of what exactly time is, St. Augustine famously replied, in his *Confessions*: "If no one ask of me, I know; if I wish to explain to him who asks, I know not."

Phenomena such as time, pornography, and coolness (to name just three) obviously require a type of knowledge that may address issues using clear terms, but not necessarily using plain, unambiguous ones, as Descartes and Leibniz have put it, a knowledge that for linguistic philosophers operates with examples, not definitions. Knowing something by seeing it means recognizing that thing in examples of it. One knows the meaning of the color red by seeing red paint; one knows the taste of a pizza margherita by eating a piece of one; one knows what beauty means when somebody points out a beautiful rose, a beautiful human being, or a work of eighteenth-century art. In all of these cases, conceptualization does not take place through the provision of a common feature or cluster of features, but by naming an example of the said conceptual category that best represents it. "Robin" is more representative of the category birds than "hen"; "murder" is more representative of the category crimes than "vagrancy." Such exemplary, representative, or even prototypical concepts are not formed via parity and disparity, but via relationships of similarity, or "family resemblances" as Wittgenstein was to call them in his later years. In logical terms they necessarily remain unsatisfactory because they involve indefinites, yet for everyday speech, for learning processes and inductive generalization, which also means for science, they are fundamentally important.[2]

They are *especially* fundamental to the phenomena of beauty and art. In his *Critique of Judgment* (§ 18 and § 46), Kant explains convincingly and momentously the strange compulsion with which an aesthetic judgment strives to spark consent, due to the specific, namely, exemplary necessity it brings with it. Within the context of aesthetics, in which rules, universal justifications, and most of all definitions are incongruous, a peremptory feeling of necessity particularly sets in. Aesthetic judgment thus provides us with the classic example of clear, yet vague knowledge. Natural beauties or works of art exemplify what beauty or art is, even though we cannot define what this is. To use another term, the cognition that allows us to realize that we are dealing with beauty or art belongs to the class of *evidence.*

In order, therefore, to clarify what "coolness" means, one should, according to my first proposal, adhere to the *method* of representative exemplification and typology. Then one need not be at the mercy of rigorous and aseptic definitional standards, nor diffuse and confusing semantics. "Cool" neither means "precisely this and nothing else," nor does it mean "everything and nothing."

The tautology that emerges when describing coolness needs to be seen as a pointer regarding not only method but also *content.* Accordingly, the concept of coolness primarily revolves around itself, largely devoid of content. What is important here, as is also the case with art and fashion, is not "what," but "how."

Against this background, systematically or analytically stringent theories are not best suited to lending this concept contours. Here philosophers with a softer theoretical touch prove more appropriate (in most cases): Lionel Trilling, Walter Benjamin, Richard Rorty, and in particular Georg Simmel and Helmuth Plessner. They bring the necessary heuristic framework to an exemplifying and typologizing analysis. With their help, it is possible to develop two hypotheses. First, coolness, with the accent on its current sense, is a phenomenon of *style* and *makeup,* meaning that it *perfects heroism, satirizes individuality,* and *aestheticizes* socioexistential *coldness.* Second, and closely connected to the first, coolness is a phenomenon currently characterized by signals in the *media* and their ability to *portray.* Together they can be summarized in a single and very simple hypothesis: coolness is a social phenomenon of *aesthetics.*

Pumpkin and Honey Bunny

"Forget it. Too risky. I'm through doing that shit." Pumpkin, a young man in a light blue, open-necked Hawaii shirt, is somewhat edgy and jittery as he says these words, smoking his cigarette in the same way.

He has got himself comfortable at a table in a simple, typically American diner, but he cannot sit still, waving his arms around as he speaks and sliding around on the leather seat. Honey Bunny, a woman of about the same age with red hair, is sitting opposite him, calm and upright (her back is playing up). She drinks her coffee and listens to what he is saying. When she speaks, it sounds like a cross between a child and a duck: "You always say that. That same thing every time: 'I'm through, never again, too dangerous.'" The two of them—both petty criminals—once again deliberate whether they should change their professional lives and work more effectively. Pumpkin believes that banks are easier to rob than liquor stores, their normal target. "Too many foreigners own liquor stores these days. Vietnamese, Koreans, they don't even speak fucking English. You tell them, empty out the register, they don't know what the fuck you're talking about. They make it too personal, one of these gook fuckers is gonna make us kill him."

He proposes robbing the joint that they are sitting in right now instead. Nobody ever robs restaurants. They do not expect to get robbed. Just like banks, these places are insured. The manager "don't give a fuck," nor do the waitresses or busboys—"some wetback getting paid a dollar-fifty an hour." Honey Bunny's expression changes. She is slowly getting the idea. When Pumpkin opens her eyes as to just how many well-filled wallets are also to be found sitting around in restaurants, she takes the bait. Her nostrils flare, her eyes light up, she smiles to reveal her teeth, and hisses: "Let's do it!" They lean over the table toward each other and kiss—once, twice, the second time more greedily. Then they sit back on their seats like two wild cats ready to pounce. They smile at each other, as united in happiness as only conspirators can be. "I love you, Pumpkin." "I love you, Honey Bunny." Then they begin. Pumpkin jumps up onto his seat, a gun in his hand, and shouts out his usual, "All right, everybody be cool, this is a robbery!" Far more rudely, Honey Bunny adds, "Any of you fucking pricks move, and I'll execute every motherfucking last one of ya!" They stand there with their guns pointing into the room. The image is held and suddenly, like the echoes of a gunshot, we hear an electric guitar.

At this point we have only known Pumpkin and Honey Bunny from Tarantino's *Pulp Fiction* (1994) for five minutes, yet we feel we know them very well. They are familiar to us from many other movies involving hypernervous, slightly hysterical, often screeching, always complaining, loud-mouthed *kids* with criminal backgrounds, always intent on being *cool* by using language that is unadorned, direct, brutal, and flippant. But they are especially familiar from that constellation that gave gangster couples a hallowed, corny, and mythical status all rolled into one, *Bonnie and Clyde*. Their story has been told and retold, most famously by Arthur Penn in 1967 (with Faye Dunaway and Warren Beatty). In the early 1930s, when America was facing the consequences of the world economic crisis of 1929, waitress Bonnie Parker and criminal Clyde Barrow cruised through Texas and its neighboring states committing a series of car thefts, burglaries, robberies, and murders before dying in a hail of bullets from six machine guns.[3]

When Quentin Tarantino's *Pulp Fiction* hit the big screen, such pairings were enjoying a minor, yet strident, cinematic renaissance. It was 1994, the same year in which Oliver Stone chased his *Natural Born Killers* all over the screen at breakneck speed, in a desolate mixture of styles including Hollywood movie, cartoon, video, and documentary, employing snatched images and distorted perspectives, all to the sound of rock 'n' roll and the narcotic-archaic music of *Carmina Burana*. One year earlier, the driving force in the movie *True Romance* was also a murdering couple, for which Tarantino wrote the screenplay, as he did for *Kalifornia*, in which Juliette Lewis once again, as in *Natural Born Killers*, triumphs as the embodiment of female *white trash*. David Lynch supplied the blueprint for these and other films in 1990 with *Wild at Heart*, depicting characters who openly dream the fairytale of true love, meanwhile passing the time by butchering people, feeling smug about their individuality (their snake-leather jackets), and adopting only (pop culture) poses. All these movies belong to the subgenre *grunge murder movies*, playing to the gloomy, somewhat psychedelic and oblique tunes of contemporary rock music such as Nirvana, Pearl Jam, and Beck. "It's better to burn out than to fade away." This famous line from a late 1970s Neil Young song epitomizes the lifestyle of the grunge generation, burnt out by life (and drugs).

Pumpkin and Honey Bunny, partners in both crime and love, are thus not alone. On the contrary, they adhere so closely to a pattern that they could be deemed copies. Their originality is mimicked and assumed, thus embodying nonsense in logical terms, and in psychological terms they are pursuing a phantasm. The same can be said of another, far more famous pairing in *Pulp Fiction*.

Vincent and Jules

Vincent and Jules are driving through Los Angeles. As always in this city it is sunny. The side windows are wide open and the limousine trundles merrily through the streets. Vincent, a white man, has got long black, greased-back hair and a little silver earring in his right ear. Jules, a black man with long sideburns, an oversized moustache and curly hair, is driving. They are both wearing black suits with white shirts and narrow black ties. Vincent is telling Jules about the hash bars in Amsterdam and the cops there who, for Americans quite unbelievably, do not have the right to search people for drugs. They amuse themselves with other little differences in Europe, like the fact that in Paris a quarterpounder with cheese is called a "Royale with cheese," and that a Big Mac is called "le Big-Mac." They are disgusted by the whole idea of eating mayonnaise on fries instead of ketchup, as is the custom in Holland.

Vincent and Jules are killers on a mission. Their boss, Mr. Wallace, first name Marsellus, would like a certain briefcase back from certain people. Vincent and Jules are professionals. They work calmly, chatting about this and that, including the point of pilot episodes for TV series and the erotic significance of foot massages. They choose their tools to fit the situation. Since they will be dealing with three, four, maybe even five men, automatics would be a good idea, yet they take shotguns. Because they reach the apartment they have been looking for too early, they go for a little walk in the hallway of the apartment block, still discussing "foot massages and sensuous things" as calmly and matter of factly, even playfully, as if on a walk or their way to work together. Their demeanor gives us no clue that several people are about to be shot dead.

The door opens and, mute and motionless like two harbingers of bad news, they stand before Mr. Wallace's so-called business partners, young men with pale faces who have just realized what is about to hit them. As they are in the middle of their breakfast, talk of hamburgers and cheeseburgers can continue, but now it becomes a brutal question-and-answer game conducted by Jules in an unmistakably threatening tone. The brutality increases when, almost casually, in the middle of one man's defensive stammerings, Jules shoots the other and then returns to his cruel trial of the first. If someone has done wrong, then he should say that he has done wrong, should tremble from head to toe. Jules underlines this emphatically with a passage from the Old Testament, cited sonorously and ending with the words: "And I will strike down upon thee with great vengeance and furious anger those who would attempt to poison and destroy my brothers. And you will know my name is the Lord when I lay my vengeance upon thee." With this he ceremoniously points his gun at the jittering boy, curled up fearfully in a ball in his armchair, and executes him with several shots in a duet with Vincent.

We know Vincent and Jules. Standing at their victims' door like two undertakers, avenging angels in the age of employment, they look as frightful as they do funny. If this happened to us "in real life," we would think we were dreaming or had somehow found our way into a movie. For this is precisely what they remind us of—movie characters. Their clothes, their set faces, their bored yet self-controlled movements, and their repertoire of recitations all let loose associations involving a meltdown of *Le Samourai* and the *Blues Brothers*. In 1980 the brothers Jake and Elwood Blues were also characterized by black-and-white outfits (albeit complemented with hats and sunglasses), a laconic manner, and a magnetic ability to bring about ridiculous situations (in turn reminding us of another famous movie couple, *Laurel and Hardy*). The Blues Brothers were also "on a mission from God," trying to save their old orphanage by raising several thousand dollars for the Chicago authorities in just a few days. Thirteen years earlier, in *Le Samourai*, Alain Delon had given the killer an epiphanic form with the face of an angel. Here, too, the killer wears plain, respectable clothes; his pale and delicate face hardly moves, he never smiles and his eyes are deeply sad. (One could see him as a chilly existentialist version of Benjamin's angel from *Theses on the Philosophy of History*: possessing neither a past nor a future.) Delon's character lives in a solitude that could not be greater ("unless perhaps it be that of a tiger in the jungle"), yet in a stylized and ritualized manner that renders him in his solitude great (outstanding, predominant).

Here two things indispensably belong together: stylization and individuality, artificiality and extraordinariness, fiction and a certain obstinacy. Director Jean-Pierre Melville always stressed that he portrayed gangsters who were fictional rather than realistic, "supermen," "men for whom honor counts." As an avowed "anarcho-feudalist" ("if there is such a thing"), Melville followed in the tradition of that "aristocratic radicalism" to which Nietzsche enthusiastically subscribed (after Georg Brandes, the literary scholar teaching in Copenhagen, had apostrophized him thus).[4] In a world completely devoid of sense, the realization of one's own lifestyle accordingly becomes the ultimate, sometimes desperate point. The individual connects himself to an ideal, which then becomes a yardstick, and living by this yardstick in turn becomes a question of honor, as for the hero of the Western.

The Hero as an Actor

This can also be expressed with a different slant. The hero gives a performance of himself, a theatrical performance, a performance of ideas and phantasms. Not only does the actor play a hero, but vice versa the (portrayed) hero is also an actor, wishing to fit a role and an image of himself. Going quite against conventional and morally diffused opinion, the definition of a hero thus includes the fact that he is an actor, parading his heroism.

As inferred by Lionel Trilling, albeit without making the distinction clear, this is meant in two different ways. Calling a hero an actor accordingly involves, first, a reference in Aristotelian terms to the realm of art, here the art of tragedy. "The Greeks were under no illusion about the actuality of a hero. Aristotle makes this plain in his comparison of tragedy and comedy: it is only in the genre of tragedy that the hero exists, for tragedy shows men as better than they really are, which is to say, nobler, more impressive, more dignified. . . . There can be no comic hero, for comedy shows men as worse than they really are, which is to say more ignoble, less impressive, less dignified."[5] There are no heroes in everyday real life. In their perfect ambiguity, heroes are artistic products: products of art and artificial. Only in the realm of art is the hero at home. Art—and this unites Aristotle and Hegel (and Danto)—is *a transfiguration of the commonplace*. Hegel is more precise than Aristotle, however. Not only, as shown in detail in the first chapter of this book, is he convinced that we gain our knowledge of heroes solely from art, but moreover that art and heroism are also in formal agreement. Just as a work of art individually *exemplifies* something universal, the hero as an individual *embodies* this universality. For Hegel both the work of art and the hero belong to times gone by: the work of art to ancient Greece, and the hero to the mythical world. Unlike his romantic contemporaries, Hegel is no longer convinced that in modern times the essence of an epoch can be expressed in an epoch. In the sober prose of the bourgeois world he sees a place for heroism only in cases where the bourgeois order is rendered inoperative, namely, in times of war and revolution.

Categorizing heroes as actors, however, means moving them not only into an *aesthetic* but also into a *modern* perspective. The hero becomes an impersonator *of himself*, or, once again in Hegelian terms, of a division between himself and the role of the hero, a role that either he assumed once, only never to escape from it again, or that he is simply trying out through a lack of emphatic conviction.

A fitting description for the first type of modern impersonator, the man trapped inside his role, is given by Robert Warshow in his essay "The Westerner" (1954). Here he dedicates a lengthy passage to the *Gunfighter*, that 1950 movie that heralded the age of the "adult Western"—adult in the sense of sober and tired—and that two years later was to find its perfect successor in *High Noon*. This type of movie does not relate how somebody becomes a hero, becomes a myth through shotgun violence, but concentrates instead on the almost hopeless consequences this entails, as the hero faces continuing rituals of violence. Gunman Jimmie Ringo (played by Gregory Peck sporting—amazingly—a moustache), as well as sheriff Will Kane (Gary Cooper with a bitter twist to his mouth) wish to leave their past behind them, leave the West that has shaped their (self-)image of struggle and honor. What to some is a *shoot out* is for others merely the defense of law and order: a lackluster game. What Warshow says about *Gunfighter* can also easily be applied to *High Noon* (and equally to *The Wild Bunch*). In each of these variations the hero knows "that he can do nothing except to replay the drama of the gunfight again and again until the moment comes in which he himself is killed. What 'redeems' him is that he no longer believes in this drama, and nevertheless he will continue to play his role perfectly: the pattern is all." In succinct terms: "A hero is one who looks like a hero."[6] A hero is one who behaves like a hero (has to behave), one who styles himself around a particular image of masculinity and violence.

Walter Benjamin provides a description of the second type of modern impersonator, the tester of a role through a lack of conviction. Benjamin interprets Baudelaire's dandyism and his frequently described contrariness, believed to be observable in his exterior and his convictions, his day-by-day change in expression and his blatantly wavering attitudes toward existence, technical progress, women, and so on, as a specific constellation of modernity taking heroism as a role model, which is fateful since in it the "hero is not provided for." The bourgeois society of modernity ties him fast "in a safe harbor," no longer permitting him to ride the "high seas." Benjamin, supported by Baudelaire's poetry, also employs familiar metaphors of sea travel in order to describe heroic existence, albeit explaining dandyism, which Baudelaire himself praises as the "last shimmer of the heroic in the age of decadence," in an obvious yet surprising way. Bourgeois society is decadent because it turns the hero over to "an eternal idleness." The hero can only react with a paradox, embodied by no other than the dandy. The latter makes a virtue out of necessity by glorifying idleness. Heroes act, and when action becomes fundamentally impossible, the spark of greatness has to come from nonaction. Not-being-able-to-act then becomes not-wanting-to-act; "you can't!" becomes "I want to do what I can't." The idling, dallying dandy presents himself as a perfectly paradoxical embodiment of the hero.

Nevertheless, this ultimate heroization displays the forced characteristics of a goodwill gesture. According to Benjamin, Baudelaire is not truly convinced. He therefore makes a virtue out of this necessity, too: "Because he did not have any convictions, he assumed ever new forms himself. Flaneur, apache, dandy, and ragpicker were so many roles to him. For the modern hero is no hero; he is a portrayer of heroes. Heroic modernism turns out to be a *Trauerspiel* in which the hero's part is available."[7] For Benjamin, the tragic drama and no longer the tragedy is the dramatic art form most appropriate to modernity, as is already recognizable in his early *The Origin of German Tragic Drama*. At the same time, it is also appropriate that the category of drama distances itself from heroism. The

hero becomes an impersonator of his own Self. He plays heroic roles because he no longer takes heroism truly seriously. In particular he plays
roles that to his mind facilitate a brusque opposition to bourgeois society,
roles that emphatically set him apart as a flaneur, a dandy, a ragman, a
lesbian for the female sex, and finally a cool criminal. For Benjamin an
apache is someone who renounces the law and retreats behind the Stoic
maxim "noli me tangere."

Individuality: Stylized and Satirized

There are thus different variations on the theme of the hero as an actor. In *Pulp Fiction* these variations conjoin. Here individuality is so much
the result of stylization, fiction so much the territory of reality, art and artificiality so much the realm in which the heroes are at home that there
seem to be no more individuals and no more heroes, just imitators and
hero impersonators. This gives rise to the first hypothesis: the cool guy is
the *perfection of the hero*, the celebrated imitation of his own Self. The cool
guy not only imitates himself in the manner of the hero, either through
compulsion or through a lack of conviction, but increases this imitation
until it becomes self-celebratory, enabling him once more, albeit at a reflective and diffracted level, to blossom in his role. The modern and aesthetic significances of heroism are thus consciously united. *Reservoir Dogs*,
Tarantino's debut as a director in 1992, also addressed this theme.

In *Pulp Fiction* the celebration of imitation is most noticeable in the
episode where Vincent is given the job of taking out his boss's young wife.
This is a job requiring caution, for as we know from the long conversation
with Jules directly preceding it (in this movie someone is always talking),
even giving this lady a foot massage with the most innocent of intentions
can have disastrous consequences for the masseur. The boss is extremely
jealous, and his stooges are burly. His wife looks just like her name would
suggest: Mia. Her dark black hair is cut in a pageboy style, her complex-
ion is white, her lips blood-red, and she has come-to-bed eyes. She is the
high-class hooker version of a femme fatale, a Queen Cleopatra from the
cocaine scene, a cartoon puss ("Kittycat"). Mia allows Vincent to drive
her to a vibrant and dazzling bar where a young man is singing who is as
charming and dashing as Ricky Nelson, where one waitress looks almost

exactly like Marilyn Monroe, and where a waiter appears who not only looks like Buddy Holly, but who also introduces himself to the guests as Buddy Holly (yet another performance of sorts).

In this establishment with its reincarnations of 1950s icons, an unforgettable event for lovers of dance movies and love stories takes place, namely, Mia and Vincent enter a dancing competition. This in itself would not be so remarkable, were it not for a movie that seventeen years previously drew crowds to the theaters in hordes, enabling a new star to be born: John Travolta. That same actor, here playing Vincent Vega, is now compelled to demonstrate his dancing skills afresh. And compulsion it is, for in contrast to *Saturday Night Fever*, in which he convincingly played a slim and supple disco king from Brooklyn in a white suit, he has now quite clearly put on a few pounds, his hair is tied back in a prankish ponytail, and his movements are considerably reduced and retarded. This is chiefly due to his new cool attitude—Mia erotically calls him "Cowboy" as he rolls himself a cigarette with a practiced hand—but it also has to do with the fact that he took a shot of heroin when getting ready to go out for the evening. In this scene Travolta looks like his own double—older, fatter, and slower—and while he is not ridiculous, the result is quite funny. He is a parody of himself. Passionate disco dancer meets cool paid dancer, and the contrast is immediately comic.

This movie is peppered with copies and parodies at every turn. This makes one of its aesthetic principles very clear, namely, the principle of nonsense comedy, perfected in the serious theater genre by Samuel Beckett. In Tarantino's work it emerges, formally at first, from the connection between two opposite poles: originality and copy, authenticity and imitation. Copied originality is logical nonsense. The copy of an original can only become an original itself if it is more than a copy, and thus different from the copied original. When someone knowingly copies an original without admitting it, the result is embarrassing or even ridiculous, but when someone copies an original without knowing it, the result is funny.

Yet the figures in *Pulp Fiction* are also individuals. Not all of them, but certainly Vincent, as well as Vincent in his combination with Jules. It is their way of walking and talking, gesticulating and acting, pulling facial expressions and remaining expressionless; it is their overall style that, despite its secondhand quality, makes them unmistakable and therefore individuals. Their stylistic law comprises combining elements taken from other movie characters, and it decrees: always act as if you were "Le Samourai" and the "Blues Brothers" rolled into one!

This unique combination gives rise to a second, no longer purely formal reason for comedy in the movie. Here we have customized killers who lend a chilly aristocratic demeanor to 1950s existentialism, while contrarily teetering on the brink of slapstick, of the comedy of clowns and adolescent boys. Never before have killers been so amusing (strange, funny, farcical), confirming once again Melville's hunch that they can exist only as products of art, as fictitious characters.

Finally, the comedy in the movie stems from a third source: the satirization attached to any instance of stylization. Stylized individuality, an own style that is exaggerated to the point of artificiality, is per se a parody of individuality. As an exaggeration, stylization lacks the substance to build up an own individuality, having to resort instead to parody and imitation. It cannot simply repeat the past; yet it has nothing new to counter it with, so it elects instead to repeat the past in a manner that is both crude and flamboyant. In summary, the characters have style, yet are stylized; they are stylized yet individual; they are individual yet spurious.

Self-creation with Rorty

In the current discussion these characters have a paternal advocate and critic in the American philosopher Richard Rorty. The combination of individualization and comedy is a waste product, quite literally a pulp-fictional product of an honorable aspect of modern thought. In the very first lines of his book *Contingency, Irony, and Solidarity*, Rorty reveals the honorable and essentially romantic tradition behind this development:

About two hundred years ago the idea that truth was made rather than found began to take hold of the imagination of Europe. The French Revolution had shown that the whole vocabulary of social relations, and the whole spectrum of social institutions, could be replaced almost overnight. . . . At about the same time, the Romantic poets were showing what happens when art is thought of no longer as imitation but, rather, as the artist's self-creation. The poets claimed for art the place in culture traditionally held by religion and philosophy, the place which the Enlightenment had claimed for science.[8]

Since then our occidental lifestyle has been determined by the two domains art and politics, at least according to Rorty's culture-historical and historical diagnosis.

Romanticism is significant for Rorty in several ways: its aesthetic of creation and the ingenious subject; its cultural centering of aesthetics; its idea of irony and perfectibility. As in the writings of Isaiah Berlin, here, too, romanticism does not join forces with liberalism in such a way as to transfer the guiding idea of (self-)creation to the public arena and politics. The consequence of this would be Napolean's empire building, or even Hitler's or Mao's, "powerful creations" arising from a spirit of uninhibited self-realization. We are now able to register soberly the genealogy of the romantic-aesthetic concept of genius for a totalitarian conception of politics directed toward a *Fuehrer* cult.[9] It is thus all the more understandable that Rorty's liberalistic reaction is *privatization of the concept of genius*. The notion of infinite perfectibility does remain in force as a political utopia that is geared toward expanding the world of solidarity ever further, but its real field of activity is the private sphere. As Rorty exemplifies using his interpretation of the *Communist Manifesto*, political perfectibility is watered down to mere hope, whereas private perfectibility remains as attractive as ever.

In his book *The Anxiety of Influence*, Harold Bloom provides the decisive impulse in this respect, which is then taken up by Rorty, albeit without its specific context of justification. This impulse is the fear that poets experience of being influenced, a horror at being potentially no more than an imitation of a great predecessor, resulting in an almost Oedipal propulsion of literature (and art in general) onward through history. The "perfect life" for a would-be poet consists in the ability to describe his thoughts using a vocabulary that is "wholly *his*," even though it is clear that he will never succeed "as complete(ly) and autonomous(ly)" in this undertaking as later romantics, in other words Nietzsche, would wish for.[10] All descriptions of the Self remain dependent on other descriptions due to our communication medium called language.

With privatization and ironic aberration, Rorty parries not only the late-romantic tendency to *glorify* genius, but also its tendency to *totalize* in two different directions: the subject encroaching on politics and vice versa. In addition, he puts a stop to efforts that claim precedence for the political. For him, the private and public spheres coexist in a balanced ratio, with irony over everything. In irony an awareness of contingency can prevail without tragedy. Being aware of contingency, of the consistent historical shaping of one's own convictions, here means never being "quite" able to take oneself seriously, at this point providing additional evidence of the degree to which the voice of (romantic) modernity can be heard from a book received as postmodern.[11]

And yet precisely this strictly equal coexistence of the private and public spheres is also the most irritating *flaw* in Rorty's conception, a flaw reflected in Habermas. For Rorty, this equal-complementaristic appreciation of romanticism is accompanied by a strategy of enclosure that is dogmatic-liberalistic and thus totally lacking in irony. The dichotomy of public-ness and private-ness facilitating an equal-complementaristic relationship to romanticism obstructs its own path. Whereas Habermas draws up a mobile model of reason based on differentiation, Rorty blocks mobility with a fundamental parallel design element and, more importantly, contradicts himself. He has no qualms in dissolving established relationships between the spheres of reason and culture in religion, philosophy, science, and art, yet firmly insists on them as soon as politics comes into play. Rorty, a critic of the dualistic thinking prevailing in the western world, for example in the pragmatism of William James and John Dewey, and enjoying a proximity to the deconstruction of Jacques Derrida, relapses into dualism himself.

The Cool Female Ironist

In matters of irony Rorty favors the female protagonist. His model to counter the metaphysicist is not "he the ironist," but "she the ironist," a tribute to Horkheimer and Adorno's "bourgeois anthropology," which always emphasizes the close correlations among masculinity, rationality, and hardened character. The (female) ironist knows about flexibility and contextuality within the rationality standard. In her eyes, what is reasonable cannot be stated definitively or even a priori independently of experience, but rather emerges in practical contexts, in the details of a situation. The ironist is a (female) expert with regard to the exactness of perception and the adequacy of a norm; her sensitive faculties and ethical knowledge go hand in hand.

Clarice Starling, the nondescript heroine in the movie *The Silence of the Lambs*, is female. She works for the FBI, in a man's world and surrounded by colleagues who appear enormous in comparison. When she is in an elevator with the men, she is, at 5' 2'', at least head and shoulders shorter than they are, standing around her in their red polo shirts like smartly packaged boxes of muscles. During an autopsy she is subjected to the skeptical, even disdainful gazes of a group of local cops in their famous or infamous black uniforms, uniforms that for some (for example, the female gangsters Thelma and Louise in the movie of the same name) are reminiscent of those worn in Germany by Hitler's SS. Starling is intelligent and strong-willed, astute in her dealings with Lector, yet with a childlike openness; she is grimly determined to hunt down the murderer of the dead women, yet sensitive in her perceptions. Cool she is definitely not.

This label has been reserved in movie history for other women: Greta Garbo, Marlene Dietrich, Barbara Stanwyck, Lauren Bacall. Coolness as a concept is not gender-neutral.[12] Yet, although women can in principle employ this concept, de facto they do so far less than men. This may be for reasons of evolutionary biology, in crude terms due to the difference between the male genetic interest in passing on his genetic material to as many available and fertile sexual partners as possible, and the corresponding female genetic interest in finding and keeping a partner who will best guarantee the survival of her offspring.

There may also be a historical explanation for the factual reticence of women in matters of coolness, however. The more her cultural role historically becomes established as that of the mother, the nurturer, and the embodiment of emotionality, the smaller her chances become of shaping the general blueprint for coolness. (To date) coolness is not compatible with bringing up children. Cinema provides no evidence of both being concurrently possible: being a mother (parent) and being cool. The fact that coolness is historically a predominantly male phenomenon does not, however, mean that coolness can be attributed to extreme masculinity. Many of the male pillars of coolness, such as 1950s icons James Dean, Marlon Brando, Montgomery Clift, and even Frank Sinatra, break with the stereotyped macho image and show clear signs of feminization.

The above-mentioned ladies of the screen are all chilly and distant in their coolness, with Greta Garbo and Marlene Dietrich additionally projecting an image of suffering and mystery (although both have another side as well, as proven respectively by Ernst Lubitsch in *Ninotchka* and George Marshall in *Destry Rides Again*, both appearing in 1939). Barbara Stanwyck is the coldest, the most profane of the group; she is a match for any man of her era so far as unscrupulous behavior, whisky, and tobacco consumption are concerned. But it is Lauren Bacall who is definitely the most ironic. The tough lady she embodies is a sculpture of female self-confidence, with a direct, fearless gaze, even features, a derisory smile, reserved rhetoric, and a ready wit. A man can never be certain whether she will beguile him or strangle him, glorify him or expose him, kiss him or bite him, love him forever or shoot him dead. Her oscillating performances earned her the moral label of the "bad good girl,"[13] a woman who seems to have evil in mind but whose actions ultimately dispel this, who discards her malicious appearance in favor of an essential integrity, without assuming a saintly stuffiness in the process. She cannot become stuffy for, like those around her, she is caught up in too many diffuse crimes; the differences between good and evil are too fluent.

The "bad good girl" is predestined for the film noir, which also cultivates such ambivalences. Here she constitutes an adequate female counterpart to a hero who has cast off heroism like a torn Second World War uniform. It was this war to which the film noir emerged as a reaction, beginning with *The Maltese Falcon* by John Houston in 1941, adapted from the novel by Dashiell Hammett and with Humphrey Bogart playing detective Sam Spade. Disillusioned to the point of fatalism, increasingly corrupt and with a cynicism intended to mask the vulnerability of his soul, here we see a leading male character who has lost his heroic stance along with his self-confidence. This type of coolness is best described as a strategy of self-preservation, to use Horkheimer and Adorno's term, namely, as a negative (never supposed to be) affirmation of the negative, that is, an affirmation that is not accommodating, but rebellious and inwardly distant.[14] The negative element increasingly takes possession of this antihero. Whereas in the first, the "romantic" phase, he is still comparatively distant toward a world intent on drawing him into its crimes; in the second phase, that of "alienation," he increasingly suffers at the hands of this world surrounding him, before in the third phase, that of "obsession," he becomes totally caught up in crime.[15] In these movies the woman is in no way inferior to the man. She triumphs as an active, driving force, including in matters of the heart. The role reversal is flagrant: she is now the seducer, and he is the seduced, the deluded one for whom love becomes a trap from which there is usually no escaping. Billy Wilder's *Double Indemnity* (1944) with Barbara Stanwyck, *The Postman Always Rings Twice* (1946), and Orson Welles's *The Lady from Shanghai* (1948) with Rita Hayworth are the best examples of this, all which perfectly exemplify the role of the femme fatale. They could not be more different from the gangster movies of the early 1930s and their open misogyny, for example, as displayed by James Cagney in *Public Enemy*.

The Blasé Attitude as Style

The cool men of the movies, the copiers of originality with their inner propensity toward stylization and satire, the specialists of individualization with an impact ranging from the ironic to the comic, are most aptly theorized by a philosopher and sociologist writing not about movies, but about the metropolis as the focal point of modernity: Georg Simmel. One hundred years on, his essay *The Metropolis and Mental Life* (1903) is still rightly deemed to be indispensable and stimulating reading for any analysis of modernity. He also provides us with the crucial keyword for any analysis of coolness: *blasé*.

According to Simmel, "There is perhaps no psychic phenomenon which is so unconditionally reserved to the city as the blasé outlook."[16] For this, as Simmel is quick to stress, "is at first the consequence of those rapidly shifting stimulations of the nerves which are thrown together in all their contrasts." The "intensification of metropolitan intellectuality" also seems to be derived from it. According to the dualistic psychological anthropology Simmel also appropriated, feelings are "rooted" in the more unconscious layers of the soul resistant to change, whereas the mind, the intellect, belongs to the conscious layers and is (thus) extremely adaptable, a skill it can and must perfect within the metropolitan environment. Life in the country or a small town is not likely to make one blasé. A blasé attitude results from a quantitative increase in nervous stimuli and a corresponding intellectualistic processing of the same. Accordingly, a blasé attitude is primarily a result of adaptation to the conditions governing modern metropolitan life, namely, a refusal to react, an attitude of refusal toward the pattern of stimulus and reaction forced on one by the metropolis and its rapidly changing, constantly new impressions. Someone who is blasé no longer reacts to what is different and new. He develops his own ethical stance.

This becomes even clearer with Simmel's second hypothesis. In addition to the "physiological source of the blasé metropolitan attitude," which "stimulates the nerves to their utmost reactivity," another source is the "money economy." "The essence of the blasé attitude is an indifference toward the distinctions between things. Not in the sense that they are not perceived, as is the case of mental dullness, but rather that the meaning and the value of the distinctions between things, and therewith of the things themselves, are experienced as meaningless. They appear to the blasé person in a homogenous, flat and grey colour with no one of them worthy of being preferred to another." This "mood," or, less romantically, this "form of existence," is the "correct subjective reflection of a complete money economy." By expressing "all qualitative distinctions" between things quantitatively in terms of "how much?" money "becomes the frightful leveller." Against this almost Marxian background of economic causality, the blasé character emerges as an attitude intent on leveling and "de-colouring," not from a *blunted* stupor, but from an *acute* perspicacity, from extremely sharp perception and intellectuality. A blasé attitude is not a refusal to perceive, but a refusal to evaluate; not an *epistemological flaw*, but an *ethical achievement*. In both senses of the word, everything becomes equable. The governing principle is calculated indifference. A kind of melancholic nihilism born of intellectual arrogance, it is conducive to "self-preservation" in modern times.

Simmel describes as "no less negative" the social behavior accompanying the blasé attitude that he discreetly calls "reserve" but does perceive as having an "overtone of concealed aversion," a "mutual strangeness and repulsion which, in a close contact . . . can break out into hatred and conflict."[17] Yet here Simmel adds a positive flipside, for metropolitan modernity facilitates a personal freedom that has no equal in kind or extent. Unlike his *Gründerzeit* rivals Emile Durkheim and Max Weber, Simmel is one of those theorists who, like Norbert Elias, Jürgen Habermas, and Ulrich Beck after him, describe modernity as a highly *ambivalent* phenomenon.[18]

Modernity permits greater subjective freedom, but also leads to a reduction in the quality of social relationships. It allows individuals to unfold their individuality on the basis of general and formal equality, as well as metropolitan anonymity, but at the same time makes it difficult for them to unfold precisely because anyone, at least in principle, is free to unfold.

The effort required to visualize, orchestrate, and differentiate in society is continually increasing. Modernity, which emerged on the back of a battle for fundamental rights, now itself sparks a battle for (social and thus also moral) visibility.[19] *Visualization*, taken in a broader sense, is its manifesto. Against this sociological background, the much talked about dominance of images and the corresponding technical media within our culture becomes slightly less lamentable. Individuals wishing to arouse attention ultimately pay homage to "specifically metropolitan extravagances of self-distantiation, of caprice, of fastidiousness," the underlying point of which "is no longer to be found in the content of such activity itself but rather in its being a form of 'being different.'"[20] When the battle for visibility becomes the social norm, the mere external form and not the content is what is crucial.

Of course, Simmel would be a bad sociologist if he did not also perceive this conduct as containing an element extending beyond mere subjectivity. For the individual is no longer concerned with shaping the external individually and incomparably. Instead the external has become the expression of a certain lifestyle choice, and here certain social lifeforms overlap. Every lifestyle choice, and therefore also its outward visible impression, always also involves a certain generality. Simmel calls this duplication of outwardness and relative generality "style." Style therefore fulfills a double function: it dissolves the old, metaphysically authenticated, universally valid convictions, yet without leaving the individual out in the cold. Its "essence" is an "unburdening and concealment of the personal," a "mitigation and a toning down" of modern "supra-individualism," a "counterweight" and (once again) a "concealment" of "exaggerated subjectivism," by spanning the typical between the poles of generality and subjectivity; for the style shown in clothes, behavior, home furnishings, and so forth is a "more general, a more typical, in short a stylized costume."[21]

At this point it seems obvious that the concept of a blasé attitude corresponds to that of style. If style per se is already a toning down of the exaggerated subjectivism of modernity, then, as a particular style, a blasé attitude amounts to an evenly mitigating toning down of our entire existence. No great interpretive powers are required to replace the concept of a blasé attitude with that of *coolness*. Coolness also means a lifestyle primarily metropolitan—the Blues Brothers and "Le Samourai," the Gunfighter and Sheriff Kane, in particular Vincent and Jules will all back me up here—and that reacts to a situation of increased nervous stimuli with a refusal to react. For the purposes of self-preservation, it therefore actually either *breeds indifference,* or, more probably, *displays indifference.* This is not meant such that behind the attitude a nontangible core of truth could assert itself, but such that permanent *acting* ultimately in itself becomes the *reality*; the form becomes the content and an appearance of impassivity can no longer be distinguished from true impassivity. In both senses of the word, namely, epistemic indistinguishableness and moral impassivity, indifference perfectly captures the Self.

The Mask of Coldness

In describing style as a concealment of the person, Simmel cued a word that he himself then elaborated on in a philosophical description of acting, influenced by Nietzsche. Some time later, in 1924, Helmuth Plessner was to expand it to a fundamental concept within his social anthropology. With *The Limits of Community*, Plessner emerged as the second definitive theorist of what we now know as coolness. This work already operates, albeit not expressly, with the *concept of roles* in a manner that was not to become universally accepted theory until much later in twentieth-century sociology.

Its point of departure is an anthropological premise that is actually modernistic, that is, historically grounded. Accordingly, human beings are creatures of "ontological ambiguity,"[22] in which "the impetus to disclosure" is in permanent conflict with the "impetus to restraint." For however much, on the one hand, they wish to be seen and must be seen in order to gain recognition and thus identity, they also, on the other hand, have to fear their identity becoming fixed since this ties them down to something that may be part of them, but that is not the whole story. Reality robs human beings of their possibilities, yet they cannot remain in the realm of possibilities. In modernity this philosophical anthropology comes into its own. In a society that is no longer traditionally structured, the conflict between self-revelation and self-concealment also becomes a general, and thus historically acute, social life form. The "struggle for a genuine face,"[23] viewed by Plessner as anthropologically given, emerges without makeup in a society in which individuals all begin by fighting to establish their positions, a fight that for some lasts a whole lifetime. In Plessner's anthropology, only modernity is as ambivalent as human beings have always been.

This ambivalence and concomitant agonal struggle are inescapable, yet they can be mitigated: through a form of social interaction by which individuals are able to present themselves, while simultaneously remaining invisible. This social form is role-play. Here Plessner addresses a humanist tradition invented by the aristocracy and only half-heartedly adopted by the bourgeoisie; for him, humanity or civilization is nothing other than the mitigation of an insoluble antagonism. It is thus intentionally one-sided to call Plessner's early, essayistic, and thus ambiguously written work, in which various lines of intellectual and cultural historical tradition cross, a "behavioral code of cold conduct."[24] Far more, he is convinced that if human beings were to take off their social masks and always say what they were thinking, "the coldness of outer space would descend upon them." It is precisely this mask that "never permits too much closeness, nor too much distance."[25] One of these masks is, of course, coolness. It, too, prevents both things: too much proximity, as well as too much distance. One is always clearly dealing with a mask, which is an element of role-play and therefore excludes intimacy and injury. In correct terms, Plessner thus provides not a behavioral code of cold conduct, but of cool conduct.

To employ Simmel's terminology once again, coolness also mitigates social coldness through stylization, or, more generally, through *aestheticization*. This is the third part of our original hypothesis. Plessner once more facilitates the specification that the cool guy is the perfect "hero-cum-actor" by completely and artificially becoming his chosen role. This sheds light on why our current concept of coolness should be a *product of the 1950s*. This was the period in which coolness entered mainstream western culture. It previously had a long historical tradition spanning English aristocratism and dandyism, romantic irony, and the courtier of the Renaissance as documented by Castiglione, even African origins infiltrating America through slavery. Thus, despite it emerging from this country, coolness is by no means a singularly American concept. According to Charles Taylor, it constitutes a specific variation on the broad western concept of self-control.

One name has been attached more than any other to the social and cultural success of coolness since the 1950s: *Elvis Presley*. He made image and attitude more important than musical ability. He also "turned rebellion into a style," possibly the best definition of coolness we have, a private oppositional stance well suited to all those who do not (cannot) dare to rebel openly. Because it is a private opposition, it can also easily be integrated in a consumer society and even be elevated to a winning pose, as had definitely happened by the 1990s.[26] Since Elvis, a cool image has become something to be taken, varied, and exploited time after time after time, most particularly through reproduction in the media. Coolness is thus an appropriate way of asserting oneself within a world "increasingly dominated by what is indicated, quoted and portrayed in the media. Coolness is exclusively a question of style, of the *look*"—"the look" is incidentally also the name given to the model Lauren Bacall—"of the mannerisms, not the psychological pervasion and transformation of a role."[27] For a good actor, role-play is not the same as self-portrayal, but for a cool guy it is. In turn, what the cool guy portrays is no more than a role.

Stressing the idiosyncratic character of role-play in which "hero" and image become identical also permits the coolness phenomenon to undergo a *sociopsychological expansion* and include a type of person who is *not* metropolitan. The best example of this within the cinematic context is the *Western hero*, and the best example from within this genre is a Western filmed by an Italian director who set out to rediscover, as well as reinvent, the America of myth and legend: Sergio Leone's *Once Upon a Time in the West*. Through extreme, almost grotesque exaggeration of the traditional features of this genre, this movie is a Western that comes across as a multiple overlapping of all those characters and characteristics that the genre has ever produced. Leone manages the paradoxical trick of staging the roles of this genre in their pure form, in this respect delivering the ultimate Western.

Because the roles are staged this way, they come across as cool. The current meaning and attractiveness of coolness stem chiefly from *self-*

reference. A "blasé guy" is often considered hollow, meaning that he displays a strong tendency to concentrate on himself rather than other matters. In psychological terms, a characteristic of the cool guy is therefore also narcissism.[28] Vincent and Jules, Harmonica alias Charles Bronson (the avenger with no name, another descendant of Odysseus who is forever denying his identity in order to preserve it), and Frank alias Henry Fonda (with steely blue eyes and an icy smirk, a villainous role turning his previous screen image on its head) would all be little more than unscrupulous or professional killers were they not visibly to embody *roles*. The role places a mitigating cloak, a mask of coolness, over the horror of social and existential coldness. At the *referential* level "cool" can be circumscribed as "chilled," "calm," "dispassionate," "nonresponsive," "indifferent," "detached," "professional," and so on. But the cool guy is not literally dispassionate or unemotional: then he would simply be "cold." Drawing on David Hickey, Greil Marcus has provided an apt description of this using the example of Cool Jazz: it is not a particular feeling that this type of music arouses, "but the memory of one." The memory hovers in the room, dislocated, just like the music conjuring it up. This music, played by Chet Baker, does not desert the one producing it, or so we learn from Marcus in the words of Geoff Dyer, but vice versa itself feels deserted by the music maker. In some respects Baker does not put anything personal into his music. It is the music of someone "who takes a few steps back and observes"; it is the "sound of a private detective," yet "more playful than the *film noir*, less melodramatic, in fact not at all melodramatic."[29] Like Hegel's seeming, the mantle of coolness points through itself to something that used to be more than just a mantle, "the substance," but is now merely represented by the mantle itself.

This is also why the *death* of modern, artificial heroes is not really a drama. It takes place in the form of a ritual as solemn as it is corny, sometimes simply funny. The long-anticipated shoot-out between Harmonica and Frank in *Once Upon a Time in the West* is an obvious example of the one version of this, a sacrificial finale in Western format. A good example of the other version is the death of aging bandit Jason in the same movie: there is a moment of surprised silence as the music, which until then had been trotting along in the rhythm of horses' hooves, stops. Jason, who has been shot, slides off his horse and then, as if it had suffered merely a minor irritation, the music starts up again. This is death as a moment to pause before life simply carries on again.

Vincent's final hour comes when he is once again in the restroom. This time his boss Marsellus has given him the job of killing Butch, a boxer (played superbly by Bruce Willis, with his famous beefy neck and little piggy eyes). Vincent waits for Butch in his house but at the precise moment Vincent goes in search of the restroom Butch returns, discovers a rapid-fire weapon in the kitchen, hears the toilet flush, and knows that someone has been sent to kill him (he broke an agreement with Marsellus to allow himself to be knocked out in his last fight in return for a large sum of money; Butch took the money and then never entered the ring). Not suspecting anything, Vincent emerges from the restroom, and all at once they are face-to-face, silently. The fatal shots ring out just as some toast pops out of the toaster (Butch was in the middle of making himself a snack). Vincent's death is thus framed by a restroom on one side and a toaster on the other. It is a fitting "death by toilet-toaster." The scene ends with Vincent lying in a corner peppered with bullets, a dime novel in his hand. The latter was no doubt intended to aid his bowel movements, one of those pulp-fiction products cynically and coquettishly acknowledged by the movie. This scene could be interpreted as a little, yet sinister, warning to the audience: "See? This is how cool guys who base themselves on pulp-fiction characters end up; this is how heroes who impersonate heroes die nowadays."

NIETZSCHE, SCIENCE FICTION,
AND HYBRID MODERNITY

Heroic Individualisms and Metaphysics

Ambivalent Criticism of Individualism

"Don't be a frog, a copy; be a prince, an original! Have the courage to use your faculty of (moral and practical) reason!" This is the motto, as much of the Enlightenment as of romanticism, that has been rediscovered by various representatives of so-called postmodern modernity, most prominently Rorty, as well as Foucault in his later works, and to a certain degree also Taylor. And always with recourse to Nietzsche. From their point of view, Nietzsche is not only an unconditional romantic but also a well-understood Enlightener. Rorty clearly stresses the first aspect; Foucault highlights the second. In Rorty's eyes Nietzsche is *the* philosopher of self-creation alongside Heidegger—a bold coupling. Since, however, Rorty specifically and correctly locates the origins of self-creation in (literary) romanticism, which he also notably links to the French Revolution, for him self-creation is a concept of political and aesthetic modernity (beginning with the French Revolution and literary romanticism), and Nietzsche is a representative of philosophical modernity.

It is indeed true to say that Nietzsche—more so than Kierkegaard, whom Rorty also names as a theorist of self-creation, and more so than Marx, whom he complementarily touches on as a theorist of justice—is a philosopher of modernity. Not that his philosophy centered around his own epoch; as we have seen, this was true of Hegel. But more so than his two older nineteenth-century contemporaries, Nietzsche is undeterred, on occasion also inconsistent, in describing and driving forward the break with metaphysics. This makes him (alongside Marx) an effective philosophical force in twentieth-century culture, for both this century's symbolic and practical dimensions. A leading hypothesis in the deliberations to follow has already been hinted at by the comment that Nietzsche drove forward the break with metaphysics more than Marx and Kierkegaard. The latter two philosophers remained bound to metaphysics, yet so did Nietzsche. I would like to prove this by taking a look at his concept of *heroic individualism as a substitute for metaphysics*. This not only amounts to a theory about Nietzsche, however, but is also exemplary of how *modernity is espoused to metaphysics*, of how attempts to legitimize it in its own right remain rooted within the very tradition it wishes to discard. Accordingly, Nietzsche's modernity would consist in an *ambivalent critique of modernity*. This intricate relationship also has an impact on a second major concept in Nietzsche's work, namely, a train of thought between philosophy and literature, between science and fiction, a train of thought that, to come right up to date and employ an alternative culture-theoretical motive, literally stands for science fiction.

Ambivalence is a marked characteristic in Nietzsche's philosophy. It will thus come as no surprise that it also characterizes his relationship to modernity. He knows that we "modern men" are "seldom unequivocal," and as an "overall insight" he notes "the ambiguous character of our modern world—the very same symptoms could point to decline and to strength." This is also visible in the artist: "Wagner *sums up* Modernity. It's no use, you need to start out as a Wagnerian, . . . " in order then, or so one could surmise, to attempt to disengage oneself from him: "attempt" because Wagner is not an unambiguous phenomenon either. He is not only "harmful," even for Nietzsche in his later years; through him "Modernity speaks its *most intimate* language" and "does not hide its good or its evil."[1]

The same ambivalence characterizes Nietzsche's relationship to individualism. In his early work on tragedy, influenced by Schopenhauer's metaphysics of the will, individualism only appears as a secondary phenomenon. Later Nietzsche criticizes it consistently and vehemently, attributing to the individual essential traits such as unity, substantiality, and autonomy. But in the political context he is prepared to differentiate. Here he occasionally makes a concession to the type of individualism that stakes a claim to "equal rights." This, then, is egalitarian individualism, declared common property with the French Revolution, one "level" of the "will to power." Here the individual is concerned with becoming "*free* from the overpowering domination by the society (whether that of the state or of the church)." The difference between egalitarian and nonegalitarian individualism is thus not one of principle, but merely a gradual one.

This means, however, that the prerequisite for nonegalitarian individualism is historic-sociological, as well as moral-psychological equality. Viewed historically and sociologically, the liberation of individuals from social domination ends in the idea of equal rights. At this level, however, an internal countermovement sets in. Since "by and large peace dominates," "many little power quanta" account for differences. The "struggle" now begins again, only "in a milder form."[2] With this comment and the theoretical concept of power underlying it, Nietzsche offers sociology no more than an extremely simplified outline, yet it is remarkable that he refers to a differentiational mechanism that was paid the greatest attention by Georg Simmel in the early twentieth century, always with recourse to Nietzsche. He, too, believed that the struggle for differentiation or distinction is one that takes place on the largely peaceful basis of democratic-political and formal-legal equality, and that feeds on those minor differences that are visible microcosms of modernity, especially in the metropolis. As already explained in my analysis of Taylor's concept of romanticism, this "qualitative" individualism, in which individuals have a real urge to be different from each other, is only possible on the basis of a "quantitative" individualism focusing on "the universal human being," "the human being itself" in the spirit of rationalism and the Enlightenment.[3]

Equality is, then, a prerequisite for inequality, also morally and psychologically. Seen like this, our task is to dominate "opponents who are our equals"; "equality before the enemy" is in fact the "first presupposition of an *honest* duel," for this is the only way to measure and increase one's own "strength." Those tackling only weak opponents (for theorists this means: small problems) will cease to "grow" as a result of these opponents (or problems), and for Nietzsche growth—or becoming—has an inherent status that one would not normally dare to presume on his behalf, namely, that of a patently fundamental category. The fact that he chooses the duel as a metaphor for this ethic of practical self-knowledge confirms his particular interest in social distinction, but also his nineteenth-century male self-perception.[4] The duel refers back to an aristocratic way of life which Nietzsche also underlined in the Greek origins of western history, including it in his canon of values under the title "the noble." For the noble, the notion of equality is not only a matter of course with regard to its social significance, however, but also to its moral one. When nobles are dealing with their own, equality is a fundamental principle. Here Nietzsche is familiar with an intersubjective, or rather interindividual generality. It is based, however, not on a universalistic, but on a particular or rather "exclusive equality."[5]

(Anti)metaphysics and Science Fiction

It seems to be quite in keeping with Nietzsche's own intentions to nominate him as the most radical and most consistent antimetaphysicist in the history of philosophy, as well as to draw a sharp dividing-line between metaphysical and nonmetaphysical theories, between the theoretical attitude of "discovering" and "inventing." Rorty brought renown to this separatist vocabulary in his recourse to Alexander Nehamas's book *Nietzsche: Life as Literature*. All the more important it is, then, to use Nehamas to disallow this. Nietzsche expressed concern that the asserted opposition between the addressed terms was "not ambiguous enough," for the simple and general reason that opposites made him suspicious per se, albeit not until his later works. Opposites characterize metaphysical thinking. "The fundamental belief of the metaphysicians," so reads the Nietzsche quotation that supports Nehamas, "is the belief in antitheses of values."[6] Nietzsche stresses not the simple opposition, but the *tension*, the strong, lasting, internal relationship between conceptions. "The tension, the expanse between the extremes" needs to be preserved.[7] Seen in this way, Nietzsche neither takes the old metaphysical voyage of "discovery," nor does he play the equally old aesthetic game of "invention." He does not research in the sense of empiricism or of (repeatedly and desperately sought) philosophical science, nor does he fantasize himself into a literary realm of fiction. What he does do amounts far more, quite literally, ambiguously and contrarily to *science fiction*. This is not only of epistemological relevance but also relevant to ethics and cultural theory, as highlighted by the figure of the hero.

Heroes in a Godless Age

Being an individual means accepting the suffering that is part and parcel of not being "in the safe hands" of a generality. It means the same as being a hero. A tragic existence is that most befitting him; driving the tragic out of life consequently means to abolish the hero. Nietzsche teaches "heroic individualism,"[8] as also defended later in terms of social theory and historical philosophy against the background of the totalitarian state by Max Weber, and especially Horkheimer and Adorno. For Weber, rationalization of all areas of life forces a standardized existence upon the individual who ultimately has no choice but to bear the inevitable consequences of modernization heroically; for Horkheimer and Adorno, liquidation of the tragic confirms the abolition of the individual as the hero of modernity.[9]

Nietzsche's motivation goes beyond this, however. He ascribes a function to heroic individualism that belongs within the extensive, yet empty framework of his postmetaphysical project, and it really is a "project," a design, a plan. God is dead and is to be replaced by new gods, new values, a new faith, yet this is not to be a faith in science, in progress, or in other ideals much extolled in the nineteenth century. One ideal eulogized by Nietzsche is that of the individual as a hero. The hero is needed to help fill the gap left by the demise of God. Like in archaic times, he himself becomes a kind of god. He bears the weighty burden of metaphysics, of establishing meaning within a world that, due to its own consistent "demystifying" and enlightening, has abolished meaning; it is no longer guaranteed by a transmundane, transindividual body. Here, too, Nietzsche is a child of his time. For him, as for most of his contemporaries, loss of faith and a worshipping of heroes go hand in hand. Viewed in terms of the history of psychology, the hero cult of the nineteenth century may be seen as a "symptom of an inner void waiting to be filled with idealized images," the basis of this theory being the more general one that "at the heart of Victorian bourgeois culture there lay a conflict" that, in Freudian terms, may be termed "ambivalence."[10] Nietzsche is also a child of his time in his figurative substantiation of the hero, with his concept of the hero being shaped by the two figures constituting heroism in the nineteenth century: the (romantic) artist and the (nationalistic) warrior.[11]

But the cry for heroism is not the last word Nietzsche has to say in this matter. Far more, the hero himself must to some degree be overcome and transformed. His ultimate form is that of the "superhero" in the ideal of the "overman." This is an artificial product, the product of a happy coincidence. The overman has relinquished the central characteristic of the hero, namely, his wanting, and shapes his life aesthetically, in the sense that his dynamic activity is joined by passivity. Nietzsche accordingly teaches a familiar three-step model. Not until the highest step is it possible to attain that satisfaction for which it is necessary that one's life has a certain style; only at this level can there be a certain reconciliation between internal peace and the "enemy within," required for the sake of one's own productivity and originality (for "the price of fertility is to be rich in contradictions"[12]). Inner turmoil and inner contentment can only be united when the enemy within is mitigated to a (mere) opponent, or, even better, an opposite *number*. Bearing this in mind, the doctrine of the overman formulates no more than the ethical-aesthetic ideal of playful self-command, a self-command subject not to rigid control, but to relaxed mastering. This is in line with the model developed by Kant in the context of aesthetic judgment as an interplay between the opposites fancy and reason, imagination and subsuming rationality, image and concept.[13] The only alternative remaining to this *systematic* solution would be a purely *temporary* one. Phases of satisfaction would then plainly alternate with those of dissatisfaction; today one feels this way, tomorrow that way. Provided it did not disassociate itself pathologically, this would still be an ego experiencing itself in its various states. Here the internal situation, tense to the point of animosity, is balanced out and integrated not by a mediating principle, but merely by time. However much the first part of the alternative, the systematic solution, may be ideal ethically and psychologically, the second part, the temporary solution, remains attractive in pragmatic terms.

Superhumans, Supermen, Cyborgs

Thus Spoke Zarathustra

"And Zarathustra spake thus unto the people: *I teach you the Superman (Übermensch). Man is something that is to be surpassed."[1] Thus Zarathustra's teachings took effect. Soon it was no longer one lesson, but many. The networks of interpretation took over, the character string looping endlessly, the meaning altered by context, the fundamental structure of an individual epoch, the nebulous interests of a social class, the substantiated interests of politicians, more of the same. A one true sense, if ever there was one, was gone forever. What remained were concepts and sentences, metaphors, and phrases. The cult, a surrogate religion to combat meaninglessness in secular times. The *Übermensch* thus became cult, too; in secular terms it became the collective projection of a better future.

The *Übermensch* as a Product of Art

Whenever utopias, futuristic visions, or human fantasies are the subject of debate, before long the *Übermensch* will be cited. Nietzsche's success story, initially assuming the discrete and then later on the far more pronounced characteristics of a cult, is closely connected with all those phrases that were quick to become first formulae and then catchphrases: "the will to power," "the eternal recurrence of the same events," "master morality and slave morality" and of course the "*Übermensch.*" The German soldiers in the First World War, or at least the more educated among them, took *Zarathustra* to the trenches with them, where it was second only to the Bible. Approximately 150,000 copies of a particularly robust edition of the book were distributed to the troops to allow them to draw mental strength from Nietzsche's celebration of the cathartic relief of war and bravery. But the *Übermensch* also had an integrating function for pronounced, sociopolitical utopias, a secular social fiction, an inner-world comprehensive life plan, for both the internationalistic left and the national-socialist right. Nietzsche's mental radicalism, his disparaging criticism, his creative self-overcoming of man was directed at a single enemy, opposed equally by both the political left and the political right: the bourgeoisie, minimal in its deeds, fruitless in its discussions, and far too comfortable in its mediocrity.[2]

Against this background, the *Übermensch* today signifies a project that, while not exactly scrapped, is certainly in decay. It stands not for a sociopolitical or biological utopia, not for the vanishing point of human society or the human species, but merely for an individual, ethical ideal. Its realizability is not a matter for the collective, but for individuals. It can only hold up as an ethical ideal if massively supported by aesthetic elements—a hypothesis that is hardly surprising in the context of a philosopher as closely bound to ethics and aesthetics as Nietzsche, but that is largely ignored with regard to the *Übermensch*. In three respects this figure is a product of art, a product of aesthetics: regarding the highest level of development (*superman*), it is a product of happy coincidence; regarding permanent self-overcoming (*overman*), it is a life form that can only be realized momentarily; regarding the "body as a great reason," it is equally the body as a great work of art.

The *Übermensch* as the Luck of the Draw

The prefix *über* ("super," "over") in the term *Übermensch* clearly opens up two threads of meaning.[3] First, there is a vertical dimension, pointing upward, to a top that as a static (complete) area of being is diametrically opposed to the bottom. The English translation of Nietzsche's *Übermensch* as "superman" expresses this meaning more clearly. It converges with the point of view favored by evolutionary biology. Accordingly, the superman is viewed as the highest level within a developmental process. Nietzsche himself repeatedly propagates this point of view, not only in *Zarathustra*. Darwin's fundamental views include humans descending from apes and worms starting things off at the bottom. Nietzsche also insists on the validity of these propositions, going on to direct an accusatory rhetorical question at the human race: "All beings hitherto have created something beyond themselves," the worm creating the ape, as we feel free to interpret his words, and the ape creating man. "And ye want, . . . " so Nietzsche continues, "rather go back to the beast than surpass man?"[4]

For the sake of accuracy, it has to be said that this question is only accusatory if creation has been deemed an ethical norm. Otherwise it is nothing other than a naturalistic fallacy. Concluding an "ought" from an "is" is only compelling if the "is" already contains an "ought," at least latently. In Zarathustra's question this is precisely the case, and for this reason its shroud is merely rhetorical. It is therefore necessary to legitimize the principle of *creation*. The overcoming of man must constitute a self-overcoming, that much is clear. But its goal is far less obvious. Generally speaking, it aims at no less than finding a substitution for God, a life-form that could occupy the vacated place of a supreme body of certainty, albeit well aware that it cannot fulfill this function totally. In philosophical terms this life-form usually bears the name *ontological affirmation*.

In recent times, Gilles Deleuze has reinforced this hypothesis most emphatically, with all the vigor of a Nietzschean thought machine, spinning and repeatedly innovative, but also unfailingly speculative. This occurs on the traditional basis of romanticism, which, inspired by Fichte's philosophy of reflection, makes the form of a reflection its content, makes self-referential thinking a principle, and thus makes eternal becoming, a becoming that has its purpose not outside itself, a purpose in its own right. Yet this process is also filtered by de Saussure's semiotics, removing from language its representative function and transporting it into a process (at least in some ways eternal) of difference production, in which meanings can no longer be pinned down (defined) in an actual or exact sense because they can no longer be pinned down (halted) in a literal sense. Affirmation cannot be separated from this semiotic edifice of negation penetrated with speculation, being indeed its precondition and its consequence; there is no affirmation not preceded by a negation, none not succeeded by a nega-tion. "The Yes which does not know how to say No," the "Yea-Yuh" of the ass, to put it in Zarathustra's words, the Christian Yes, as Nietzsche is forever reminding us, is merely a distortion of the Dionysic, the "pure" affirmative, which implies destruction as active obliteration and makes reference to orgiastic experiences. (It is true that this Christian Yes is also a distortion brought about by Nietzsche himself. In his "Sources of the Self,"[5] Charles Taylor demonstrates how much the modern "affirmation of normal life" can also be attributed to Christian religious tradition, ac-cording to which God, as the creator of being, also affirms it. Nietzsche here proves to be the opposite, the heir to Christianity, a philosophy of on-tological affirmation as the transformation of a body of religious thought into a nonreligious conceptuality.) Pure affirmation is essentially an act of creation: "Affirmation is to create—not to bear, to assume, to shoulder a burden." It *is* being because (or more cautiously: to the extent that) being is becoming, a process of creation, of construction and destruction, in this sense destruction.[6]

Unlike Derrida and the deconstructivist versions of events he in-spired, Deleuze, whose 1962 book on the subject was to make Nietzsche accessible for the postmodern philosophical version of events, was not accused of ignoring the "positive" creative elements of this work, of be-lieving himself capable of doing without *Zarathustra* altogether or con-tenting himself with only addressing the (problematic) fourth part.[7] In the rough conflict between a metaphysical interpretation of affirmation and a critical one, Deleuze provides if not (strict) arguments, then at least good argumentative material for the second stance, according to which creation in no way stands for a will to power that has become indepen-dent, for an empowerment of subjectivity to command what is being, as is maintained most emphatically by Heidegger, but far more for refraining from the concept of externally given being, as founded in epistemology.[8] Being is consequently to be viewed only as something to be created and constructed and, to this extent (and only to this extent, not in the sense of a metaphysical ontology), as a creating and a constructing, as something that creates itself (by being created).

Despite this structure of the eternal, Nietzsche nevertheless chooses to present self-overcoming aimed at affirmation of the ontological, rather than the factual being, in other words affirmation of a becoming that includes affirmation and denial, position and negation, in a stepwise structure as well. Yet this is not a contradiction, for the structure of the eternal does not take hold until the top step. On this step "evolution as a linear event ends," leading into that "self-reference" that Nietzsche interprets not idealistically but according to the power theory, as "wanting to have power over oneself," and materialistically, as "the great reason of the body." This self-reference "absorbs the dynamics of the *over* by replacing a linear vertical development with a circular movement, and through the activity of creating-beyond-oneself strives to stretch the self eternally."[9] In order to get to that top step, to become superhuman, mankind must accordingly surmount two other steps first, namely, those of the "ought" and the "want," ultimately arriving at the "is" (affirmation): "Higher than 'you ought' is 'I want' (the heroes); higher than 'I want' is 'I am' (the Greek gods)."[10] In this comment Nietzsche attributes to the Greek gods the highest form of being; in *Zarathustra* he uses a child to symbolize a step of the "spirit," an intellectual life-form that emerges from the "metamorphoses" completed by camel and lion, from the symbols of a spirit initially heavily loaded, bent double with factual respect, and then heroic, the "you ought" having been replaced by an "I want." The child, characterized by new beginnings and play, by affirming creation, is the emblem of the *Übermensch*, in its achievement heir to both the ancient gods and the Christian God. "Dead are all the Gods: now do we desire the Superman (*Übermensch*) to live." Or, linked to the metaphor of sea voyage, another favorite with Nietzsche: "Once did people say God when they looked out upon distant seas; now, however, have I taught you to say, Superman (*Übermensch*)."[11]

But Nietzsche also employs the *aesthetic* tradition to explain or dissect the whole that is concentrated within the concept of the *Übermensch*. Faithful to his historical genealogical view of things, he aims at an "overcoming of previous ideals," pertaining to "philosophers, artists, saints." He replaces the artist, "the genius," with "the man who creates mankind beyond himself,"[12] in other words, the *Übermensch*. The *Übermensch* is art that has stepped into, or stepped back into life. Then Nietzsche answers the logically consistent question of what he regards as art very traditionally. For the *Übermensch* is the man who is able to put the "hero-will" out of his mind again and who is thus able to appreciate chance, in other words what literally comes along by chance, as favor, luck, or mercy. In the tradition of classical idealism, the model for this is beauty. "Unattainable is beauty by all ardent wills." Furthermore, beauty demands that one stand with one's "relaxed muscles," that one lets and permits rather than wills and wants. When a perceptive "power," or in neutral Kantian terms phenomenon, becomes "gracious," when, again to use Kant's terms, a "favor" is shown to us or at least appears to be shown to us, then this, for Nietzsche as for Kant, is "beauty." For the hero the "last self-conquest" thus consists in shaping his life aesthetically, in the sense of allowing passivity to enter his dynamic and forward-driving activity, an element that Derrida, in the tradition of Heidegger, is currently emphasizing, or even overemphasizing, and that Rorty—to name a current contrasting example—is criminally neglectful of in his Nietzschean conception of self-creation. Just as an aesthetic experience cannot be forced, neither can happiness in life be forced. The "superhero" is more than a hero because he refrains from doing exactly those things that usually characterize a hero: wanting, struggling, fighting.[13]

Thus for Nietzsche, even for Nietzsche, it is first necessary to learn to want, or in other words to learn to deny the "ought," in order then to put wanting behind oneself again. Like other philosophers before him (being those whom he tended to denigrate as his adversaries), he teaches a traditional three-step model. If we comprehend the concept of the *Übermensch* in the sense of a superman, then only on the top step can a satisfaction— to return to the debate about the aphorism "giving style to one's life"—be achieved that is borne not by bourgeois compromise and comfort, but by ontological affirmation. To put it another way, the *Übermensch* lives the principle of the as-if, stressed by Kant as the heuristic rule of science, as well as, and in particular the constitutive rule of aesthetic evaluation, and legitimized by Nietzsche himself from the outset, since his *The Birth of Tragedy*, as a fiction governing knowledge and action, or in traditional terms: as a life-permitting illusion. The *Übermensch* knows to take all things and events *as if* he himself wanted them to be just as they are. In this respect he really does manage to change all the "it is so" into an "I wanted it thus."

The *second* thread of interpretation within the concept of the *Übermensch* is that of the *horizontal*. It signifies a horizontal movement, an across rather than an up, a dynamic aimed not upward but forward, expressed in English by "overman." The self-overcoming of man toward the overman is here an eternal self-becoming. In this interpretation it is most obvious that the *Übermensch* is not to be established as a type of being into which the individual or the species could develop and in which it could dwell. The overman might be a utopia, but not one located in the future, at the end of our history to date. Far more it refers to the temporal modality of the moment and is realized, if at all, only momentarily and only within the history of an individual. However much it might be true, on the one hand, that the overman can only be understood "as a becoming state," "never as an achieved state within being," that he "is and will remain utopian," it is equally true, on the other hand, that this categorical statement requires precision: the overman can never be understood as a *definitively* achievable state within being, but can be understood as an *instantaneously* achievable state within being; it does produce itself "in each case now in the individual completion of an immanent self-transcendence, momentarily, not permanently." "Accordingly, Nietzsche admits: 'Aim: to *achieve* the overman for an instant.'"[14] To achieve it means to have recognized for a moment the meaning of one's own life, the "meaning of the earth," of which Zarathustra speaks right at the outset, "earthed" signifying not located in a hereafter. This meaning can, however, only ever be temporary since the "horizontal" movement of self-transcending and thus of generating meaning cannot end.

This moment of recognizing the meaning as a realization of the overman in man is for Nietzsche, however, always also a reference to the *aesthetic* level of experience. Nietzsche himself does not forge a link between the concept of the overman and that of the aesthetic moment, yet if we remember what Nietzsche adopted from Schopenhauer's aesthetics, as well as the extent to which he elevates the aesthetic to a model of constructivism, then forging the above-mentioned link does not require any extensive interpretatorial effort. From Schopenhauer's *The World as Will and Representation* Nietzsche accordingly adopts the temporal structure of suddenness, explicitly in *The Birth of Tragedy*. It has the character of an aesthetic entity, with "horror" and "blissful rapture" seizing man when "suddenly" his imagination makes that he "loses his way" due to the cognitive shape of an appearance, in other words when he believes the cognitive shapes of space, time, and causality, as well as the "Apollonic" principle of individuation and identification, to be annulled and takes a "glimpse" into the delimited realm of the Dionysian.[15]

Later Nietzsche does attribute a nonpassive significance to this so-called contemplative act by Schopenhauer. What appears as contemplation is in reality "poetry," something created by mankind, the result of an epistemic activity, not something that is being per se, and this claim is also a fiction, an epistemic achievement of synthesis, to be sure, as Nietzsche had to concede and can concede, a useful and inevitable fiction for pragmatic reasons, and thus a fiction both true and convincing. The human being who writes poetry, in other words a human being who recognizes, who sees, who hears, who senses, has adopted a *"vis creativa,"* a "whole eternally growing world of valuations, colors, accents, perspectives, scales, affirmations, and negations."[16] This is precisely where the model character of aesthetic creativity lies for cognition. For Nietzsche, learning from artists also means using their powers of worldly creation as orientation. Discovering the meaning of one's own life therefore means inventing it and, in order to do this, corresponding to the horizontal interpretation of the superhuman, again and again, always afresh, a creative effort that finds its model in the artistic powers of creation.

Yet the *Übermensch* does not only comprise a vertical and a horizontal interpretation; it can be seen as the *tension* between these two levels of interpretation. The concept that, according to aesthetics, unites this inner tension is the *"great reason of the body."* Even if the effect is always simplifying and somewhat embarrassing when central philosophical ideas are pressed into geometric diagrams, this procedure is not always distorting. In the case of the *Übermensch,* the twofold "über" can be plotted as two axes at 90° angles, one of which points vertically upward and refers not only to the idea of the *superman* but also and especially to the spiritualism that pervades our cultural history and that is protected by Christianity and its concern for the soul. The other points horizontally sideways and refers not only to the idea of the overman but also to the hedonistic materialism so successfully suited to everyday life, for example, that of the "last man" with his concern for the body alone. The steeper the middle line or resultant, symbol of the *Übermensch* in this third interpretation (just as its utopian content could be symbolized in the two previous interpretations by one axis each), is as it distances itself from the axes, "the stronger the tension which has to be borne, and with each step taken" (not to be forgotten), "the two axes grow in the same ratio."[17] Man becomes *Übermensch* to the same extent as he is able to bear the growing tension between his spiritual and materialistic sides and, following the example of the tightrope-walker mentioned by Nietzsche in his prelude to *Zarathustra*, balance between them.

Nietzsche also describes this precariously tense relationship using the formula (the expression, the short apt phrase, the mathematical, scientific, and thus diagrammatic definition) of the great reason of the body. Here, too, a contradiction is open to interpretation. On the one hand, this formula defines reason as an organ within the body; on the other hand, the body is an instrument of reason. If, as seems almost to be a matter of course, "all human achievement is always also the expression or yield of the human body," then the achievement of reason is also "connected" to the human body, also belongs to the "structure" or "disposition" of the human body.[18] If, by contrast, the body does not act reasonably of its own accord, but reason—as the ability to recognize, distinguish, and conclude—instead "extends far beyond" what the body is capable of, which in particular can be seen in the way it can be directed *against* "the body" in the form of tiredness, pain, desire, or fear, then, according to classic terminology, reason is what "dominates," "rules," and makes the body its tool.

In general, the solution to this "contradictory" or "paradox"[19] hypothetical context is the field of art and philosophical aesthetics. Kant, in particular, was pioneering in his definition of aesthetic evaluation as (four) paradox expressions: pleasure with disinterest, universality without concept, purposiveness without purpose, and subjective necessity. Yet a direct link between Nietzsche and Kant in this context cannot be established: at best an indirect one via Schiller, the "poet of his youth whom he cites more frequently in his *The Birth of Tragedy* than Goethe or Wagner."[20] Deducing an aesthetic meaning from Zarathustra's formula of the great reason of the body and thus finding a new aesthetic justification for the concept of the *Übermensch* is, however, suggested in this context through the way that the body is to be perceived "following the analogy of the artist," as the "creative basis" from which all activity, shaping and creativity stems. The corresponding term for this unconscious production, originally employed by Kant and then driven romantically onward by Schelling and Schopenhauer, is that of genius.[21] The great reason of the body is thus one of the body's great *works of art.*

Science Fiction and Film

The most popular experimental ground for the figure of the *Übermensch,* or, more specifically in this context, artificial human, is the literary and cinematographic genre of science fiction. The world of science fiction, and with it the "cinematic image" of the artificial human being, falls "into two complementary visions": that "of something which looks like a human being but 'in reality' is a machine"; and that "of something which looks like a machine but can think and even feel like a human being."[22] The latter category is familiar to us in the guise of robots or computers, the most famous movie examples being HAL in *2001—A Space Odyssey,* Robby in *Forbidden Planet,* and the adorably funny pair C3PO and R2-D2 in *Star Wars.* Representatives of the former category are known as androids, replicas, or cyborgs; are a more recent, for obvious reasons a more dangerous, invention; and can famously be seen in *Blade Runner* and *Terminator.*

The artificial human being, or, more appropriately, the human machine, represents a central element within iconography and thus also when defining the science-fiction genre. Definitions are a delicate matter, to be treated with care. Since science fiction, like most linguistic terms outside the sciences, cannot be defined as a formula or by establishing a common characteristic, yet a definition cannot be disposed with altogether, we have to content ourselves either with establishing a *cluster* or constellation of characteristics, most or ideally all of which apply in the face of the phenomenon in question, or—more modestly—with finding an exemplary case, a prototypical representative or characteristic example in line with Wittgenstein's idea of a "family resemblance."

In the case of science fiction, one such constellate feature—apart from spaceships, previously undiscovered planets, and scientific laboratories—is the artificial human being. This figure does not occur in all works of science fiction; if one is to be found in a movie or a book, however, this would be a reason to categorize that movie or book as belonging to the science-fiction genre. *A* reason, not *sufficient* reason, otherwise a novel such as Mary Shelley's *Frankenstein*—or its classic adaptation by James Whale, including Boris Karloff in his unforgettable role as the artificial creature—would have to be assigned to this genre without further ado. The *prototypical* definition illustrates even more clearly how unconvincing this is, whatever some people might maintain. More representative of the genre than, say, *Frankenstein* is undoubtedly a novel such as Aldous Huxley's *Brave New World* or a movie like Stanley Kubrick's *2001—A Space Odyssey*. This manner of definition, which is usually applied intuitively, is the result of a multitude of experience overlapping in a pattern of resemblances and which cannot be comprehended by adhering to a logical opposition of identity and difference, nor as the crystallization of a merely partial identity, a gradually realized equality. Yet, as we should not forget, both types of definition come with a historical catalog: a constellation of defining characteristics can be altered through a restructuring process or through the introduction of a new characteristic, while a currently representative example can (continually) be called into question by the emergence of new examples.

In addition to the *iconographic* definitional element, there is also the simple point of the *genre* to be taken into account. Science fiction is a genre at home in both novels and movies. Nevertheless, like America in the eyes of the European immigrants before it, *film* now gradually seems to have become the Promised Land. It apparently places the quest for a New World within its most suitable framework, the reason being that *film* is itself able to present *(new) worlds* better than any other aesthetic medium, due to the illusion of realism that it alone can provide. As a genre, science fiction urges toward the new and the unknown. This is another one of its definitorial, narrative characteristics. This is, of course, usually also true of the horror and fantasy genres. It would therefore be more specific to science fiction to say that it crosses the borderline of familiar *knowledge*. The will to knowledge, the desire to shift cognitive boundaries, is far more important in the science-fiction genre than in either of its two fiercest competitors. Whereas horror movies resolutely unhinge the world of scientific rules, and fantasy movies subject this world to magic or to the childlike force of make-believe, science-fiction movies acknowledge this world by working relentlessly to extend it and perfect it.[23] The motto of the TV series *Star Trek*: "To boldly go where no man has gone before," could be a brilliant motto for science fiction itself. It marks the advance of both the nineteenth-century belief in scientific and technical progress and the deeply American myth of the *frontier*, most popularly portrayed in Westerns. In the context of science fiction it was first brought to the big screen in the major productions of the 1950s, in the shape of a scientific and technical optimism that depicted the future as a world of sparkling chrome cleanliness free of all signs of perspiration, as if the movies had been directed by the rediscovered housewifely culture of that decade. This urge toward the (cognitive) unknown is, of course, no less ambivalent than that of gaining land by conquering the Wild West. In the latter case heroic pioneers render themselves redundant by aiding the advance of civilization; in the former case space patrols reduce with every "mission" they successfully undertake that endless expanse driving them on like an innermost promise. The *space cowboys* work hard to make themselves unemployed. They too will at some stage no longer be needed and will find themselves washed up on one of the planets they were once responsible for annexing.

In order to limit the limitless in this ambivalent way, science-fiction movies (incidentally here, too, horror and fantasy movies) use the means that for an essential part define film in general: imagery, visibility. Movies tend to convey an optical illusion of movement by speeding through a catalog of images. *Movies*, as the very name suggests, provide moving pictures, or, as they have been known since Deleuze, "moving images" (unlike "time images" *in*direct representations of time, understood not in the everyday sense of a homogenous and linear movement from one now, one state of being, to the next, or in cinematographic terms: from one photographic recording to the next, but as an affective intensive form of perception bringing differences to the fore, not spreading extensively, spatializing, that is, reducing complexity through the singular standpoint of the Self, cinematographically responding best to the technology of montage, to the compilation of different points of view, observations, chronological perceptions; it is not a single photo that constitutes the semantic unit used in film, but rather a sequence of cuts or shots; in philosophical terms film thus realizes the primate of becoming over being, which is contrary to our everyday perception).

The generation of an optical illusion, namely, that of movement through space and time, is essential to the medium of film, and illusionism is therefore its foremost characteristic. In a nonstatic way, movies both *show* the visible (for example, in documentaries) and *render* visible (for example, in computer animations). Their ability to present the world means a proffered system of symbols (Cassirer, Goodman), a life-world (Husserl, Heidegger), a mutual referential context of signs or experiences, paving the way for certain interpretations, ideologies, and thus ways of living. As has often been noted, the manner of this presentation is based on a combination of pictures, words, sounds, music, and body language, a multimediality that reveals film to be the synthesis of all other art forms, a technically reorganized, all-over work of art (and thus an unexpected successor of opera). In other words, it is based on a combination of visual, acoustic, and indirectly tactile perception (triggering physical reactions), the visual part of which in turn largely consists of movement, that is a permanent relocation of the camera, technically and artificially acting as the endlessly agile eye of the cinema-goer. This is precisely what generates the illusion of reality, remaining specific to film to the present day and lending it such suggestive power.

For science-fiction movies, recognizing the unknown thus means rendering the *invisible visible*. Yet it is important to be clear about the *ambivalence* of this process. Accordingly, in their will to knowledge, science-fiction movies are, on the one hand, aimed, in the sense of Foucault (Nietzsche and Heidegger), at safety through dominance, at power in its negative, repressive sense, yet on the other hand, they make possible precisely what provokes the human need for safety, as a "space" full of meaning, as an unpinpointable "meaningfulness." This is it in a nutshell, the emphasis obvious within the context: a "world of space," in both the practical everyday and the philosophical phenomenological senses. Relationships of power, as Foucault stresses in a provocative (and therefore necessarily partly thoughtless) generalization, also reveal a positive, productive side and as a negative entity do not, in accordance with a conventional dualistic pattern, simply assume the existence of a positive entity that is then left to be repressed. They open up a space for the visible (and a dimension for the speakable), lay down rules, without doing so explicitly, to dictate what is perceived (and what spoken).

Science-fiction movies not only illustratively bring an element of control to what was previously without limits or illustration but also encourage the emergence of the same, whether for the first time. Not only in the manner of a Hegelian dialectic of limitation, of a definitorial determinism that repeatedly produces an undetermined as well, but also in the manner of a metaphysically critically (Heidegger) or first "archaeologically" and then genealogically (Foucault) structured analysis of the fundamental types of knowledge (*episteme*), laying down in advance the conditions governing the possibility of what is speakable and visible, the "understanding of being." What Foucault describes in *The Will to Knowledge*, using the compulsion to confess, as a discursivation spreading explosively throughout the course of history can similarly be seen in science-fiction movies as an untiring motivation to illustrate the unknown, as well as a continued differentiation of the same.

The attraction continued to grow with the technical possibilities provided by the image machine known as cinema. The special effects in *2001—A Space Odyssey*, filmed in the late 1960s, were so good that at the time it was said that anybody wishing to top them cinematographically would have to film the real thing, that is, in space itself. In *Star Wars*, just ten years later, the flight curves of the depicted spaceships and combat aircraft were simulated so precisely that the cinema-goer really had the feeling of participating in a night battle of the skies and of diving at supersonic speed into the phenomenal depths of space. After watching these scenes it is easy to believe that the movie's director, George Lucas, dreamed as a boy of becoming a Formula 1 racing driver. "For the first time in the history of cinema," enthused the coproducer, "we have reached the point where scriptwriters can write whatever they like, producers have every option open to them and directors are limited only by their own imaginations."[24]

Yet this was not merely an expression of enthusiasm at a new technology; it was also a premonition that the human race was on the verge of a *cultural* change of revolutionary dimensions. For movies and the science-fiction genre this meant that from now on they would be inextricably allied. The gloating way in which cinema at the start of the twenty-first century is spoken of as a cinema without limitations is more than just a metaphorical reference to the infinity of space, iconographically laid claim to by science fiction. The relationship between the two has become an alliance because a *new aesthetic principle* has come into force, a principle as follows: everything that can be imagined can be realized in film; everything that fiction can invent and the imagination can dream up can also be filmed and thus transported to a credible illusion of reality. That means: since *science fiction* encourages the imagining of future worlds and life-forms, and since *film* has become the perfect machine for creating imagery and realizing the imagined, then film is also the paradigmatic aesthetic science-fiction medium.

The New Episteme: The Creative Being

There is, of course, a dark, seemingly tiny fleck in the midst of all this enthusiasm about unlimited possibilities. It is said that directors are only restricted by their own imaginations. What appears to be a *quantité négligeable* is actually qualitatively crucial. For imagination, responsible for limiting the subject matter that can be addressed by professional directors, is in turn limited by precisely those epistemic principles that a philosopher like Foucault, interested in epistemology and the social sciences, was so keen to analyze. From the point of view of cultural theory, the question here is which *epistemic principle* the genre of science fiction and, more generally, the culture surrounding it are controlled by. It is also a question of what exactly is driving this cinematographic discursivation of the unknown so relentlessly onward.

When a certain theme or an iconographically and symbolically significant image is continually repeated and used in the cultural sphere of art and cinema, psychologists and (particularly structuralistic) cultural anthropologists suggest that, in the manner of a myth, this theme or image is hiding an unsolved, maybe even insoluble problem, a fundamental contradiction requiring solution but quite possibly continually standing in its own way. This suggestion is particularly powerful in the case of the artificial human being. It is an image that can be seen as a semantically compressed intersection of three "grand narratives," to use Lyotard's phrase, as a concentrated overlapping of three cognitive formations in which western culture finds much of its legitimization: Christian religion, science, and bourgeois anthropology.[25]

First, for Christian cultures the creation of artificial human beings is a project that amounts to blasphemy. The image of the artificial human being is attractive because it is *forbidden*, attractive since the biblical story of Adam and Eve, tempted by the Devil in the form of the serpent. Wanting to be like God is a sin that must be paid for with banishment from Paradise, with a life of plight, disease, and shame, with human mortality. Thinking along these lines, taking the paradisiacal temptation even further and attempting to be like God by imitating the act of human creation can only end badly. In a hypertrophic undertaking of this kind, the hand of the Devil must be involved.

Second, for scientists the project represents a substantial challenge to take part in a contest that sensationally touches the very core of scientific self-perception. For science sees itself as a kind of methodically verified knowledge, as the area of knowledge with an exemplary claim to accuracy. This obligation toward verification also harbors a metaphysical tendency to penetrate to the very bottom of a phenomenon, with a major part of science defining itself in this way, at least until the twentieth century. Exposing the biological basis of the human being is therefore a natural and internally set goal for scientists who are accordingly specialized. The appeal of the image of artificial man is here that of *scientific self-assurance*: science provides itself with permanent and ultimately definitive proof of its own ability. Yet not even science is free of religious and mythical elements. As the subdisciplines of medicine and psychology, its goal to alleviate human beings of their physical ailments and mental suffering is permeated by the religious motif of deliverance from all mortal evil. For all this Prometheus stands as a mythological example. "The New Prometheus" is tellingly the subtitle of Mary Shelley's *Frankenstein*.

The third "grand narrative" running through the traditional history of the artificial human being is that of bourgeois anthropology, in which the sexual being man dreams of his own creation, or, to put it more scientifically, of his autogenesis or autopoiesis and reproductive autarky. In the archives of fiction it is nearly always men who attempt to create a human, usually a male, being. In this context, *Frankenstein*, although written by a woman, can also hold up as a good example. In the novel, as well as in its numerous movie adaptations, the act of creation is completed without a woman; a man generates a man, commenting enthusiastically: "with my hands, with my own hands." On closer inspection,[26] this act of creation is built not only on a virile monism, undermining the traditional dualism of male and female, but also on a form of necrophilia, on generating from the dead, from body parts (of dead men). The artificial being, the new man, is to this extent a stillbirth: a deadly form and the creation of a man, of the scientist Frankenstein, who can only create life from dead material. *Frankenstein* is accordingly the story of a man (as the product of western bourgeois culture) who creates a new man from himself, that is, from the parts of dead men, who in turn then kills men, women, and ultimately himself.

From a psychoanalytical point of view, the Oedipal structure at work here is obvious. The artificially created son directs his libidinous desire at the future wife of his creator-father and ultimately becomes his murderer. At least in the novel, this is partly due to the fact that the creator-father rejects him as a deformity, as an aesthetic failure, filled with disgust, disappointment, self-contempt, and ultimately with the wish to see the creature he has created dead, an affective chain of reactions expressing all too clearly the disappointed love of the male creator for his male creature, a virile-narcissistic and homoerotic insult. Withheld emotional nurturing, a topic with which Mary Shelley remains true to the educational theory prevalent at the time of the Enlightenment, produces emotional cripples who then take revenge for their suffering in manslaughter and murder, ultimately becoming stigmatized for their actions as monsters. (The movie adaptation by Whale, by contrast, draws on the biologistic paradigm that had been increasing in popularity since the last decades of the nineteenth century: here the brain of a criminal, which has unknowingly been implanted in the creature, is the cause of his violent actions.) The second justification for killing is also Oedipal: Frankenstein breaks the promise he made to his male creature to give him a female creature for company. He is inwardly driven to break his promise because otherwise he would ultimately restore to the female sex that sexual function required to preserve the species that the technological act of creation had supposedly rendered superfluous. The desire to create life in a nonnatural way is a "male fantasy" that is certainly older than the bourgeois society of the nineteenth century, but it was during this period that it really took off, remaining strong to the present day. Even this bourgeois anthropological tradition conceals a twisted but clear motif from Christian religion. Two thousand years after, according to the Bible, Mary the woman created a child without a man, man has now responded by turning the tables and creating a child without a woman. It is almost as if he had this need to work through an ancient humiliation and attack the very essence of woman, her ability to give birth.

The fact that this image of an artificial human being has captured the human imagination unrelentingly, that in particular it has lastingly inspired aesthetic imagination during the past two hundred years and cinematographic imagination during the past one hundred years, is not only due, however, to the powerful threefold tradition of the Christian monotheistic history of creation, the scientific logic of research, and bourgeois anthropology. It also has an *epistemological philosophical* reason, which can be revealed with the help of Foucault. In his book *The Order of Things*, Foucault investigated the formation of the humanities, that is, sciences such as philology, psychology, and sociology, across three successive epochs, namely, the Renaissance, the "classical" rationalistic age, and modernity. The condition of the possibility of these sciences is established, in his eyes, in what he calls the "episteme" of an epoch and that could, in the words of Thomas Kuhn, be deemed a "paradigm," a conceptuality underlying both the sciences and everyday knowledge, laying down what is speakable and recognizable; accordingly, any change in this area brings with it completely new questions, perceptions, and scientific methods, which, in the words of Heidegger, allow not only the (known) world to be seen in a new way but also a new world to be seen. During the Renaissance the cognizability of the world was founded on the episteme of "similarity," for in this epoch—Don Quixote being the famous literary example—words and things were linked by similarity, as were words to things, and thus easily confused. In contrast, the rationalistic age was built up around the epistemological principle of "representing," imagining, or illustrating things using signs (words and pictures). It replaced the natural link between signs and the signed, regulation through similarity, with an artificial link, but one that still staked claim to correctness, finding its marked expression in the metaphor of mirroring nature. The act of representation is, however, capable of representing everything except the representing entity itself, that is, the representing Self under the heading of subjectivity.

The Maids of Honor by Velázquez provides a stunning and now famous example of this. According to Foucault's interpretation of this work, Velázquez portrays the Spanish royal couple, seen toward the back of the painting in a small mirror, but which during the scene portrayed must be standing in the area of the room toward which the gazes of all the persons depicted, the little princess with blonde curls, the maids of honor, a female dwarf, a court jester, as well as that of the painter himself are directed, and in which we ourselves, as observers of the painting, must be standing. This point outside the painting, at which all the gazes converge, is for Foucault the centre of representation that in itself cannot be represented.

Art historians may well be critical of this interpretation. One could support the hypothesis that Velázquez, who depicts himself in the painting as the painter, wished to produce not a portrait of the royal couple, but precisely the painting that we have before us as observers, showing him at work painting the maids of honor. From the room shown in the painting, as well as from the little princess, who appears in several of Velázquez's works, we know that everything portrayed is back to front, meaning that the painting itself represents a mirror. Thus all the persons depicted are located outside the picture, on the same side as us, the observers. Accordingly, the royal couple is not the true center of the picture and its representation, but rather the painter is. In this painter the three functions of representation analyzed by Foucault overlap, for he is not only the producing/representing subject but also the represented object and the receiving subject; in other words he is what, according to Foucault, is impossible in the classical age of rationalism: a subject capable of self-representation.[27]

Of course, the role played by the royal couple is once again the most problematic in this hypothesis, since if their portrait is taken as being a small mirror image within a large "mirror picture" then they must both be standing inside the painting, in an area visible within the space shown, which is not the case. To this extent Foucault's somewhat different hypothesis retains its stake within the truth-oriented game of interpretations. But the crucial factor here is not whether his interpretation of the painting is correct from an art historian's point of view, but instead what he, albeit contrafactually, is able to disclose with the help of the picture. His saving grace could ultimately be formulated in the subjunctive, namely, if his hypothesis about Velázquez's painting were the correct one, then the result of his interpretation would be no less than astonishing in its content and ingenious in its form. Yet if it should actually turn out to be incorrect, then first he would merely have selected the wrong example to illustrate his theory on epistemology and the history of science, and second this would still not discount it altogether, for it could, *for the sake of argument*, still hold up as a demonstration object. After all, Foucault was not intent on finding scientific evidence to prove that no work of fine art from that epoch was capable of portraying self-representation, but merely on finding an example of the same.

Staying with his interpretation, the modern episteme arrives on the scene, indicated by Velázquez's painting. "The human being," subjectivity as a duplication into a simultaneously empirical and transcendental aspect, then adopts the position that in Velázquez's works remains vacant, namely, the position located outside the picture occupied by the royal couple having its portrait painted, where both Velázquez himself in real life and the virtual recipient of the picture are standing. It is the position of the self-observing observer, simultaneously inside the picture, that is, empirical, and outside the picture, that is, transcendental, simultaneously represented and representing. But for Foucault, and not just for him, this fundamental epistemic figure proved to be an aporetic doublet, the untenability of which was already developing, in the structuralistic "counter-sciences" conceived of by Lévi-Strauss, de Saussure, and Lacan, into a new way of thinking. This is only vaguely suggested, however, and but one thing can be stated with certainty, namely, that the principle of modernity, the human being, is, as declared poetically and prophetically in the last sentence of the book, "disappearing like a face in the sand of an ocean beach."

Foucault was forced to remain vague about a possible episteme for this newly emerging, postmodern philosophy. Yet the answer could be more obvious than he would have liked to admit, he who in his *Order of Things* does not even draw the line at criticizing Nietzsche and the romantic infinite subjectivity discovering the unconscious. For it is precisely the *romantic* reinterpretation of subjectivity that is to encourage one particular episteme, heralded as early as the Renaissance: that of the *creative being*. What Rorty underlines with his theorem about exemplary artistic self-creation and what Charles Taylor (as before him Isaiah Berlin) addresses with his theorem about romantic expressivism being one of the greatest sources of modern identity, is for Foucault in his last works the "esthetics of existence." But the real heuristic pioneer in this area was Hans Blumenberg, with his 1957 essay "'Imitation of nature.' Towards a prehistory of the idea of the creative being." In this essay, Blumenberg formulates the hypothesis that, historically speaking, modern subjectivity lays claim to the attribute of creativity with such vehement pathos because it has had to fight for it, up against an almost overpowering ontological and theological tradition. For almost two thousand years, starting with Aristotle, it appeared as if the definitive answer to the question of what human beings are capable of in their own right were to lie in "art" (*téchne*) as an imitation (*mimesis*) of nature. The corresponding idea that man is essentially incapable of accomplishing anything new under the sun (under nature) was not revised until the beginning of the modern age and philosophers and researchers such as Nikolaus von Cues (with his *idiota* figure of a layman carving a wooden spoon, producing something new), Copernicus, and Descartes, ultimately becoming heroically established during the transition from German idealism to romanticism. Artistic, ingenious creativity now appears to be the only completely self-determined and thus exemplary human activity.[28]

It is a transition that takes place *within* the mentalistic paradigm of subjectivity, but which eminently *shifts* its meaning, for subjectivity now *admits* to having two faces, to being simultaneously the solution to all puzzles, yet remaining a puzzle in itself. The puzzle of the puzzle-solver has to remain unsolved. As a late romanticist, Nietzsche also tellingly incorporates this within his *Übermensch*, the human being who unceasingly (manically) exceeds his own capabilities because he constitutively cannot know who he is in a substantialist sense. To use the language of German idealism: The constitutive principle of cognition and action eludes that cognition. According to this philosophy, this is no ultimately satisfactory solution. The only satisfactory solution would be complete self-knowledge.

Romanticism turns its back on this "hybrid," haughty undertaking[29] by putting some distance between itself and it; it admits ironically or tragically to the aporias linked with this undertaking. But by doing precisely this, it takes a step beyond mere self-empowerment and opens up a second track alongside the modern power-based will to knowledge. Modernity, as shown by Foucault in his *Order of Things*, is an anthropocentric project centered on subjectivity, which in turn is subject to a fundamental self-contradiction analyzed by Kant, namely, that the subject is to ensure an objectivity that used to be guaranteed by metaphysics, that it is to maintain a correspondence between itself and the objects of the world and function as a representation of those symbols it has destroyed through its self-reflection, by referring the representing subject to itself. The subject thus reveals itself to be an entity that is just as intelligibly infinite as finite, just as transcendental as empirical, but, since Kant, this has been precisely its strength. The limits of its finite cognitive faculty simultaneously house the transcendental conditions for infinitely advancing objective knowledge, making it precisely the finity of the subject that enables it to assume the position of the referred center of representation, the absolute. But, as Foucault states in a spirit of existentialism, this amounts to systematic overtaxing, which in turn can be seen in the infinite dynamics displayed by the cognitive process. To put it another way, the aporia of this type of knowledge is only superficially avoided by launching itself into a tireless process of knowledge acquisition. The "Will to Knowledge," which Foucault analyzes exclusively and generalizingly in a later work in connection with the power theory, is still an effect of the central aporia of the philosophy of consciousness described in his *Order of Things* and finds expression in the cognitive disciplines of the humanities, whose claim to universally valid knowledge thus conceal the mere will to the power of the Self, of the *humanus*.

Yet, if we take the romantic reinterpretation of subjectivity seriously, this is only *one* strand of the history (of knowledge). The other strand points not at a will to *knowledge*, but at a will to *creation*. It remains an effect of the aporia underlying the subjectivity theory and, in its restless drive to create, is expression of this fundamental self-contradiction. It also remains, as will be shown more precisely later, an element of the "axis" of subjectivity intersecting with that of the power systems; in other words, not merely is it, on the one hand, an effect of the power, but it also, on the other hand, cannot (totally, autonomously) elude it either.[30] Nevertheless, the will to (self-)creation has its own history, a history that in its peculiarity Foucault chooses not to pursue any further. He is far too caught up in the romantic, restless dynamic circling the inner contradiction of subjectivity, only seeing in the corresponding "types of knowledge" variations of one and the same aporia. To the same extent with which he rightly comprehends the modern age as an epoch essentially characterized by romanticism, he fails to recognize the momentum that it assumes with the firm introduction of creative productivity. The order of things now becomes a "superhuman" task, no longer in a literal sense, but in a Nietzschean one. It is not superhuman because it attempts the impossible in a heroic, rebellious manner and becomes submerged in its hubris, but because it accepts that postmetaphysical and posttranscendental thinking has to be—following the logic of justification—ultimately groundless, believing itself capable of making up for the "death of God," the end of certainties independent of experience and free of context, purely through the mortal ego, with its powers of creation and desire to configurate. The Self (*Ich*) therefore remains the hero of philosophy, but by creating itself time and again in line with artistic and romantic examples, free of the burden of having to rescue truth through the Self, objectivity through subjectivity, the pathos of despair also becomes foreign to it. The way in which the latter still rings out from Nietzsche's works only goes to show, once again, how he never felt relaxed with metaphysics.

Accordingly, the human being, the principle of modernity, does not disappear like a face on a sandy beach when the tide comes in, but instead shows a new face, only slightly changed, yet considerably different. The old paradigm of *subjectivity* has not been cancelled out completely, but with the attribute *creativity* a new element comes to the fore that prohibits, even more vehemently than is true of the subjectivity theory episteme anyway, this subjectivity from being inextricably linked to the paradigm that has become known, especially in the context of Habermas's deliberations, as that of a "philosophy of consciousness." Instead, the episteme of the creative being proves itself open to approaches from the fields of intersubjectivity theory and linguistic philosophy. It is *transverse* to the paradigms of the philosophies of "consciousness" and "language"; it cannot be attributed to the "mentalistic" or "linguistic" paradigm.

All the same it should be noted that in the *Order of Things* Foucault's analysis concentrates on the mentalistic paradigm, to stay with this terminology, and on the one hand differentiates it threefold in the described manner (unless one takes the epoch of the Renaissance and its corresponding episteme of similarity to be part of the "ontological" paradigm conceived of in antiquity) as well as, on the other hand, hinting at transforming it toward the linguistic paradigm, which, however, appears not as a liberating solution to the problems of the previous paradigm, but far more as its continuation in a different form; neither the "formalizing," logical, and language analytical conceptualization of the language, nor the "interpreting," hermeneutic version represented by Marx, Nietzsche, and Freud, nor even the "romantic literary" variation represented by Mallarmé can claim to overwhelm the modern episteme engraved in the humanities.[31] The *linguistic turn* does not bring a turn for Foucault as regards the humanities. Not only the episteme of the creative but also that of the human being itself refuses to be assigned to either the paradigm of consciousness philosophy or that of language philosophy. With the reaccentuation, with the episteme of creative subjectivity, this becomes a whole lot clearer. The fact that philosophers whose arguments are based on language philosophy and intersubjectivity theory, such as Rorty and Taylor, work so intensively with the model of creative subjectivity is merely a welcome external confirmation of this.

Foucault fails to recognize the intrinsic value of creative subjectivity, as can also be shown within the framework of his genealogical method, with which he revokes the structuralistic premise of his "archaeology" of the humanities. The structuralistic method of analyzing historical formations of knowledge from the inside out implies the primacy of these formations of knowledge over the various practices. Accordingly, it is discourse that links technical, economic, social, and political factors to a network of practices, which in turn sustain its own reproduction. Yet Foucault is faced with the problem that analyzing the rules of a discourse archaeologically only serve to render it comprehensible quasi-transcendentally, in the historical conditions governing its possibility, but not in the actual way it works. For there are no rules that could regulate their own application.[32] That is one of the reasons why Kant, in his epistemology based on transcendental philosophy, sees himself systematically forced to make room for the concept of judgment as a force (*Kraft*). The rules governing psychopathological discourse, for example, do not provide sufficient explanation for the nondiscursive practices of the mental asylum. In his work *Discipline and Punish* Foucault therefore reverses the primacy ratio and attempts to explain the emergence of knowledge using the network of practices now associated with the concept of power.

Accordingly, if we contemplate the history of philosophical aesthetics and the concept of subjectivity it helped to render valid against the backdrop of Foucault's hypothesis that in the modern age disciplining (so the new leading term) enforces itself as subjectivization, that the new type of control is that which enables the controlled to be subjects through (self-)control, that modern subjects are submissive and useful for particular functions precisely because they are capable of autonomy, then the aesthetic concept of subjectivity initially seems to fit completely into the power theory framework he erected.[33] For the "aesthetic turn" taking place during the mid-eighteenth century consisted in viewing art no longer as a medium for representing royal sovereignty, to use Foucault's terminology, but as a medium for producing and reproducing subjectivity.

The role of the avant-garde attributed to philosophical aesthetics for idealistic philosophy and the humanities has been emphasized in leading philosophical histories, including recent works, for example in Alfred Baeumler's *Irrationalitätsproblem in der Ästhetik und Logik des 18. Jahrhunderts* and Ernst Cassirer's *Philosophie der Aufklärung*, as well as Luc Ferry's *Homo Aestheticus* and Terry Eagleton's *The Ideology of the Aesthetic*. What the aesthetic concept of the subject does is to overcome the rationalistic dualism of sensoriality and reason. For Baumgarten, being able to appreciate beauty and being able to think strictly logically were no longer mutually exclusive in the way they were for Pascal and Descartes. The subject was far more a channel for "harmonizing" these contrary skills, for bringing them into agreement (*zusammenstimmen*). As a "science of sensory recognition," as Baumgarten states in the very first paragraph of his work *Aesthetica*, aesthetics is the science of a recognition analogous to that of intellect. Accordingly, not only intellect but also sensoriality is an active skill. The scope of what can be attributed to the ability and actions of the subject is thus extended to include the entire subject. Yet not really the entire subject, for the analogy theory does have its limits. In this newly perceived concept of sensoriality, the otherness and uncontrollability factor that Descartes and Pascal, following idealistic dualistic and Christian tradition, attribute to sensoriality in general is in turn rendered valid in the concept of force, which opposes that of method. Baumgarten's reinterpretation reverberates all the way down to Kant. He too saw the powers of imagination, and especially of judgment, as a skill that has to be *practiced*, precisely because we cannot dispose of it at will.

For Foucault's hypothesis of subjectivization as submission this signifies a *double* ambiguity, however: not only, with the concept of submission, does it underline the flipside of the Enlightenment and autonomization process, but submission itself can also be interpreted in different ways: if it rationalistically means the creation of a specifically modern, self-imposed dominance over the Self for the purpose of increasing effectivity, then aesthetically it means the acknowledgment of a necessary, immanent limitation to dominance. In the "power" (*Kraft*) of the subject, that which, once again ambiguously, it owes itself to and at the same time cannot direct, the disciplinary power encounters something that cannot totally be made submissive. To put it deconstructivistically: the proviso of the possibility of self-dominance, subjectivization *as* submission, is simultaneously the proviso of its impossibility; the proviso of disciplinary power, the self-disciplining subject, is at the same time exactly what poses limitations to this power. If the subject is, from the point of view of the power theory, the source of a productivity that can only be organized efficiently because the subject organizes itself efficiently, then from an aesthetic point of view, as well as according to the episteme of the creative being, it is the authority of an ultimately undisciplinable *creativity*.

According to this reinterpretation of Foucault's power theory, aesthetic creative subjectivity is neither just a randomly pliable element within disciplinary power, nor a further instance of disciplining subjectivization, nor a fundamental alternative, the Great Refusal, or even the "totally other." It is far more one of those instances of "resistance" that Foucault pursues or implicitly enlists in all his works but seldom names. This is noticeable, for example, in his work *The Will to Knowledge*. The definition of power cited in this work already brings him closer to the aesthetic reinterpretation of his theory. Power is "the multiplicity of force relations" that crystallize in institutions, social groups, industry, the family, and so forth.[34] By using the concept of force to define power, Foucault immediately, from an aesthetic point of view, furnishes power with an element of resistance. It is then easy to understand and accept the brief assertion: "Where there's power, there's resistance." For where there is power, there are forces, and for the aesthetically expanded rationalistic philosophy of the eighteenth century, forces cannot be totally controlled. They are not subject to the same methodical inevitability as mathematical deductions. Foucault obviously does not adhere to this philosophical rationalistic concept of power, but more to a physical one. For recognizing the subject as a force should also have led him to restrict his own theory on disciplinary power.

In language oriented toward the physical, resistances are "the other side" of power relationships, "the counterpart which cannot be ignored." For in circumstances where forces confront each other, it is clear that one force has to oppose the other. Society as a totality, as an infinite referential context of different forces is per se a nonregulable dynamic dimension. Turned around, this implies that a resistance cannot occur "purely," cannot stem "from just any, completely different principles." It is always also determined by all the relations it finds itself in and moves within. Taking this power-theory premise, the Nietzschean saying, "Everything is power" loses some of its scandalous and inconsistent monism. It then means no more than: "Practical and discursive conditions are conditions of force." Of course, the extent to which they really are this remains questionable. Are they, the weaker version, *not free* from the effects, or do they, the strong version, become *completely* consumed by them? Can they be explained *not without* the effects or *only through* them?

Foucault's works include wordings in both of these senses. Admittedly they are only consistent in the weaker version. Yet the power-theory conceptualization of subjectivity provides two advantages in this context. On the one hand, this subjectivity avoids a criticism that Derrida rightly aims at Rorty's version of subjectivity. The latter is namely conceived according to the principle of (self-)invention or (self-)creation and is thus too rooted in a "technical epistemic anthropocentric dimension." Derrida opposes this "dreamily" with an "invention of the other," or in theological vocabulary the "entirely other," an invention in which it is important—again theologically but also in the sense of Heidegger—to "allow that which is different to arrive," echoing the *advenire* in the "event" of Advent. Here the invention is not so much an achievement due to activity as far more to passivity.[35] On the other hand, Foucault's conceptual subjectivity avoids the danger that Derrida is exposed to, namely, that of placing the different beyond the relations of power, beyond the range of validation of deconstruction. With Foucault, at least, there is no assertion of a (pure) hereafter or an immaculate utopia.

Last but not least, this places him in critical opposition to the latest Utopian guise, known in its theoretical context as "heterotopia" and that has recently crystallized as a permanent appeal to that context itself, going by names such as a "discourse of difference," a "patchwork identity," or a "culture of hybridity." The discourse of difference is fundamentally and critically opposed to that of identity. Against the culture of the same it brings into play that of the different, of that deviating from the norm. Yet, reversely accentuated, that means that it excludes everything that insists on a (fixed) identity. Anyone adopting a firm stance, not adapting smoothly, not reacting "flexibly," is antiquated. From the viewpoint of Foucault, to this extent the discourse of difference itself establishes a new "dispositive" of power. It is important to remain aware of this metacriticism, especially in the light of a position that is permanently changing, in the spirit of romanticism and vitalism, like no other and that propagates the primate of becoming over that of being: namely, that of Deleuze and Guattari. Their pointed way of describing the exuding cosmos of romanticism and vitalism with the metaphor of the machine, a success since early modernity (but which the two authors do not accept as being a metaphor), does at least cast a clear light on the ambiguity whereby a vision of aimless and, teleologically as well as logically, unbound recombining can also be a true image of the way in which capitalism functions. *Anti-Oedipus* and *A Thousand Plateaus* belong to the analytical context of *Capitalism and Schizophrenia*, as their subtitle implies, but they do not bow to the dualism of affirmation and negation. Deleuze and Guattari are aware that the criticism of identity, of compulsively halted assignation of meaning, is itself not free of that criticized, but this fact has been lost in the reception of their works. Therefore it must again be emphasized: even a culture that sees sense in wildly combining the elements, even a *hybrid* modernity is not the solution to all the problems thrown up by the modern age.

The question that sparked these contemplations, namely, that of what is behind the cinematographic will to picture-knowledge, what endlessly motivates it to think up new images, has thus been philosophically answered. A reorganization of the paradigm of subjectivity in the sense of creativity can be seen in the solution: from imitation to imagination! From mimicking nature to producing it, from mimesis to autopoiesis. The ego finally wants to become an infinite ego, that which it already structurally is so far as idealism and romanticism are concerned. It no longer wishes to be a mere copy in an unchangeable cosmos set out in advance by divine intervention. The solution for movies, especially science-fiction movies, is therefore: from portrayal of the visible to production of the visible, from representation (of one reality) to a vision (of possible realities)! This is the solution that, following the end of the plain "human being" episteme, cannot cease to be a driving force toward a vivid discursivation of the invisible.

Heroes of the Future

"The Will," thus spoke Zarathustra referring to redemption, is "the emancipator." It is a mental force characterizing the hero. Yet "the Will itself is still a prisoner," for it cannot "break time," it is "impotent towards what has been done." "To transform every 'It was' into 'Thus would I have it!'—that only do I call redemption!"[1] Science fiction, in both its literary and cinematic forms, puts this to the test. The test results are positive in both cases, albeit with different test persons. Various types of hero have been employed by the genre in its search for the redeemer figure since the 1980s: the philosopher (later a priest), the warrior, the artist (who knows how to make the best out of life). This can be illustrated in detail on the basis of three movies from this period.

The World as Will, Faith, and Representation: *The Matrix*

After it was released in 1999, *The Matrix* rapidly achieved cult status, provoking not only jubilant comments from faithful science-fiction and action movie fans but also the interest of usually more aloof intellectuals. Particularly those well versed in philosophy were able to recognize instantly the epistemological and sociocritical problem underlying the movie, presented in an elegant combination of Descartes and Putnam, on the one hand, and Adorno and Foucault, on the other. In its own way it readdresses that fundamental doubt that occupied Descartes as a philosopher and founder of the principle of subjectivity on the threshold to modernity, and that was more recently updated by Putnam: Could it not be that we are being deceived in all things by an almighty, evil spirit of Godlike proportions? That there could be radical uncertainty not only about the existence of the material world, including our own bodies, but also about the teachings of the sciences, particularly of mathematics? Could it not be, following Putnam's thinking, that our brains are really lying in tanks filled with a nutrient-enriched solution and connected to a supercomputer, supplying them so perfectly with electronic impulses that we are deluded into thinking that everything is completely normal? We would still "see" and "feel" our hands rising once we had decided to raise them; we would still "experience" our familiar environments and everyday situations, from having breakfast to riding a bicycle to working at a computer screen, in the normal way; we could even sit in a theater and watch a movie about an amusing and somewhat absurd notion that our brains could be awash in a special solution, their nerve endings connected to a supercomputer giving us the false impression of sitting in a theater, whereas in reality we are merely receiving computer-generated electronic impulses. The sociotheoretical consequences of this epistemological hypothesis have been addressed by theoreticists such as Adorno and Foucault. They believe dominance to have become more or less total and totalitarian, "power" to be just as omnipresent as it is intangible; they believe that the Enlightenment, intended universally, has turned into a "universal blinding" that only individual dissidents, be they esoterically or anarchically minded, are able to see through and break through.

In contrast to Descartes and Putnam, *The Matrix*'s answer to the question of whether we as human beings could be fooled in such gigantic dimensions is a loud "yes." The movie is able to do this because the philosophers' "no" leaves a trail of doubt. As is well known, Descartes's riposte to the universal uncertainty regarding our perception and thoughts is that an evil power might be able to deceive me about the content of what I am thinking, but not about the fact *that* I am thinking or doubting. Accordingly, there can be no doubt about the "I think." Of course, the Cartesian substantiation of certain knowledge is itself based on certain prerequisites.[2] "I think," for example, forms a special and unusual premise within the argument "I think, therefore I am"; it is, in contrast to sentences such as "I go for walks" or "Josef Früchtl thinks," beyond doubt. Second, it provides its own verification as one has to do no more than just complete that thought, whereas the sentence "I go for walks" requires one to establish that one actually has a body and can move. Third, it is self-evident because it does not have to be rendered evident by another sentence or a special reflection; whenever I think, I can also grasp that I am thinking, whereas in the sentence "The author of the book *The Impertinent Self* thinks" it is not at all self-evident that I am that author. This special status of the premise "I think" leads us, however, to the conclusion "I am." The term "I" must refer to an actually existing, thinking entity, a "bearer" of the act of thinking, for otherwise this premise would be doubtful, not self-verifying, and not self-evident. For Descartes, the proof that I cannot be the product of deception by an evil spirit therefore depends on how convincing the premise "I think" appears to be.

In contrast, Putnam's refutation of doubting skepticism and the demon hypothesis draws on the philosophy of language. For this he, too, naturally requires certain premises, which he takes from the reference theory. In Crispin Wright's short version of this refutation,[3] the first premise states, seemingly evidently, that in the language that I speak the word "brain" refers to brains. When I speak of brains, I also *mean* brains. The second premise states, however, that in the language of a brain that has been lying in a vat, the words "brain" and "vat" do not refer to brains and vats. For both premises Putnam draws on the "causal theory of reference," according to which we can only refer to objects with which we causally interact. A brain in a vat cannot have any causal contact to real brains or real vats. It can only reference a virtual substitute, a series of bits in the supercomputer creating a vision of a brain or a vat. My language, or so the logical conclusion states, is therefore different from that of a brain in a vat, and therefore I cannot be a brain in a vat. According to the reference theory, the (critical) sentence: "We are (nothing but) brains in a vat" is impossible and therefore nonsensical—providing that we believe the causal theory of reference to be correct and can claim the "I" from the first premise to be true without resorting to circular arguments.

It has to be said that the weaknesses existing within this philosophical argumentation correspond to those found in the movie *The Matrix*.

Above all, in its dualism of an apparent and a real world it propagates unquestioningly a stale form of metaphysics. It employs Foucault's concept of power as naturally as it ignores Derrida's undertaking of deconstruction. Instead of breaking down the prominent contrast between appearance and reality, illusion and truth, into many small, internally regenerated pairs of opposites, it reinforces it. Accordingly, being is divided in two. It comprises two incompatible types of entity: for Plato the idea (archetype) and the image, for Aristotle the form and the material, for Descartes the *res cogitans* and the *res extensa*, for Kant the intelligible and the empirical. As we know, this binary form of metaphysics has found a culturally powerful equivalent in Christian religion, which is also to have consequences in *The Matrix*.

The main figure of the movie, known respectfully in the hacker scene as Neo, works as a programmer for a software firm, yet the movie introduces him with some typically philosophical wounds, as somebody who has got "splinters in his head," who cannot rid himself of a feeling that "something is not right with the world," who is suffering from Cartesian Doubt, unable to be sure if he is awake or dreaming, and who ultimately follows the battle cry of the Enlightenment: "Wake up!" His awakening is brought about by a character bearing the name of an ancient Greek god, Morpheus, who could enable forms (*morphé*) to appear to those who dream. Morpheus knows what is not right with the world already, and he is keen to pass on this knowledge to Neo. So the two of them meet one night, in thunder and lightning, in a shabby, bare room, depicted in the style of a Gothic novel. As Neo is about to hear, the world is an "imaginary world which you are led to believe in, in order to distract you away from the truth"; it is a "prison which you can neither touch nor smell," a product of what in the computer world is known as the "matrix," a network of intersecting points in the midst of the electronic signals. The present everyday world is in reality a ubiquitous matrix that our senses fail to grasp, a technological substitute for the God of Christianity or his devilish adversary, just as omnipresent as it is absent. The computer-generated world is a "prison" in which people only seemingly live their lives in self-determination: in truth they are "slaves."

Morpheus follows his theoretical enlightenment with the far more complex practical aspects. This concerns no longer just the spirit but also physical experience, or, as Plato states in his cave analogy, the entire soul. True enlightenment is not merely an extension of knowledge, a lengthening of our informational chain; its fulfillment is also a reversal, in theological terms a conversion, in the sense of German idealism and critical theory an instance of self-reflection, the unity of recognition and interest, insight and liberation. Accordingly, spiritual one-dimensionality is linked to a (physical and ethical) attitude. Just as Plato's cave dwellers had to be liberated in a manner painfully exposing them to the truth, Neo has to undergo the same process. He has—and these images are undoubtedly some of the most impressive in the entire movie—to be liberated from the fields of generated human beings, from the unforeseeably vast networked system that interlocks (connects and drains) human bodies through tubes in order to exploit them as sources of energy, in a reversal of the original man-machine relationship, as batteries to maintain the system, the machines, and thus the matrix. Therefore no matrix, no world of illusion without the "energy," the material resource provided by the human beings themselves. Without realizing it, they are collaborating with the cocoon of illusion that holds them prisoner.

Yet the movie does not hold true to this comprehensive concept of enlightenment. More precisely, it ultimately portrays enlightenment as an idealistic project leading back to religious faith. In this respect, too, it initially follows Plato.[4] Just as the latter's philosophy describes an ontological sphere of the essential kind, an actual reality, in contrast to which a sensually perceptible reality can only be categorized as an imitation (*mimesis, imitatio*), a seemingly beautiful human being only as a reproduction (of the idea) of beauty itself, tasty food only—literally—as an aftertaste (of the idea) of pleasure, sensually experienced love only as a reflection (of the idea) of love itself, and so on, so too in *The Matrix* is that which we perceive as reality just a "simulation" or "mental projection," albeit in the contemporary context of computer technology. (However, here true reality is not a pure and abstract kingdom of shapes, but gloomy, dirty, ugly, and life-threatening, a "desert," as Morpheus puts it using the words of anti-Platonist Nietzsche.) So-called reality, as Morpheus goes on to explain, consists of no more than electronic signals, which the mind interprets, but which are transmitted to the people via the system. Reality is therefore a twofold construction, a construction of the mind as well as the machines, one that is both mentally and computer generated.

Neo thus receives a lesson in idealism and constructivism (a constructivism not of the sober and mathematical kind, but of the radical kind pertaining to the science of culture, based on the assumption that there is no such thing as knowledge devoid of consciousness, that everything which is perceived and recognized is a construction of this perception and recognition). If a computer program is behind reality, then we only have to "rewrite" the program in order to attain a new reality. Reality is thus not what "stands in our way" like the "object" in subjective-idealistic epistemology and opposes us (its cognitive definition and practical alteration), but what fits in with our constructive arbitrariness. It stands to reason that this panders equally to the omnipotent fantasies of the empirical species computer programmer, deeply rooted in this constructivism and thus awkward around enlightenment, and to those of postmodern theoreticists for whom, according to their smooth formula, everything is "text." *The Matrix* takes this neurotically crooked yearning and turns it into a redemption program.

Neo is the reincarnation of a man who was born when the matrix was created by intelligent machines and who, as Morpheus explains, had the ability "to change whatever he wanted." His will and his desires could be realized without delay. "He could reshape the matrix according to his wishes." In other words, in this world governed by appearances he was a being close to God. It was also him who liberated the first human beings and disconnected them from the vast machine of illusion. *The Matrix* thus provides a mythical and religious answer to the question that remained unanswered in Plato's cave analogy, namely, that of the first liberator. The main character in the movie is clearly meant to be a redeemer. His very name makes this clear: Neo, pointing toward the new, the coming, and also an anagram of "one," the chosen one. Neo is the hero as a thinker, in whom the divide between the sciences and the arts closes.

To make a finer critical point: he is a smart and pale intellectual, revealing once more what an affinity there is between computer science and mysticism. Mysticism insists that insights can only be gained through personal experience and not simply through teaching and the providing of evidence. This form of mystical teaching, which today is primarily encountered within Asian culture, is an element just as existent in our present understanding of experience as historically in ancient philosophy.

The wise man or master, inspired as a result of practice, is not a thinker in the theoretical sense. Far more he perceives thinking, philosophy, as the highest form of life. This mystical element, whereby one has to create one's knowledge *oneself*, functions as a link between science, common sense, religion, argumentative discourse, everyday practical experience, and unreserved faith.

The type of religion *The Matrix* extols is, however, a *mixtum compositum* of various existing major religions and their tendencies, primarily Tibetan and Zen Buddhism, Gnosticism, and Christianity.[5] Buddhism involves an attitude of categorizing the perceived world as an illusion, of working toward liberating the spirit, of placing emphasis on continual training toward this goal, and of trusting in the reincarnation of Buddha. For Gnosis, too, ignorance and a belief in illusion (not sin) are fundamental human problems, but it also cultivates a firm separation—totally alien to Buddhism—between good and evil, light and dark. In political terms, this Gnostic view of the world is equivalent to the conspiracy theory, a popular tradition within works of science fiction anyway, in which "dark" powers, enemies of human beings and humanity, here intelligent machines, have deviously overpowered the laws of action. In psychoanalytical terms this is once again equivalent to the theory of the superego as an omnipotent controlling body, like the reverse image of an imagined life that is indestructible in the manner of a cartoon or fantasy movie, in which even flying bullets can be willed: directed by the fingertips of the Almighty, they fall at his feet like golden rain.

Thankfully, *The Matrix* does not take its religious and mythical elements seriously all the time. When at the end of the movie the laws of gravity within the matrix and pseudo-world no longer apply to Neo, the image conjured up could in a religious and steadfast way be that of the Ascension of Christ, but it could also ironically be that of Superman, the *Übermensch* in a vertical, superlative sense. (Unfortunately, with each installment of its trilogy the movie increasingly loses its self-irony, ultimately purveying the redemption cult with a holy seriousness. We observe the science-fiction genre mutating to fantasy, scientific laws becoming the playthings of magic, or, in the words of Freud, the material to fulfill childish and adolescent desires.)

From the perspective of ideological criticism or deconstructivism, a further interesting aspect of this movie is that it does not conceive of the future purely as an extension of the present. This, however, requires a dimension that does not submit to deductive thought, to a chain of proof where one link is clearly attached to the next, namely, the dimension attributed by the romantics to the realms of *imagination*. The imagination produces pictures, myths, and utopias. Alteration, the creation of another world, takes place according to rules that cannot be the existing ones. The latter would principally reproduce the same things over and over again. In pictures, myths, and utopias, these rules are progressive, unfinished, experimental, exaggerated, and vague. Their *two faces* can also be seen in *The Matrix*.

The central myth brought back to life in *The Matrix* is the freedom of the will and the spirit. Despite what is claimed by materialists and naturalists, most prominently by La Mettrie, the human being is not determined, is not a machine. The hero of the matrix era is a thinker, not only in the spirit of the western, ancient, and Asian worlds, but also that of the idealists and constructivists, for whom the world is divided into will and representation—not Schopenhauer, but Fichte—and for whom the only things that are real are those which have been mentally constructed according to certain rules.

On the one hand, this entails the familiar western metaphysical and religious message that the spirit should free itself from material things. In this context Agent Smith voices a general truth when he describes how disgusted he is by human bodies. It also entails the scientific and mathematical message that sensually perceptible phenomena are in reality constructed according to a clear rule or numerical series. In an artificial, computer-generated world, superiority can therefore not be proven physically, only mentally. Thus naturalism generates a new, steep idealism. Neo (at least in the first part of the trilogy) has completed the last step in his learning process when, in his final showdown with the agents, with intelligent programs, with the protectors of the matrix, and especially with Agent Smith, he recognizes that it is all a code, an ontological statement, an ordered numerical series. As a trained computer programmer and mathematician he is able to see through the body of the agent, viewing him as a fluorescent green column of numbers. His opposite's body becomes a kind of computer screen. Now that the code can be read, it can also be cracked.

The body into which Neo dives in a last attempt to be liberated is nothing more than a computer program. Blasting one's opposite apart from the inside, excellently portrayed in the movie with action and special effects, amounts for a Hegelian-Marxist system critic to sizing up the system according to its own criteria and then bringing it down from the inside. For a computer specialist it would mean introducing a virus and crashing the program that way. In *The Matrix* a last victory for the humanum is thus achieved. For, as Agent Smith notes, the virus is the organism that has most in common with the human being. The human being, a decadent disease in the Nietzschean sense, uses this disease to overcome itself in a superhuman manner. Its weakness is also its strength: the machines would like to wipe it out like a virus, but as a virus it is ultimately and reversely triumphant over its virtual (potential and artificial) destroyers.

The flipside of such traditional metaphysics, however, is once again that the future cannot be predicted, only created. The romantic tradition may have demonstrated from its outset that the pathos of creation is founded on the loss of a sure distinction between true and false, the real and the imagined world, yet it can also, as *The Matrix* shows, be linked to a retained distinction between these worlds. It remains unclear whether Neo is the chosen one until he believes it himself, namely, at precisely the moment when he concentrates all his mental energies on saving his friend Morpheus. The future, according to the movie's *hyperideological,* and therefore *ambivalent* message, is a self-fulfilling prophecy. The suggestive message is: "All you have to do is believe in what you would like the future to hold!" *This* belief cannot simply be the equivalent of a religious message about the saving grace of God and a system of dogmas. Far more it pertains to how we *act,* and that is crucial for all those who see history as a dimension of possibility.

Battle of the Terminators: Masculinity Versus Mimesis

Terminator 2, like its predecessor of the same name and numerous other science-fiction movies, takes Nietzsche's redemption formula literally. Traveling back in time is an implementation of the retrospective power of (historical) interpretation, a philosophical theory employed neatly by the genre. "Every great human being exerts a retroactive force," for he or she is able to reinterpret what is irreversible and thus seemingly unalterably passé, to illuminate as the "sunshine" the dark continent of the past (in keeping with Plato's ancient image for the concept of truth from his cave analogy, but reversing the Platonic intention) and thus bring to light, in other words bring into existence, events previously "undiscovered."[6] In this indirect way historians thus have at their disposal the power to bring about change. The more exactly and more originally they examine their entire material, the more they can change previous knowledge about history, in other words change history itself, in other words change ourselves, whom we view as the protagonists of a sure and morally intentional tradition. Once again the "it was" is open to the redeeming "thus would I have it." The science-fiction movie takes this historical heuristic literally and embarks on a journey through time. *Terminator 2* introduces an additional Jewish-Christian aspect. For the Jewish-Christian tradition, adopted in philosophy by Benjamin, Horkheimer, and Adorno, human activity, with all its suffering and unhappiness, is factually irreversible, a thing of the past, only healable in the comprehensive salvational sense from the point of view of redemption, or in the theological sense from the point of view of soteriology. Only the Last Judgment can facilitate retroactivity, and *Terminator 2* takes this theme literally, too; it becomes, as its subtitle heralds, a *Judgment Day*, a secularized Day of Judgment.

In *Terminator 2* the future is ruled by a supercomputer and the fighting machines it has developed. In order to settle the apocalyptic war between it and the human race, it sends a terminator, a cyborg, a killing machine in human form back into the past to liquidate the future human commander. The latter, however, sends another terminator after it in order to protect himself and the human race from this same apocalyptic war, incidentally the same terminator who was supposed to kill the commander's mother in the first installment of the movie to prevent him from being born, but which is now reversely programmed to protect him, currently an adolescent hanging around in amusement arcades. The mission is successful; as in *The Matrix*, here too the human beings beat the all-powerful computer at its own game.

Terminator 2 is also a continuation of the three great stories: Jewish-Christian religion, science (finalized with military means), and the bourgeoisie. As a replacement father figure, the terminator played by Schwarzenegger holds together a sacred bourgeois family that has long begun to break apart. The mother, Sarah, the biblical ancestor of the chosen people of Israel, is leading a promiscuous life, is training in guerrilla camps to fight against the military-technical-complex, and is ultimately held against her will in a psychiatric clinic. Her son John, whose surname is Connor, giving him the initials J.C., the same as those of Jesus Christ (and also the movie's director James Cameron), is growing up with foster parents who are unable to assert their authority over the boy. Only when Schwarzenegger's terminator arrives is the mother able to claim: "Of all the fathers who have come and gone over the years, this machine, this 'thing' was the only one who was up to it," up to being a fatherly friend, a guardian one can rely on. In this science-fiction movie the machine, the artificial human being, once again proves to be the better human being, or at least the artificial man proves to be the better man. In the course of the action the mother might function as a driving historical force, but she is not Amazon enough; at the crucial moment, an attempt to shoot the inventor of the fateful computer chip, she once again has to be called to order as an hysterical woman by a man, by the "cool dude" already inside her son ("Mom, Mom! We have to be a bit more constructive here, okay?"). At the end, the fatherly terminator sacrifices himself for the sake of the human race like a God made of steel and flesh. He already has implanted within him the chip that will lead, or, seen retrospectively, has led to the dominance of the supercomputer. Only the destruction of this chip can prevent the apocalyptic future that has already taken place in the movie. Only this deed, in human terms a deed heroic and self-sacrificing, can save the future, in two senses of the word: as the survival of the human race and as the dimension of action.

Terminator 2 thus becomes *Judgment Day* in the sense of the Last Judgment: the end of all time for this intratemporal, black utopia consists in the fact that time is again possible. The future is open once again, not predetermined. It arrives not as an unavoidable fate, but once more full of intentional or unexpected events. "No fate" is the imperative that Sarah vicariously and aggressively holds on to. She wants to save or win back the competence to act in the name of humanity. In the struggle between historical determinism and the freedom of the will, *Terminator 2* (like its predecessor) clearly comes down on the side of freedom. (Not until the third and seemingly last installment is atomic war on the agenda, bringing about the eradication of billions of people in one fell swoop, demonstrating without much ado that all the martial efforts within the first and second installments were ultimately in vain, with Fate winning in the end after all. If there were to be a next installment, it could, no longer hampered by the problems of time travel and fate, take up the story of the war that has now broken out in the present-day plot between the computer-controlled machines and the people surrounding John Connor, and use this as another demonstration of free will, acting to its full advantage. Narrative fiction, unbound by the accusations of contradiction that would be hurled at philosophers in a similar case, can settle a theoretical antinomy such as that between determinism and freedom in favor of one side on one occasion and in favor of the other side the next.)

In *Terminator 2* the redeemer is, as he is called from the outset, a "warrior." He is not in the least unfeeling like a machine but, to use an expression favored by John and the kids of the 1980s and 1990s, "cool," a human machine superior to human beings in its mental and physical capabilities, its cognitive intelligence, and its physical invulnerability, bordering on immortality, indestructibility. The machine is not only human through its cognitive powers but also in its capacity for grasping moral lessons. The first commandment taught to it by John is "Thou shalt not kill!" The strong protector is thus initially the moral protégé who first has to be taught right from wrong, and in this way becomes humanized. This raises it above its technically perfected successor, a prototype made of "mimetic polyalloy," a quicksilver transformation machine, a creature of liquid metal that can change its exterior to match that of any material or person that touches it. This latter terminator is introduced in the form of a policeman (the embodiment of a state under the rule of law, in hard contrast to the rocker and outlaw outfit of Schwarzenegger's terminator, serving the dramatization as a reversal of good and evil), but it also adopts other shapes as required, even that of Sarah Connor, in order to tempt the boy into its arms.

For researchers of the sexes, this multisexuality and ambiguous appearance (slim figure, delicate and narrow face) are evidence of a barely "encrypted homosexuality," whereas Schwarzenegger's terminator comes over as "archetypally hypermasculine,"[7] as an archaic example of male superhumanness, a supermasculinity that is shown to be a fusion of premodern virile body image and highly modern, filigree technology, a "techno-gladiator."[8] In this merger, which historically is that between technology and nature, cybernetics and organism, as found in the coin-age "cyborg," masculinity can also be seen in *Terminator 2* as a product of the Frankenstein dream: male self-creation. For John creates himself a replacement father and male protector, first by teaching him and then, as an adult and leader in the battle against the machine-run system, by programming him and sending him back in time to save both his mother and himself. The feminist touch that at first glance the movie appears to have is dubious. Sarah may act as a driving force within human history, hurling accusations familiar from the women's movement at the scientific inventor of the highly complex and later independent computer program, a man, yet she tends toward hysteria, in accordance with the established Freudian image, and she can only hold her own as a warrior by making herself masculine; she not only smokes and drinks whisky but also does bodybuilding, "steeling" her body in the manner of the cyborgs, and knows how to handle a weapon. She too thus assimilates what her son has demonstrated: creating (oneself as) a man with the help of a machine.

This technically perfect terminator is underdeveloped, however, not only morally, in its antihumanism and multifaceted sexuality, but also with regard to the theory of rationality. In this respect it may be seen as the embodiment of the difference principle, the walking nonidentity, or in other words: as the unsurpassed realization of the ancient European notion of mimesis. Precisely because of this it in turn succumbs to a form of dialectics: its strength proves simultaneously to be its weakness. For, bound to the onto-theological tradition extending from Plato until far into modernity, it cannot create anything essentially new. Thus the old terminator model might be technically inferior to the new one (and in the ultimate showdown gradually turn into a robot fit for the scrapheap, full of dents, rusty, and squeaking), but in Foucault's sense it is epistemically superior. It represents, albeit within its all too visible cybernetic limits, no less than the New European principle of creative subjectivity.

Yet the movie does not convey this as its message. Far more, it is only enjoyable with its fantasy redemption world because it does not take itself too seriously. This is guaranteed by the inept learning steps of the old terminator model, its machinelike funny naivety (which is also lent appropriate expression by Schwarzenegger's wooden Austrian-American accent) and its corresponding self-centered comments ("I need a holiday"), but even more so by the medley of special effects throughout. The permanent battle between the cyborgs is nothing other than a war game between two computer programs that could go on forever. Since the cyborgs are (almost) indestructible, the battles between them grow to such monstrous and grotesque proportions that all one can do is laugh in the face of the incredible (of what is beyond the anthropologically and technologically viable) and enjoy the action (the movie as a moving picture) for its own sake. Of course the result remains dubious. The movie feeds far too much on what it condemns: technology and violence. A fear of ever-developing technology becoming independent, as well as of raging violence, is coupled with a never-ending desire for technology and violence. Dystopia and utopia are inextricably intertwined. To this extent the movie demonstrates a performative contradiction: what it propagates as content, it refutes in its performance. The message is not to leave the development of technology to itself, nor to the research logic of the corresponding sciences, but to subject it to moral boundaries. Yet the movie cannot, especially as a science-fiction movie, convey this message without laying claim to precisely what it is warning against. The performative contradiction, or, in postmodern terms, the paradox consists in the fact that a movie from the science-fiction genre, which survives on a fascination for technology and which employs a whole barrage of special effects, is rejecting this technical aspect of itself. It amounts to no less than a wish to destroy the fascination of its own pictures. To use Vivian Sobchack's language, the special *effects* take away from the special *affects*; as viewers we are amazed by the effects and to the same extent feel bereft of affects. The "demonic shadow" that the *Terminator* movies conjure up as a dystopia to our technological utopia, another side of our true self, is then no more than a fleeting pretty picture on the screen.[9]

The More Human Artificial Human Beings:
Blade Runner

The most human, least ambivalent, yet still multifaceted and extremely fragile figure of redemption is provided by *Blade Runner*, that science-fiction movie that in the early 1980s raised the genre to a new aesthetic level, marked by the film noir and the *no-future feeling* of the punk generation. Like *The Matrix* it met with enthusiasm from both science-fiction fans and distinguished intellectuals. A bibliography dedicated to this movie alone would include hundreds of articles, scientific essays, and books. Even today it may still be regarded as one of the best (most intelligent, most complex, most sensitive) movies of its genre. Like *The Matrix* and the *Terminator* movies it creates a dystopia. As Morpheus remarks bitterly, and presumably in an allusion to Nietzsche, the true world, the "real thing" behind the simulation in which the apocalyptic battle between human beings and intelligent machines is taking place, is a "desert." Life in this subterranean world eternally bereft of light is the price to be paid for knowing the truth. To this extent *The Matrix* provides a variation on the ancient myth of the expulsion from Paradise. The children of the computer generation have once more "eaten from the Tree of Knowledge," have taken the red pill instead of the blue one, with the result that they now recognize the world for what it truly is: an inhospitable place lacking in sensuality.

The world is no less bleak in *Blade Runner*. It, too, is set below an arch of cosmic darkness and the smog of a gigantic industrial landscape. It never stops raining as the people push their way through the city streets, past brightly lit advertising slogans. The future in this movie is initially a recycling product, a collage of shabby scenes from the Los Angeles of 1982 when the movie was made.[10] The space opened up by the frontier, that border extended further and further by the American pioneers, heroes of the Westerns, has now imploded. In such negative utopias the science-fiction movie leads the tradition of the Western to its predictable, albeit only temporary end, postponed both temporally and spatially.

It is the job of Blade Runner Deckard, a kind of detective and bounty hunter, to eliminate replicants, artificial people who have been constructed to work as slaves in outer-space colonies and who have now come back to Earth without permission. But in the course of his hunt he becomes increasingly unsure about what he is doing. For the creatures he is hunting not only appear to him to be more human than he himself or the other hunters, they also force him to pose the anthropologically fundamental and increasingly modern age question of identity: How can I know that I am me? The movie *Blade Runner* addresses this question primarily by concentrating in this context on the metaphor of the eyes and vision, thus also reflecting on its own medium, film.

From the outset of the movie, the central significance of the eye motif is hard to miss, with the camera moving into a dark world charged with flashes of fire, passing over a nighttime urban Moloch and gliding toward a huge building, a kind of pyramid that turns out to be the headquarters of the so-called Tyrell Corporation, the enterprise dominating the business of replicant production. A large blue eye appears on the screen, reflecting the whole scene. The association with a divine eye that sees everything also comes to mind with the triangular pyramid shape. In addition, the man who gave his name to this gigantic building, Tyrell, is later referred to as the "God of biomechanics." In cinematographic terms this is the eye of the all-seeing camera or the viewers. But it could also be the eye of a replicant. The decisive test to distinguish between a genuine and an artificial human being is an eye-reaction test, in which a Blade Runner confronts the test person with questions and hypothetical situations and observes the reactions of the eye on a detector screen while the answers are being given. In this way the eye becomes the proverbial window to the soul; it reveals the innermost part, the identity of a person. Now and again, however, for example, the first time it is demonstrated on the replicant Leon, the scientific test results contrast conspicuously (visibly) with the emotional behavior of the persons involved. The experimental mechanical procedure exposes the person tested; that person is not what he or she appears to be, namely, a normal (not artificially manufactured) human being. The whole procedure in turn exposes the tester, however. The tester performs his task routinely and cynically, like a cold and sadistic machine, whereas his object, the replicant, is a human, an all-too-human, bundle of feelings, marked by uncertainty, tension, nerves, fear, and ultimately a panic that gives way to deadly violence.

When Deckard tests the replicant Rachel, the situation is initially reversed, with the test results corresponding to the behavior of the test person. With her dark hair up, her lips red and curvy, her face impassive and pale, her posture erect, a cigarette elegantly tucked between her fingers, and her answers as calm as they are precise, she is the perfect embodiment of the type of woman left to our collective consciousness by the film noir, the shop-window mannequin version of the femme fatale. Yet as she gradually realizes that she, too, is artificial, she amazingly begins to acquire more and more clearly human traits. After she has saved Deckard's life (Leon was just about to kill him—by pushing out his eyes) and the two of them are starting to fall in love, she accompanies him back to his flat. There before our eyes her outward appearance changes to such an extent that the appropriate word both theologically and aesthetically would be a transfiguration. She unleashes her hair, and thus in a way also the corset keeping a tight hold on her sensuality and her feelings. She sits down at a piano and plays. An aura of softness surrounds her. She almost herself becomes one of the old framed photos that she is looking at, coming across as the incarnation of all the dreamlike female figures of the nineteenth century. The difference between (human) original and (humanoid) copy has disappeared. The more the artificial people show their feelings, the harder it is to "see" them, to recognize them as something other than human. In reverse, the human beings, with their indifference and cynicism, appear as machines. Deckard admits that his former wife used to call him "sushi, cold fish." His name is a philosophical reminder of Descartes, the father of modern philosophy who divided the world up into just two substances, *res cogitans* and *res extensa*, enabling material to be described using the metaphor of the machine, but not the thinking ego opposed to it. A smiling female replicant quotes him by saying "cogito ergo sum," whereas Deckard, by contrast, arouses suspicions that he himself could be a replicant; the ego can no longer be distinguished from the machine.

The extent to which the differences become blurred and the assessments change over is shown as the climax of the movie in its final scene. The leader of the replicants, Roy, a Nietzschean example of self-discipline and predatory intelligence, his face daubed with blood (and eyes darkly outlined), now begins to hunt Deckard like a city Indian, a wolf in human form, or a "Siegfried in the world of tomorrow,"[11] blond and blue-eyed with his body half bare. The hunter has become the quarry, a motif (of fear) often found in the science-fiction genre, faithful to the age-old theme of creatures one day turning against their creator. The replicants are our overdeveloped "shadows," representing an uncontrollable fear that technologically improved things "will be better *than* us, rather than better *for* us."[12] The final scenes of *Blade Runner* demonstrate with symphonic pathos the extent to which they are better. For instead of doing what a replicant would easily be capable of doing, namely, killing Deckard, the replicant saves him from plummeting from a great height. Furthermore, he saves Deckard's life at the very moment his own draws to an end. What is special about the series of replicants to which Roy belongs is that over time they are able to develop their own feelings. Since this involves a risk to human beings, these replicants are only equipped to function for or given a "life expectancy" of four years. They have come back to Earth to demand "more life" from their creator Tyrell, "more" in a quantitative, but also a qualitative sense, a free life, no longer that of a "slave," of a creature held in permanent fear.

The biblical Christian symbolism running through *Blade Runner* concentrates at the end on its central element, Christ dying and then being resurrected. Before he saves Deckard, the replicant has already driven a nail through his own hand, and now he sits collapsed in the pouring rain, bathed in a bluish night light that is becoming brighter by the minute, and lets various images, "memories," pass through his mind. There is one moment that is moving in its sublimity: "I've seen things you people wouldn't believe," he begins, "attack ships on fire off the shoulder of Orion. I've watched C-beams glitter in the dark near the Tannhauser Gate. All those . . . moments," he continues weakly, close to death, "will be lost in time," he pauses, "like . . . tears, . . . " another pause, "in rain." Then he smiles and says slowly, "Time to die." A white dove that has been perched on his arm flies up into a sky that, for the first time in the director's cut of this movie, is blue. If he were a human being, we would say it represented the departure of his soul. This scene escapes coming across as corny due to the way it disposes us to hover between feelings. Just a short time after he was feeling helpless and afraid for his life, Deckard, and with him the viewers, witnesses with astonishment and increasing respect a conversion, a voluntary metamorphosis of a murdering machine into a vulnerable and irreplaceable existence that, as a result, acquires moral dignity. The rising dove might be a symbolic reference to the Holy Ghost, but the sky that opens up to (and above) the replicant is that of the *Übermensch*. The replicant represents Christ as a rebel, a "prodigal son"—as he calls himself in allusion to the New Testament—who murders his "father," the "God of biomechanics" (by completing an act which is both Old Testament— "an eye for an eye"—and Oedipal, pressing in first the eyes and then the skull[13]), because he refused to give him the life he wished for. Despite this, he gives the enterprise's slogan "more human than human," which was meant in a technical and perfectionist sense, a moral slant. The artificial human being is more moral than the genuine human being. The former shows a sensitivity his Lord and Master lost a long time ago, when he became set in his ways as a mixture of bioengineer, company boss, and agent. As also happened in the light of Schwarzenegger's terminator, here the "ecce homo," the crucifixion of Christ, claimed even by that dedicated anti-Christian Nietzsche, receives an additional meaning: Behold the man of the future in all its artificiality![14]

This is the second vision of the future in *Blade Runner*, the positive one. The future is no longer a mere collage assembled from the dirty, bleak, and bizarre late twentieth-century present. Forming a collage or a hybrid to some extent in itself becomes the solution: the newly manufactured human being morally stands for a new beginning, which then, however, turns out to be familiar, namely, the old values of individuality and dignity, of mortality and self-determination. Roy's last words are carried by a metaphysical melancholy because they cite the individuality of an existence that inherently has its own view of the world like one of Leibniz's monads, a view inevitably lost with this existence. At the same time, however, this metaphysics of individuality is undermined by a postmodern, or rather hybrid-modern suspicion. For it could be possible that even Roy's memories, like Rachel's, are only implants, displaced parts that can be taken from one or more sources and then used again in other replicants. Roy in particular is characterized by a conflict that the modern age has helped to constitute, lending it particular expression in its romantic and hybrid version: a claim to particularity while simultaneously being dependent on humanity in general. In order to be an ego, the ego needs others, but in so doing it always runs the risk of denying one side of itself, namely, individuality, for the sake of the other side, namely, equality. Instead of being an original, it becomes a mere copy. Like no other replicant, Roy embodies a claim to uniqueness. It is telling that he (in the laboratory of an old Chinese eye engineer) quotes the poet, painter, and engraver William Blake and thus refers not only to his own ontological interim status but also to the significance that art has for him. (The same poet assumes a central metaphoric role in *Dead Man* by Jim Jarmusch. The youthful hero of this movie, played by Johnny Depp, answers to the name of Bill Blake and is thought to be the poet in question by an Indian who laughingly maintains that his own name is "Nobody." The motif of naive innocence, of the purely foolish, solidarily encounters that of the nobly wild and contrasts sharply with that of the civilizatorily corrupt. They unite in a hero who, merely driven, is no longer a hero.

The movie portrays a slow death, and with it that of the genre. The world of the Wild West is for Jarmusch a world that in its mythical oppositions is wrong, self-embracing, and ironic. *Dead Man* thus provides us with the paradox of a Western that no longer is one, a showpiece Western for the contemporaries of a hybrid modernity.) The artificial human being is like the ego of the "postmetaphysical," "postmodern," hybrid-modern age: created with a fixed lifespan, determined from the outside, yet also from within, with obvious strengths, but also with "inbuilt" weaknesses, no longer a whole, but composed of various parts, a life-form that has a recognizable predecessor in Frankenstein's monster and a recognizable vanishing point in Deleuze-Guattari's "Schizo." From this French perspective, schizophrenia is seen as a neurotic ailment arising from an incompatibility between the eternal, romantic "desire to desire" or in former times "covet" and the (linguistic-symbolic and capitalistic) law that demands the crystallization of a uniform ego. This ability to recognize the hybrid-modern ego in the android of the *Blade Runner* cosmos fundamentally explains the movie's success.[15] Once again in the sense of Deleuze and Guattari, as well as Foucault (and, of course, Nietzsche and Freud), it represents identification with a life-form that is at once glorified and exterritoralized, transfigured, and excluded. One element presupposes the other: real exclusion presupposes imaginary transfiguration.

In the artificial human being the hero becomes a superhero who accepts the "it was" as if he had wanted it like it is, who no longer says

"I want," but just "I am." He thus becomes an artist to Nietzsche's taste, one who is no longer interested in works of art, but in making his own life art, a celebration of ontological affirmation: "It is good exactly as it is, because I have made it like I ultimately wanted it, even if it was only due to the repercussions of my intuitive mind. Affirmation means creation. And living means playing." "If you don't live," the replicant calls out to Deckard during their showdown, "then you can't play." "And if you don't play . . ." Deckard is closer here than ever before to understanding this way of acting, as well as the life-form pervading it, to understanding the "other one," which here proves to be the other one (side) of himself. He too has learned from what has happened. His comment contains the ethical essence of the movie: "Maybe he loved life more than ever before in these last moments, not only his life, but the life of anyone, my life. All that he wanted were the same answers as we all want: "Where do I come from?" "Where am I going?" "How much time have I got left?'" Loving life, loving being for what it is, yet still taking these questions seriously, knowing that there are no definitive answers to be had, that is the answer the movie gives us to our fundamental ethical question. The "Blade Runner," symbolic of running without stopping, that romantic unrest in which the Self is permanently drifting away, becomes a pivotal image. The hubris of the subject, the principle of modernity, cures itself by recognizing itself as a hybrid, as self-elevating (haughty and arrogant, believing itself capable of too much), even as assembled from alien pieces.

Accepting one's own limitations instead of puffing them up into the ideology of the frontier means accepting what is not at our disposal, what does not conform to planning and technical rationality. That in turn is nothing new, but a project that has accompanied modernity, viewed in all its complexity, since its beginnings. Following the Hegelian tradition, critical theory calls this "self-reflection." That is also what this book has been an attempt to emulate.

Notes

INTRODUCTION

1. Adorno 1978, p. 49 (par. 29).
2. Wicke 1998, pp. 253 and 254.

CHAPTER 1

1. Hegel 1969 onward, vol. 20, pp. 123 and 120.
2. Here I underline a definition by Hembus: "Westerns are movies about conflicts at the American frontier" (1997, p. 8).
3. Hegel 1969 onward, vol. 12, p. 113.
4. Cf. Hembus 1997, pp. 8–9; the quotation from Thoreau is taken from *A Week on the Concord and Merrimack Rivers* (1849).
5. Cf. Frank 1982, p. 73.
6. Cf. Cassirer 1956, esp. pp. 105, 123; Horkheimer/Adorno 2002, pp. 12, 35, 52–53; cf. also Frank 1982, pp. 107–8; Seesslen 1991a, p. II.
7. Cf. Barthes 1964, esp. p. 85.
8. Cf. Frank 1982, pp. 77, 81, 111, also the quotation to be found there by Cassirer.
9. Cf. Freud 2001a, pp. 261, 548–49; Freud 2001b, pp. 16–17, 118, 127, 135–36.
10. Cf. Lévi-Strauss 1967, pp. 222, 226.
11. Cf. Habermas 1984, pp. 46–47, with reference to Godelier and Malinowski.
12. Blumenberg 1990, pp. 9, 10, 127, 685; cf. Wetz 1993, p. 85; cf. also Horkheimer/Adorno 2002, pp. 10–11.
13. [Translator's note: For this reason I shall adhere to the German term *Heimat* throughout this section.]
14. Cf. Seesslen 2000a.
15. [Translator's note: The dated German term *Lichtspiel* for moving picture translates literally as "light-play."]
16. Cf. Bronfen 1999, pp. 334–35, cf. also p. 355.

17. Cf. Bronfen 1999, pp. 336 and 344–45, with reference to J. A. Place, *The Western Films of John Ford*, New York, 1974; cf. also Slotkin 1998, pp. 462, 466; he places *The Searchers* halfway between the ideology of the cold war and the civil rights movement.

18. Cf. Budd 1998, p. 142.

19. Bronfen 1999, p. 361.

CHAPTER 2

1. Hegel 1975, pp. 185, 181, 188.

2. Cf. Hegel 1967, pp. 67 (§ 93) and 219 (§ 350); cf. fundamentally p. 64 (§ 82).

3. Cf. Schnädelbach 1999, pp. 14, 42.

4. Gamm 1997, p. 98; on Mead and Habermas, cf. Habermas 1992.

5. Hegel 1975, p. 183.

6. Hegel 1975, pp. 182–83.

7. Cf. Hegel 1967, p. 184 (§ 280); Hegel 1975, p. 197.

8. Hegel 1975, pp. 185, 187, 188.

9. Hegel 1975, p. 188.

10. Hegel 1975, p. 184.

11. Hegel 1969 onward, vol. 12, p. 48.

12. Hegel 1969 onward, vol. 18, pp. 514 and 507.

13. Hegel 1969 onward, vol. 18, p. 514.

14. Hegel 1969 onward, vol. 12, p. 285.

15. Hegel 1975, pp. 1205, 1218, 1223; cf. also p. 195.

16. Hegel 1975, p. 192.

17. Hegel 1975, p. 193.

18. Hegel 1975, pp. 191, 192–93; this aspect is emphasized by Heinz Schlaffer, with a view to the French Revolution, in a literary study instructed by Hegel (and Lukács) and thus founded in the philosophy of history, yet extended to include some historical sociohistorical material. Following the example of Jean Paul, Goethe, and Lessing, this study reproduces in powerful (and often rapid) strokes the contradictions within the concept of bourgeois individuals as heroes.

19. Hegel 1969 onward, vol. 7, pp. 492–93; cf. Avineri 1976, p. 231.

20. Böhringer 1998, p. 32, with reference to René Girard's victim theory.

21. Seesslen (1991b), p. VIII.

22. Hembus 1997, pp. 568 and 502.

23. Marcus 2008, p. 15, cf. pp. 123, 175.—In addition to a "desire for peace of mind," Marcus sees in this "obsessiveness" a "cornerstone" of rock 'n' roll (p. 15). He cannot contemplate Elvis Presley without thinking of Herman Melville (cf. p. XI). His book *Mystery Train* from the mid-1970s is "an attempt to view rock 'n'

roll not as a youth culture or an anticulture, but plainly and simply as American culture" (p. 4).

24. Hegel 1975, p. 593.

25. Cf. Bayertz 1981; in an essay since then (2003), Bayertz has progressed beyond the confines of commentary to good honest theory, as it were.

CHAPTER 3

1. Cf. Frevert 1998, p. 324, also regarding the conversational dictionaries.

2. Cf. Seeba 1993, p. 39.

3. Cit. in Taylor 2003, p. 4.

4. Cf. Carlyle 1966, pp. 155, 164, 171, 174, 200–202; cf. also Frevert 1998, p. 324.

5. Cit. in Schlaffer 1973, p. 126.

6. Cf. Frevert 1998, pp. 326–27, 330.

7. Frevert 1998, p. 332; cf. on the preceding pp. 328–29, 336–37.

8. Cit. in Meuter/Otten 1999, p. 12; cf. Frevert 1998, pp. 340–1.

9. Gay 1995, p. 165; cf. also pp. 9–10; cf. Maurer 1996, p. 33.

10. Cf. Frevert 1998, p. 339; cf. also pp. 338, 342–43; cf. likewise Westfehling 1988, p. 146.

11. Cf. regarding the following Kocka 1995, pp. 9–22; cf. also Maurer 1996, pp. 32, 63; Habermas 1990, pp. 18, 24.

12. Mann 1995, p. 453.

13. Mann 1995, p. 456.

14. Frevert 1991, p. 16.

15. Mann 1995, p. 634.

16. Mayer 1996, p. 410.

17. Lukács 1971, p. 29.

18. Hegel 1975, p. 31; cf. Avineri 1976, pp. 139, 185, 282.

19. Lukács 1971, p. 36.

20. Lukács 1971, p. 41.

21. Lukács 1971, p. 61.

22. Horkheimer/Adorno 2002, p. 35.

23. Adorno 1979, para. 97; regarding Nietzsche and his famous theory about the soul as a "social structure of drives and affects," cf. Zitko 1991, p. 100.

24. Adorno 1979, para. 17.

25. Horkheimer/Adorno 2002, p. 123; regarding the entrepreneur as a yardstick for individuality, cf. in summary Schroer 2000, p. 58.

26. Weber 2001, p. 60.

27. Weber 2001, p. 67.

28. Weber 2001, pp. 111 and 105.

29. Horkheimer/Adorno 2002, p. 43.
30. Adorno 1979, para. 36.
31. Cf. in detail Früchtl 1986, esp. pp. 13, 184–85.
32. Adorno 1979, para. 40.
33. Adorno 2001, p. 104.
34. Schnädelbach 1992, pp. 166 and 168.
35. Honneth 2000a, pp. 81 and 83.
36. Honneth 2000b, pp. 731 and 732.
37. In his lecture on *The Construction and Dissolution of History Following Nietzsche*, Emil Angehrn underlines the parallels among Nietzsche, Foucault, and Derrida regarding this matter, but he also points out a difference. For while it remains unclear with Nietzsche how the three types of historical observation are to be brought together, deconstruction involves the theory that they necessarily complement one another. Such complementarity for the different and opposing models of critique would, of course, first have to be proven.
38. Cf. Horkheimer/Adorno 2002, p. 99; Adorno 1979, para. 131.
39. Cf. Früchtl 2003.
40. Horkheimer/Adorno 2002, p. 62.
41. Cit. in Hembus 1997, p. 71; cf. on the following also p. 411; and Scheel 1991, p. 860.
42. Scheel 1991, p. 855.
43. Benjamin 2002, p. 108.

CHAPTER 4

1. Habermas 1987, p. 106.
2. Habermas 1990, p. 30; cf. 33–34.
3. Habermas 1998, pp. 195, 198; regarding the following citations, cf. 211, 227–28, 231.
4. Cf. Habermas 1984, pp. 216–17; cf. also Klinger 1995, pp. 10–11.
5. Habermas 1984, pp. 73, 363; Habermas 2007, p. 19.
6. Regarding this accusation cf. Klinger 1995, pp. 15–16.
7. Cf. Habermas 1994, esp. pp. 11, 16.
8. Menke 1996, p. 73.
9. Habermas 2002, p. 178.
10. Hembus 1997, p. 286; cf. p. 22.
11. Cf. Hembus 1997, pp. 516, 773.
12. Regarding "professional plot," cf. Wright 1977, p. 85; Seesslen 1995, p. 135.
13. Hembus 1997, p. 516.
14. Cit. in Hembus 1997, p. 286.

CHAPTER 5

1. Izenberg 1992, p. 6, cf. pp. 8.
2. Klinger 1995, p. 157; Hegel 1975, p. 593.
3. Cf. Kremer 2001, pp. 1, 44, 90.
4. Cf. Gamm 1997, pp. 62–63.
5. Givone 1998, p. 216.
6. Cf. Frank 1986, esp. pp. 30, 60.
7. Cf. Früchtl 1996, p. 326.
8. Peitz 1995, p. 70.
9. Cf. Korte 1995, p. 48.
10. Peitz 1995, p. 80; also cf. Faulstich 1995b, p. 278.
11. Faulstich 1995b, p. 273; Faulstich's analysis of the identity issue with regard to the viewers appears to be too simple, however. Cf. p. 277.
12. Peitz 1995, p. 83.
13. Peitz 1995, p. 81.
14. Cf. Korte 1995, pp. 47, 51.
15. Cf. Tudor 1989, esp. pp. 102, 215; on film noir, cf. Schrader 1976, p. 471; and following on Werner 2000, p. 53.
16. Kettner 1999, p. 280, referring to Noël Carrol's *The Philosophy of Horror*.
17. Cf. Sobchack 1999, p. 32.
18. Peitz 1995, p. 87; cf. 85.
19. Cf. Slotkin 1998, p. 63, esp. p. 71.
20. Cf. Peitz 1995, pp. 85–86, with recourse to Elizabeth Young, professor of English and film studies.
21. Cf. Hembus 1997, p. 85.
22. Cf. Slotkin 1998, pp. 10, 612.
23. Cf. Slotkin 1998, pp. 10, 594, 610; cf. also Hembus 1997, p. 568.
24. Hembus 1997, p. 195.
25. Cf. Erhart 1997, p. 344.
26. Erhart 1997, p. 347; cf. pp. 332, 344.
27. Seesslen 1995, p. 229.
28. Benjamin 2003, p. 392.
29. Berlin 1996, p. 76.
30. Berlin 1996, p. 78.
31. Berlin 1996, p. 79.
32. Taylor 1989, p. 376; on St. Augustine, Descartes, and Locke, cf. pp. 127, 143, 159.
33. Cf. Taylor 1989, pp. 429, 498–99.
34. Cf. Taylor 1989, pp. 106–7, 495–96, 498.
35. Simmel 1995, pp. 49, 52; cf. Schroer 2001, pp. 309–10.

36. Simmel 2002, pp. 18–19.

37. Simmel 1993, p. 383.

38. Simmel 2002, p. 19.

39. Simmel, cited in Schroer 2001, pp. 315 (comment p. 23), 319, 326; on the "hybrid" life-form, cf. pp. 324–25, 327.

40. Cf. Taylor 1989, pp. 8, 510, 512.

41. Taylor 2003, p. 66; cf. pp. 14, 33, 56; on the relationship between authenticity and individuality, cf. Früchtl 1998.

42. Taylor 2003, p. 91.

43. Warshow 1998, p. 35; cf. regarding the following pp. 35–36, 38, 40, 47; Warshow 1948, p. 243.

44. Warshow 1998, p. 36; Warshow 1948, p. 240.

45. Warshow 1948, p. 243.

46. Warshow 1948, p. 244; cf. 1998, p. 36.

47. Warshow 1998, p. 37.

CHAPTER 6

1. Marcus 1998, p. 21.

2. Cf. Gamm 1994, p. 310.

3. Cf. Freitag 2001.

4. Jean-Pierre Melville, cited in Hahn/Jansen 1998, p. 157; regarding Brandes cf. Gerhardt 1992, p. 57.

5. Trilling 2006, pp. 86–87.

6. Warshow 1998, pp. 42 and 47.

7. Benjamin 2003, p. 60.

8. Rorty 1989, p. 3.

9. Cf. Rorty 1989, p. 66; Berlin 1996, p. 82; Klinger 1995, pp. 149–50.

10. Rorty 1989, p. 97; cf. p. 43.

11. Rorty 1989, p. 73; cf. p. XV.

12. Cf. regarding the following, Pountain/Robins 2000, pp. 22–23, 138–39.

13. Cf. Werner 2000, p. 34.

14. Cf. Poschardt 2000, pp. 10–11, 16, 43, 131 , 329; on the historic-sociologic explanation of the film noir as a reaction to the Second World War and subsequent anticommunism, cf. Schrader 1976, p. 463; Werner 2000, pp. 27–28, 37–38, 53–54.

15. Cf. Werner 2000, pp. 27, 37, 53.

16. Simmel 2002, p. 14; cf. also Simmel following citations.

17. Simmel 2002, p. 15.

18. Cf. Simmel 2002, p. 11; cf. Schroer 2001; Habermas is not appropriately acknowledged by Schroer.

19. Cf. Schroer 2001, p. 308.

20. Simmel 2002, p. 18.

21. Simmel 1997, p. 216.

22. Plessner 1999, p. 109.

23. Plessner 1999, p. 103.

24. Lethen 1994, pp. 75, 120; Essbach/Fischer/Lethen 2002, p. 9.

25. Plessner 1999, pp. 163 and 164.

26. Cf. on the following Pountain/Robins 2000, pp. 12–13, 19, 23, 28, 49; the authors counter the theory that coolness is first an ethnic, namely, African American (and male) phenomenon, second an age-specific, namely, adolescent, phenomenon, and third a phenomenon of U.S. culture, as maintained in studies by Richard Majors/Janet Mancini Billson, Marcel Tadesi, and Peter Stearns. They are closer to accepting the studies by Thomas Frank on the "hip consumerism"of the 1960s and by Herbert Gold on the artistic bohemians of the same period. It is telling that all these studies were performed in North America in the 1990s (cf. pp. 10–11); cf. also, with a slightly different emphasis, Marcus 1998, pp. 24–25.

27. Schreckenberg 1998, p. 129.

28. Cf. Pountain/Robins 2000, p. 26; the authors complement this characteristic with those of irony and hedonism.

29. Marcus 1998, pp. 24 and 27; cf. pp. 27–28.

CHAPTER 7

1. Nietzsche 2006, p. 132; Nietzsche 2005, pp. 233–34; Nietzsche 1977, vol. III, p. 624; cf. in general also Zitko 1991.

2. Nietzsche 1988, vol. 12, p. 502.

3. Simmel 2002, p. 12.

4. Cf. Frevert 1991, p. 16.

5. Gerhardt 1995, p. 173.

6. Nehamas 1996, p. 232; Nietzsche 2006, p. 8.

7. Nietzsche 2005, p. 212.

8. Thus Thiele's accurate expression in 1990, p. 3; the internal difficulties of this conception are, however, insufficiently clear to him.

9. Cf. Horkheimer/Adorno 2002, p. 124.

10. Gay 1995, pp. 159 and 178. Gay also remarks, however, that the "hero worshipers did not have it all in their own way" (159) and in part "abated" (165).

11. Cf. Frevert 1998, pp. 324, 327, 334, 337–38.

12. Nietzsche 2005, p. 173.

13. Cf. Früchtl 1998, p. 124.

CHAPTER 8

1. Nietzsche 1997, p. 6.
2. Cf. Aschheim 1996, pp. 131, 168.
3. Cf. Pieper 2000, p. 93.
4. Nietzsche 1997, p. 6.
5. Cf. Taylor 1989, part III; Rohner (2004) attempts to show how far this religious source is from being obsolete, even under modern conditions such as those formed by Nietzsche; those who desire "complete" happiness cannot disregard the concept of redemption.
6. Cf. Deleuze 1983, pp. 185–86, cf. p. 190.
7. Cf. short summary by Aschheim 1996, p. 52, n 4.
8. Cf. Thomä 1998, p. 142, with additional reference to Wolfgang Müller-Lauter as an advocate of critical interpretation. Thomä is keen to show that ontological affirmation is not an end in itself, not a celebration of a continuing act of creation, but refers to a point outside itself, to an affirmed moment, from which the coherence of life has to be (re)constructed (cf. p. 150).
9. Pieper 2000, p. 111.
10. Nietzsche 1977, vol. III, p. 425; cf. Nietzsche 1997, p. 21.
11. Nietzsche 1997, pp. 75 and 82.
12. Nietzsche 1988, vol. 10, p. 503.
13. Nietzsche 1997, pp. 115–16.
14. Pieper 2000, pp. 106 and 112.
15. Nietzsche 2000, p. 22.
16. Nietzsche 1974, pp. 241 and 242.
17. Pieper 2000, p. 105; cf. p. 103.
18. Gerhardt 2000, pp. 126 and 127; cf. p. 129.
19. Gerhardt 2000, pp. 133 and 134.
20. Gerhardt 2000, p. 137; cf. also Pieper 2000, p. 107.
21. Gerhardt 2000, p. 152; cf. p. 153
22. Seesslen 2000b, p. 30.
23. Cf. Sobchack 1999, pp. 26, 43, 55, 88.
24. Quoted in Giesen 2000, p. 8.
25. Cf. Seesslen 2000b, pp. 13, 14, 20.
26. Cf. Kettner 1999, p. 287; Seesslen 2000b, p. 19.
27. Cf. Marx 1999, referring to H. U. Asemissen.
28. Cf. Früchtl 1999.
29. Habermas 1987, pp. 263 and 264.
30. Foucault 1990b, p. 4.
31. Cf. Foucault 1994, p. 296.

32. Cf. Habermas 1987, p. 267, with reference to Hubert L. Dreyfus/Paul Rabinow, *Michel Foucault: Beyond Structuralism and Hermeneutics.*

33. Cf. Menke 2003.

34. Foucault 1990a, p. 92; regarding the following quotations, cf. p. 95.

35. Cf. Thomä 1998, p. 138.

CHAPTER 9

1. Nietzsche 1997, p. 138.

2. Cf. regarding the following Perler 1998, pp. 82, 143.

3. Cf. Müller (2003).

4. Cf. also Irwin 2002, p. 13.

5. Cf. Brannigan 2002; Bassham 2002.

6. Nietzsche 1974, p. 104 (section 34); on the theological soteriological aspect, cf. Rohner 2003.

7. Derry 1997, pp. 299 and 301.

8. Oberender 1993, p. 11.

9. Rushing/Frentz 1995, p. 193, referring to Sobchack, cf. p. 184; cf. Oberender 1993, p. 18.

10. Rushing/Frentz 1995, p. 145, referring to Sobchack.

11. Koebner 1999, p. 131.

12. Rushing/Frentz 1995, p. 149; cf. p. 5.

13. Cf. Rushing/Frentz 1995, p. 156.

14. Cf. Koebner 1999, pp. 131, 133; Faulstich 1995a, p. 113.

15. Cf. Faulstich 1995a, p. 114; Rushing/Frentz 1995, p. 145; Koebner 1999, p. 131.

Bibliography

Adorno, Th. W. (2001). *The Culture Industry: Selected Essays on Mass Culture.* Routledge Chapman & Hall.

Adorno, Th. W. (1978). *Minima Moralia. Reflections from Damaged Life.* London/ New York: Verso.

Andersen, A. (1999). *Der Traum vom guten Leben. Alltags- und Konsumgeschichte vom Wirtschaftswunder bis heute.* Frankfurt and New York: Campus.

Angehrn, E. (2001). *Konstruktion und Auflösung der Geschichte im Anschluß an Nietzsche.*

Aschheim, St. E. (1996). *Nietzsche und die Deutschen. Karriere eines Kults.* Stuttgart/Weimar: Metzler.

Avineri, S. (1976). *Hegels Theorie des modernen Staates.* Frankfurt/M.: Suhrkamp.

Barthes, R. (1964). *Mythen des Alltags.* Frankfurt/M.: Suhrkamp.

Bassham, G. (2002). The Religion of *The Matrix* and the Problems of Pluralism. In *The* Matrix *and Philosophy: Welcome to the Desert of the Real,* ed. W. Irwin. Chicago and La Salle: Carus Publishing Company. 111–25.

Bayertz, K. (2003). Zur Ästhetik des Western. *Zeitschrift für Ästhetik und Allgemeine Kunstwissenschaft* 48, no. 1. 69–82.

Bayertz, K. (1981). Hegel und der Wilde Westen. In *Dialektik 2: Hegel—Perspektiven seiner Philosophie heute.* 138–41.

Behler, E. (1989). *Unendliche Perfektibilität. Europäische Romantik und Französische Revolution.* Paderborn: Schöningh.

Benjamin, W. (2003). *Selected Writings. Volume 4: 1938–1940.* Trans. E. Jephcott, and others, ed. H. Eiland and M. W. Jennings. Cambridge, MA: The Belknap Press of Harvard University Press.

Benjamin, W. (2002). *Selected Writings. Volume 3: 1935–1938.* Trans. E. Jephcott, H. Eiland, and others, ed. H. Eiland and M. W. Jennings. Cambridge, MA: The Belknap Press of Harvard University Press.

Berlin, I. (1996). Revolution der Romantik. Eine grundlegende Krise in der neuzeitlichen Geistesgeschichte. *Lettre International* 34. 76–83.

Blumenberg, H. (1990). *Arbeit am Mythos.* Frankfurt/M.: Suhrkamp.

Böhringer, H. (1998). *Auf dem Rücken Amerikas. Eine Mythologie der neuen Welt im Western und Gangsterfilm.* Berlin: Merve.

Brannigan, M. (2002). There Is No Spoon: A Buddhist Mirror. In *The* Matrix *and Philosophy: Welcome to the Desert of the Real,* ed. W. Irwin. Chicago and La Salle: Carus Publishing Company. 101–10.

Bronfen, E. (1999). *Heimweh: Illusionsspiele in Hollywood.* Berlin: Volk & Welt.

Budd, M. (1998). A Home in the Wilderness: Visual Imagery in John Ford's Westerns (1976). In *The Western Reader,* ed. J. Kitses and G. Rickman. New York: Limelight Editions. 133–48.

Cassirer, E. (1956). Sprache und Mythos. In *Wesen und Wirkung des Symbolbegriffs,* by E. Cassirer. Darmstadt: Wissenschaftliche Buchgesellschaft.

Deleuze, G. (1983). *Nietzsche and Philosophy.* Trans. H. Tomlinson. New York: Columbia University Press.

Dery, M. (1997). Der Cyborg: Von posthumanen Wesen und der Politik des Körpers. In *Cyber. Die Kultur der Zukunft,* by M. Dery. Berlin: Verlag Volk & Welt. 257–361.

Erhart, W. (1997). Mythos, Männlichkeit, Gemeinschaft. Nachruf auf den Western-Helden. In *Wann ist ein Mann ein Mann? Zur Geschichte der Männlichkeit,* ed. W. Erhart and Britta Herrmann. Stuttgart/Weimar: Metzler. 320–49.

Eßbach, W., Fischer, J., and Lethen, H. (2002). Vorwort. In *Plessners "Grenzen der Gemeinschaft." Eine Debatte,* ed. W. Eßbach, J. Fischer, and H. Lethen. Frankfurt/M.: Suhrkamp. 9–14.

Faulstich, W. (1995a). Der neue Science-fiction-Film: *Blade Runner* (1982). In *Fischer Filmgeschichte. Vol. 5: Massenware und Kunst 1977–1995,* ed. W. Faulstich; H. Korte (Hg.). Frankfurt/M.: Fischer. 107–19.

Faulstich, W. (1995b). Der neue Thriller: *Das Schweigen der Lämmer* (1991). In *Fischer Filmgeschichte. Vol. 5: Massenware und Kunst 1977–1995,* ed. W. Faulstich; H. Korte (Hg.). Frankfurt/M.: Fischer. 270–87.

Ferry, L. (1992). *Der Mensch als Ästhet. Die Erfindung des Geschmacks im Zeitalter der De-mokratie.* Stuttgart/Weimar: Metzler.

Figal, G. (1999). *Nietzsche. Eine philosophische Einführung.* Stuttgart: Reclam.

Foucault, M. (1994). *The Order of Things: An Archeology of the Human Sciences.* New York: Vintage Books.

Foucault, M. (1990a). *The History of Sexuality. Vol. 1: An Introduction.* Trans. R. Hurley. New York: Vintage Books.

Foucault, M. (1990b). *The History of Sexuality. Vol. 2: The Use of Pleasure.* Trans. R. Hurley. New York: Vintage Books.

Frank, M. (1986). *Die Unhintergehbarkeit von Individualität. Reflexionen über Subjekt, Person und Individuum aus Anlaß ihrer "postmodernen" Toterklärung.* Frankfurt/M.: Suhrkamp.

Frank, M. (1982). *Der kommende Gott. Vorlesungen über die neue Mythologie.* Frankfurt/M.: Suhrkamp.

Freitag, S. (2001). Amerikanisches Ballett—Die Geschichte von Bonnie Parker und Clyde Barrow. In *Mord und andere Kleinigkeiten. Ungewöhnliche Kriminalfälle aus sechs Jahrhunderten,* ed. A. Fahrmeir and S. Freitag. München: Beck. 227–43.

Freud, S. (2001a). *The Standard Edition of the Complete Psychological Works. Vol. IV: The Interpretation of Dreams.* London: Vintage Books.

Freud, S. (2001b). *The Standard Edition of the Complete Psychological Works. Vol. XXI: The Future of an Illusion, Civilization and its Discontents and Other Works.* London: Vintage Books.

Frevert, U. (1998). Herren und Helden. Vom Aufstieg und Niedergang des Heroismus im 19. und 20. Jahrhundert. In *Erfindung des Menschen. Schöpfungsträume und Körperbilder 1500–2000,* ed. R. van Dülmen. Wien u. a. 323–44.

Frevert, U. (1991). *Ehrenmänner. Das Duell in der bürgerlichen Gesellschaft.* München: Beck.

Frisby, D. (1989). *Fragmente der Moderne. Georg Simmel—Siegfried Kracauer—Walter Benjamin.* Rheda-Wiedenbrück: Daedalus.

Früchtl, J. (2003). Aufklärung und Massenbetrug oder Adorno demonstriert etwas uncool für den Film. In *Wieviel Spaß verträgt die Kultur? Adornos Begriff der Kulturindustrie und die gegenwärtige Spaßkultur,* ed. G. Seubold and Patrick Baum. Bonn: DenkMal. 145–65.

Früchtl, J. (1999). Die Idee des schöpferischen Menschen. Eine Nachgeschichte zu ihrer Vorgeschichte. In *Die Kunst des Überlebens. Nachdenken über Hans Blumenberg,* ed. F. J. Wetz and H. Timm. Frankfurt/M.: Suhrkamp. 226–43.

Früchtl, J. (1998). Spielerische Selbstbeherrschung. Ein Beitrag zur "Ästhetik der Existenz." In *Was ist ein gutes Leben? Philosophische Reflexionen,* ed. H. Steinfath. Frankfurt/M.: Suhrkamp. 124–48.

Früchtl, J. (1996). *Ästhetische Erfahrung und moralisches Urteil. Eine Rehabilitierung.* Frankfurt/M.: Suhrkamp.

Früchtl, J. (1986). *Mimesis—Konstellation eines Zentralbegriffs bei Adorno.* Würzburg: Königshausen & Neumann.

Gamm, G. (1997). *Der Deutsche Idealismus. Eine Einführung in die Philosophie von Fichte, Hegel und Schelling.* Stuttgart: Reclam.

Gamm, G. (1994). *Flucht aus der Kategorie. Die Positivierung des Unbestimmten als Ausgang aus der Moderne.* Frankfurt/M.: Suhrkamp.

Gay, P. (1995). *The Naked Heart: The Bourgeois Experience, Victoria to Freud.* New York and London: W. W. Norton & Company.

Gerhardt, V. (2000). Die "große Vernunft" des Leibes. Ein Versuch über Zarathustras vierte Rede. In *Friedrich Nietzsche. Also sprach Zarathustra,* ed. V. Gerhardt. Berlin: Akademie Verlag. 123–64.

Gerhardt, V. (1995). *Friedrich Nietzsche.* München: Beck.

Giesen, R. (2000). Künstliche Welten im Film. In *Künstliche Welten. Tricks, Special Effects und Computeranimation im Film von den Anfängen bis heute,* ed. R. Giesen and Cl. Meglin. Hamburg and Wien: Europa Verlag. 7–9.

Givone, S. (1998). Der Intellektuelle. In *Der Mensch der Romantik,* ed. F. Furet. Frankfurt and New York: Campus. 215–51.

Habermas, J. (2007). Philosophy as Stand-In and Interpreter. In *Moral Consciousness and Communicative Action,* by J. Habermas. Trans. Chr. Lenhardt and Sh. Weber Nicholson. London: Polity Press. 1–20.

Habermas, J. (2002). Fundamentalismus und Terror. Antworten auf Fragen zum 11. September 2001. *Blätter für deutsche und internationale Politik* 47, no. 2. 165–78.

Habermas, J. (1998). Konzeptionen der Moderne. Ein Rückblick auf zwei Traditionen. In *Die postnationale Konstellation. Politische Essays,* by J. Habermas. Frankfurt/M.: Suhrkamp. 195–231.

Habermas, J. (1994). On the Pragmatic, the Ethical, and the Moral Employments of Practical Reason. In *Justification and Application. Remarks on Discourse Ethics,* by J. Habermas. Trans. C. P. Cronin. Cambridge, MA: MIT Press. 1–18.

Habermas, J. (1992). Individuation Through Socialization: On George Herbert Mead's Theory of Subjectivity. In *Postmetaphysical Thinking: Philosophical Essays,* by J. Habermas. Trans. W. M. Hohengarten. Cambridge, MA: MIT Press. 149–204.

Habermas, J. (1990). *Strukturwandel der Öffentlichkeit. Untersuchungen zu einer Kategorie der bürgerlichen Gesellschaft,* mit einem Vorw. z. Neuaufl. 1990. Frankfurt/M.: Suhrkamp.

Habermas, J. (1987). *The Philosophical Discourse of Modernity. Twelve Lectures.* Trans. F. G. Lawrence. Cambridge, MA: MIT Press.

Habermas, J. (1984). *The Theory of Communicative Action. Vol. 1: Reason and the Rationalization of Society.* Trans. Th. McCarthy. Boston: Beacon Press.

Hahn, R. M., Jansen, V. (1998). *Die 100 besten Kultfilme. Von "Metropolis" bis "Fargo."* München: Heyne.

Hegel, G. W. F. (1975). *Aesthetics: Lectures on Fine Art.* Trans. T. M. Knox. Oxford: Clarendon Press.

Hegel, G. W. F. (1969 onward). *Werke in zwanzig Bänden.* Ed. E. Moldenhauer and K. M. Michel. Frankfurt/M.: Suhrkamp.

Hegel, G. W. F. (1967). *Hegel's Philosophy of Right.* Trans. with notes by T. M. Knox. New York: Oxford University Press.

Honneth, A. (2000a). Über die Möglichkeit einer erschließenden Kritik. Die "Dialektik der Aufklärung" im Horizont gegenwärtiger Debatten über Sozialkritik. In *Das Andere der Gerechtigkeit. Aufsätze zur praktischen Philosophie*, by A. Honneth. Frankfurt/M.: Suhrkamp. 70–87.

Honneth, A. (2000b). Rekonstruktive Gesellschaftskritik unter genealogischem Vorbehalt. Zur Idee der "Kritik" in der Frankfurter Schule. *Deutsche Zeitschrift für Philosophie* 48, no. 5. 729–37.

Hembus, J. (1997). *Das Western-Lexikon*. Extended new edition by B. Hembus. München: Heyne.

Horkheimer, M., and Adorno, Th. W. (2002). *Dialectic of Enlightenment: Philosophical Fragments*. Ed. Gunzelin Schmid Noerr, trans. Edmund Jephcott. Stanford: Stanford University Press.

Irwin, W. (2002). Computers, Caves, and Oracles: Neo and Socrates. In *The Matrix and Philosophy: Welcome to the Desert of the Real*, ed. W. Irwin. Chicago and La Salle: Carus Publishing Company. 5–15.

Izenberg, G. N. (1992). *Impossible Individuality: Romanticism, Revolution, and the Origins of Modern Selfhood, 1787–1802*. Princeton, NJ: Princeton University Press.

Kettner, M. (1999). Eine Projektion der Moderne: Mary Shelleys *Frankenstein*. In *Filmästhetik*, ed. L. Nagl. Wien: Oldenbourg. 268–99.

Klinger, C. (1995). *Flucht Trost Revolte. Die Moderne und ihre ästhetischen Gegenwelten*. München/Wien: Hanser.

Kocka, J. (1995). Das europäische Muster und der deutsche Fall. In *Bürgertum im 19. Jahrhundert. Bd. I: Einheit und Vielfalt Europas*, ed. J. Kocka. Göttingen: Vandenhoeck & Ruprecht. 9–75.

Koebner, Th. (1999). Herr und Knecht. Über künstliche Menschen im Film. In *Der Frankenstein-Komplex. Kulturgeschichtliche Aspekte des Traums vom künstlichen Menschen*, ed. R. Drux. Frankfurt/M.: Suhrkamp. 119–37.

Korte, H. (1995). "Die Eskalation des Horrors": *Halloween—Die Nacht des Grauens* (1978). In *Fischer Filmgeschichte, vol. 5: 1977–1995*, ed. W. Faulstich and H. Korte. Frankfurt/M. 38–55.

Kremer, D. (2001 [1997]). *Romantik*. Stuttgart/Weimar.

Leone, S. (1997). An den Grenzen des Irrealen: Der Western. In *Das Western-Lexikon*, ed. J. Hembus. Extended new edition by B. Hembus. München: Heyne. 6–7.

Lethen, H. (1994). *Verhaltenslehren der Kälte. Lebensversuche zwischen den Kriegen*. Frankfurt/M.: Suhrkamp.

Lévi-Strauss, Cl. (1967). *Strukturale Anthropologie*. Frankfurt/M.: Suhrkamp.

Lukács, G. (1971). *The Theory of the Novel*. Trans. A. Bostock. Cambridge, MA: MIT Press.

Mann, Th. (1995). *The Magic Mountain.* Trans. J. E. Woods. New York: Alfred A. Knopf.

Marcus, G. (2008). *Mystery Train: Images of America in Rock 'n' Roll Music.* New York: Plume.

Marcus, G. (1998). Birth of the Cool. In *Make it Funky. Crossover zwischen Pop, Avantgarde und Kunst, Jahresring* 45, ed. U. Groos. Köln. 21–32.

Marx, R. (1999). Foucaults Irrtum. Die Repräsentation der Repräsentation: Was in der *Ordnung der Dinge* durcheinandergeraten ist, in Frankfurter Rundschau, April 24.

Maurer, M. (1996). *Die Biographie des Bürgers. Lebensformen und Denkweisen in der formativen Phase des deutschen Bürgertums (1680–1815).* Göttingen: Vandenhoeck & Ruprecht.

Mayer, H. (1996). Der Zweikampf zweier Zivilisten. Das Nichtduell zwischen Settembrini und Naphta im *Zauberberg* von Thomas Mann. In *Das Duell. Der tödliche Kampf um die Ehre,* ed. U. Schultz. Frankfurt/M.: Insel. 403–15.

Menke, Chr. (2003). Die Disziplin der Ästhetik. Eine Lektüre von "Überwachen und Strafen." In *Kunst als Strafe. Zur Ästhetik der Disziplinierung,* ed. G. Koch and others. München: Fink. 109–22.

Menke, Chr. (1996). *Tragödie im Sittlichen. Gerechtigkeit und Freiheit nach Hegel.* Frankfurt/M.: Suhrkamp.

Meuter, G., Otten H. R. (n.d.) Einleitung: Der Bürger im Spiegelkabinett seiner Feinde. In *Der Aufstand gegen den Bürger. Antibürgerliches Denken im 20. Jahrhundert,* ed. G. Meuter and H. R. Otten. Würzburg: Königshausen & Neumann.

Müller, O. (2003). *Hilary Putnam und der Abschied vom Skeptizismus oder Warum die Welt keine Computersimulation sein kann.* Paderborn: Mentis.

Necakov, L. (1987). The Terminator: Beyond the Classical Hollywood Narrative. In *Cine Action!* Nr. 8. 84–87.

Nehamas, A. (1996). Nietzsche, Modernity, Aestheticism. In *The Cambridge Companion to Nietzsche,* ed. B. Magnus and K. M. Higgins. Cambridge: Cambridge Univeristy Press. 223–51.

Nietzsche, F. (2006). *Beyond Good and Evil.* Filiquarian Publishing.

Nietzsche, F. (2005). *The Anti-Christ, Ecce Homo, Twilight of the Idols and Other Writings.* Ed. A. Ridley and J. Norman. Trans. J. Norman. Cambridge: Cambridge University Press.

Nietzsche, F. (2000). *The Birth of Tragedy.* Trans. with an Introduction and Notes by D. Smith. New York: Oxford University Press.

Nietzsche, F. (1997). *Thus Spake Zarathustra.* Trans. Th. Common. Introd. by N. Davey. Hertfordshire: Wordsworth.

Nietzsche, F. (1988). *Sämtliche Werke. Kritische Studienausgabe* in 15 Bänden (KSA). Ed. G. Colli and M. Montinari. München, Berlin, and New York: dtv/de Gruyter.

Nietzsche, F. (1977). *Werke in drei Bänden.* Ed. K. Schlechta. München / and Wien: Hanser.

Nietzsche, F. (1974). *The Gay Science.* Trans. with commentary by W. Kaufmann. New York: Vintage Books.

Oberender, Th. (1993). *Zwischen Mensch und Maschine. Reflexionen über James Camerons Film "Terminator 2" im Licht der Philosophie von J.-F. Lyotard.* Siegen: MuK, no. 88.

Peitz, Chr. (1995). *Marylins starke Schwestern. Frauenbilder im Gegenwartskino.* Hamburg: Klein.

Perler, D. (1998). *René Descartes.* München: Beck.

Pieper, A. (2000). Zarathustra als Verkünder des Übermenschen und als Fürsprecher des Kreises. In *Friedrich Nietzsche. Also sprach Zarathustra,* ed. V. Gerhardt. Berlin: Akademie. 93–122.

Plessner, H. (1999). *The Limits of Community.* Trans. A. Wallace. Humanity Books.

Pountain, D., and Robins, D. (2000). *Cool Rules. Anatomy of an Attitude.* London: Reaktion Books.

Rohner, M. (2004). *Glück und Erlösung. Konstellationen einer modernen Selbstverständigung.* Münster: LIT.

Rorty, R. (1989). *Contingency, Irony, and Solidarity.* Cambridge: Cambridge University Press.

Rushing, J. H., and Frentz, Th. S. (1995). *Projecting the Shadow: The Cyborg Hero in American Film.* Chicago: University of Chicago Press.

Sayre, R. F. (1985) (Ed.). *A Week on the Concord and Merrimack Rivers; Walden; The Main Woods; Cape God.* New York.

Scheel, K. (1991). "Die Wahrheit der Legende. John Ford und der Abschied vom Western. *Merkur* 45, nos. 9/10, *Kultur? Über Kunst, Film und Musik.* 854–61.

Schlaffer, H. (1973). *Der Bürger als Held. Sozialgeschichtliche Auflösungen literarischer Widersprüche.* Frankfurt/M.: Suhrkamp.

Schnädelbach, H. (1999). *Hegel zur Einführung.* Hamburg: Junius.

Schrader, P. (1976). Notizen zum Film noir. *Filmkritik* no. 238. 463–78.

Schreckenberg, E. (1998). Was ist postmodernes Kino? Versuch einer kurzen Antwort auf eine schwierige Frage. In *Die Filmgespenster der Postmoderne,* ed. A. Rost and M. Sandbothe. Frankfurt/M.: Verlag der Autoren. 118–30.

Schroer, Markus (2001). *Das Individuum der Gesellschaft. Synchrone und diachrone Theorieperspektiven.* Frankfurt/M.: Suhrkamp.

Seeba, H. C. (1993). Schwerterhebung. Zur Konstruktion des heroischen Subjekts. *Daidalos* 49. 37–51.

Seeßlen, G. (2000a). Wie der Stahl geheiligt wurde. Warum und zu welchem Ende wollen Maschinen "Ich" sagen? *DIE ZEIT* no. 7 (February 10).

Seeßlen, G. (2000b). Traumreplikanten des Kinos. Passage durch alte und neue Bewegungsbilder. In *Künstliche Menschen. Manische Maschinen. Kontrollierte Körper*, ed. R. Aurich u. a. Berlin: Jovis. 13–46.

Seeßlen, G. (1995). *Western. Geschichte und Mythologie des Westernfilms.* Marburg: Schüren Presseverlag.

Seeßlen, G. (1991a). Mythos und Film. Eine mögliche Annäherung an das populäre Kino. *medien praktisch* no. 3. II–V.

Seeßlen, G. (1991b). *Red River.* Ein Film rebelliert gegen den Mythos. *medien praktisch* no. 3. VIII–XI.

Simmel, G. (2002). The Metropolis and Mental Life. In *The Blackwell City Reader*, ed. G. Bridge and S. Watson. Oxford: Blackwell. 11–19.

Simmel, G. (1997). *On Culture: Selected Writings.* Ed. D. Frisby and M. Featherstone. Los Angeles: Sage.

Simmel, G. (1995). Die beiden Formen des Individualismus. In *Aufsätze und Abhandlungen 1901–1908, Bd. 1, Gesamtausgabe Bd. 7*, ed. G. Simmel. Frankfurt/M.: Suhrkamp. 49–56.

Simmel, G. (1993). Das Problem des Stiles. In *Aufsätze und Abhandlungen 1901–1908, Bd. II, Gesamtausgabe Bd. 8*, ed. G. Simmel. Frankfurt/M.: Suhrkamp. 347–84.

Sloterdijk, P. (1999). Regeln für den Menschenpark. Ein Antwortschreiben zum Brief über den Humanismus—die Elmauer Rede. *DIE ZEIT* no. 38 (September 16).

Slotkin, R. (1998 [1992]). *Gunfighter Nation: The Myth of the Frontier in Twentieth-Century America.* Norman: University of Oklahoma Press.

Smith, H. N. (1970 [1950]). *Virgin Land: The American West as Symbol and Myth.* Cambridge, MA: Harvard University Press.

Sobchack, V. (1999). *Screening Space. The American Science Fiction Film.* 2d ed. New Brunswick, NJ: Rutgers University Press.

Taylor, Ch. (2003). *The Ethics of Authenticity.* Cambridge, MA: Harvard University Press.

Taylor, Ch. (1989). *Sources of the Self: The Making of the Modern Identity.* Cambridge, MA: Harvard University Press.

Thiele, L. P. (1990). *Friedrich Nietzsche and the Politics of the Soul: A Study of Heroic Individualism.* Princeton, NJ: Princeton University Press.

Trilling, L. (2006). *Sincerity and Authenticity.* Cambridge, MA: Harvard University Press.

Tudor, A. (1989). *Monsters and Mad Scientists: A Cultural History of the Horror Movie*. Oxford: Basil Blackwell.

Warshow, R. (1998). The Westerner (1954). In *The Western Reader*, ed. J. Kitses and G. Rickman. New York: Limelight Editions. 35–47.

Warshow, R. (1948). The Gangster as Tragic Hero. *Partisan Review* 15, no. 2. 240–44.

Weber, M. (2001). *The Protestant Ethic and the Spirit of Capitalism*. Trans. T. Parsons, with an Introduction by A. Giddens. London and New York: Routledge.

Werner, P. (2000). *Film noir und Neo-Noir*. München: Vertigo.

Westfehling, U. (1988). Helden, Anti-Helden, anonyme Helden. In *Triumph und Tod des Helden. Europäische Historienmalerei von Rubens bis Manet*, ed. E. Mai and A. Repp-Eckert. Milano: Electa Spa. 139–50.

Wetz, F. J. (1993). *Hans Blumenberg zur Einführung*. Hamburg: Junius.

Wicke, P. (1998). *Von Mozart zu Madonna. Eine Kulturgeschichte der Popmusik*. Leipzig: Kiepenheuer.

Williams, D. (1998). Pilgrims and the Promised Land: A Genealogy of the Western. In *The Western Reader*, ed. J. Kitses and G. Rickman. New York: Limelight Editions.

Wood, R. (1998). Rio Bravo & Retrospect. In *The Western Reader*, ed. J. Kitses and G. Rickman. New York: Limelight Editions.

Wright, W. (1977). *Sixguns and Society: A Structural Study of the Western*. Berkeley: University of California Press.

Zelle, C. (1995). *Die doppelte Ästhetik der Moderne. Revisionen des Schönen von Boileau bis Nietzsche*. Stuttgart: Metzler.

Zitko, H. (1991). *Nietzsches Philosophie als Logik der Ambivalenz*. Würzburg: Königshausen & Neumann.

Index of Names

Cultural Memory | in the Present

Dan Zahavi, *Husserl's Phenomenology*

Rodolphe Gasché, *The Idea of Form: Rethinking Kant's Aesthetics*

Michael Naas, *Taking on the Tradition: Jacques Derrida and the Legacies of Deconstruction*

Herlinde Pauer-Studer, ed., *Constructions of Practical Reason: Interviews on Moral and Political Philosophy*

Jean-Luc Marion, *Being Given: Toward a Phenomenology of Givenness*

Theodor W. Adorno and Max Horkheimer, *Dialectic of Enlightenment*

Ian Balfour, *The Rhetoric of Romantic Prophecy*

Martin Stokhof, *World and Life as One: Ethics and Ontology in Wittgenstein's Early Thought*

Gianni Vattimo, *Nietzsche: An Introduction*

Jacques Derrida, *Negotiations: Interventions and Interviews, 1971–1998,* ed. Elizabeth Rottenberg

Brett Levinson, *The Ends of Literature: Post-transition and Neoliberalism in the Wake of the "Boom"*

Timothy J. Reiss, *Against Autonomy: Global Dialectics of Cultural Exchange*

Hent de Vries and Samuel Weber, eds., *Religion and Media*

Niklas Luhmann, *Theories of Distinction: Redescribing the Descriptions of Modernity*, ed. and introd. William Rasch

Johannes Fabian, *Anthropology with an Attitude: Critical Essays*

Michel Henry, *I Am the Truth: Toward a Philosophy of Christianity*

Gil Anidjar, *"Our Place in Al-Andalus": Kabbalah, Philosophy, Literature in Arab-Jewish Letters*

Hélène Cixous and Jacques Derrida, *Veils*

F. R. Ankersmit, *Historical Representation*

F. R. Ankersmit, *Political Representation*

Elissa Marder, *Dead Time: Temporal Disorders in the Wake of Modernity (Baudelaire and Flaubert)*

Reinhart Koselleck, *The Practice of Conceptual History: Timing History, Spacing Concepts*

Niklas Luhmann, *The Reality of the Mass Media*

Hubert Damisch, *A Childhood Memory by Piero della Francesca*

Hubert Damisch, *A Theory of /Cloud/: Toward a History of Painting*

Jean-Luc Nancy, *The Speculative Remark (One of Hegel's Bons Mots)*

Jean-François Lyotard, *Soundproof Room: Malraux's Anti-Aesthetics*